WAGNER
AND THE
NEW CONSCIOUSNESS

Wagner
and the
New Consciousness

Language and Love in the *Ring*

Sandra Corse

Rutherford • Madison • Teaneck
Fairleigh Dickinson University Press
London and Toronto: Associated University Presses

Associated University Presses
440 Forsgate Drive
Cranbury, NJ 08512

Associated University Presses
25 Sicilian Avenue
London WC1A 2QH, England

Associated University Presses
P.O. Box 488, Port Credit
Mississauga, Ontario
Canada L5G 4M2

The paper used in this publication meets the requirements
of the American National Standard for Permanence of Paper
for Printed Library Materials Z39.48-1984.

Library of Congress Cataloging-in-Publication Data

Corse, Sandra.
  Wagner and the new consciousness : language and love in the Ring /
Sandra Corse.
    p.   cm.
  Includes bibliographical references.
  ISBN 0-8386-3378-1 (alk. paper)
  I. Wagner, Richard, 1813–1883.   Ring des Nibelungen.   II. Title.
ML410.W15C73   1990
782.1′092—dc20   88-46186
                                                            CIP
                                                            MN

PRINTED IN THE UNITED STATES OF AMERICA

CONTENTS

ACKNOWLEDGMENTS

I would like to thank Brent Weaver, who read and commented helpfully on several chapters of the manuscript. My special thanks to Larry Corse for preparing the musical examples.

WAGNER
AND THE
NEW CONSCIOUSNESS

INTRODUCTION

The *Ring* cycle holds a peculiar fascination for modern audiences, a fascination resulting from what Thomas Mann characterized as the "miraculous world of sound and its peculiar intellectual magic."[1] Mann goes on to say that in Wagner's works the music is more than just music, and the poetry is more than just poetry. Rather, the text is musical and, especially, the music is literary: the music

> seems to shoot up like a geyser from the precivilized bedrock depths of myth (and not only "seems": it really does); but in fact—and at the same time—it is carefully considered, calculated, supremely intelligent, full of shrewdness and cunning, and as literary in its conception as the texts are musical in theirs. Resolved into its primal elements, the music is designed to throw into high relief philosophical propositions that have been embodied in myth.[2]

The literary quality of the music, the infusion of myth with philosophy, and the peculiarly compelling quality of the whole that Mann finds in all of Wagner are particularly evident in the *Ring* cycle, perhaps Wagner's most interesting work because the mixture of these elements is so complete. The *Ring* cycle works, in part, because of the perfect balance of these elements, whereas in *Tristan* and *Parsifal* the philosophical ideas sometimes overshadow the drama, and in the earlier works the dramatic technique and theory have not been developed to the high level found in the *Ring*. Yet in many ways the *Ring* cycle does not seem to work. Its final meaning remains obscure, as it apparently was to Wagner himself; he changed the text of the ending several times before reaching the version we have now. This confusion, which might be considered a weakness of the *Ring*, results from the same source as its strengths: the diversity of ideas and techniques Wagner tried to incorporate into a single whole.

When he began to write the text for the *Ring*, Wagner had come to see the music drama as the instrument by which to develop the new social and political ideas that were a subject of lively discus-

11

sion in Germany at the time, ideas that Wagner enlarged upon from his recent reading of Feuerbach and Hegel (he had not yet discovered Schopenhauer). In developing the ideas that became the *Ring* (and also *Oper und Drama* and "The Art-Work of the Future"), he came to see himself as an artist version of the Hegelian hero, a world-historic figure; he saw in German and Norse mythology the basis for an allegory that would explore, through what he felt were the unique expressive capabilities of music and drama together, a new, modern concept of the self and of history, a concept he drew in part from his philosophical sources and from ideas that were "in the air" at the time, in part from his own proclivities already evident in such works as *The Flying Dutchman* and *Lohengrin,* and in part from the literary and musical traditions in which he worked. In the *Ring* he tried to devise not only a plot but also specific musical techniques that would express and explore this new concept of the self. He posited an audience, the German people, whose spirit would be objectified in the *Ring* cycle, and this spirit, so objectified, would allow his listeners to find in the new work the instrument for creating in themselves this new concept of the self, which might, in the romantic revolution he still believed in at the time, lead to the creation of a new world. Thus a strong utopian element colors the intent of the *Ring* cycle.

Wagner's idea of a redefinition of selfhood was a romantic project, certainly—part of the general romantic revolt against the Enlightenment—but he found in his reading of Hegel the idea in somewhat altered form, because Hegel emphasized reason, as necessity or spirit, while other romantic writers tended to emphasize intuition and the subconscious as a natural force rather than consciousness as a social force. Wagner also imbibed at least in part the Hegelian notion of history. And he found in Feuerbach a writer who led the way in moving the concept of the self from metaphysics, where Hegel, in spite of his emphasis on history, left it, to a realm of sensuous material reality. Feuerbach rejected idealism and celebrated the diversity of physical reality and social relations, especially in love. Wagner took the importance of sensuous reality quite seriously, but he looked through Feuerbach to his source in Hegel for many of the details of the notion of self-realization as well as for the idea of necessity as the moving spirit of history, reflected, however, in the individual need for love that Wagner substituted for the Hegelian absolute spirit.

For Hegel, the gap between subject and object—a traditional concern of philosophy that implies the status of the individual and of physical reality—was a problem of modern culture, which could be overcome through a dialectical understanding of history.[3] Hegel's great advance over previous philosophies, according to Andrew Feenberg, was "his concept of being as continuous becoming."[4] Wagner picked up this idea and emphasized the continuous becoming of the individual and society in the *Ring* cycle. But in so doing he made it difficult to determine just who is the "hero" of the *Ring:* the heroic individual who reflects self-consciousness achieved through a combination of sensuality and rationality in love (Wagner's concept, which combines elements of Hegelian and Feuerbachian thought) is Wotan (early and late), Siegmund, Sieglinde, Siegfried, and Brünnhilde—not any of them singly but all of them collectively. Brünnhilde, however, reaches a level of self-awareness the others do not, but it is a level impossible without their contributions. Brünnhilde would not have come to her loving self-sacrifice—presented as the highest act of humanity in the *Ring*—without the experiences of the others. This concept of the self as *becoming,* as object of history as well as subject, is what makes the *Ring* cycle so compelling.

Although Wagner derived many of his ideas concerning the self from Feuerbach, he certainly knew that Feuerbach's ideas came largely from Hegel, and he was aware that some of these ideas were more rigorously developed in Hegel than in his follower and critic. Wagner was already interested in love before he read either philosopher, of course, and he had in several of his earlier operas emphasized the self-sacrifice of love that is his own version of the mutual recognition of individuals Hegel finds necessary. But from his reading of Hegel and Feuerbach Wagner gained a theoretical and psychological basis for this idea. For Wagner, however, caught in the very ideology of domination he attempts to criticize, Hegelian mutual recognition finally means giving up the self rather than realizing it, and the *Ring* cycle becomes, in spite of itself, a document of the failure of love in patriarchal society. Wagner, at the end of *Götterdämmerung,* can only reiterate his earlier concept, in which the loss of self in love is understood as death, a loss that Wagner seems to have regarded as positive but is difficult to read positively today.

Wagner's concept of love and self-sacrifice in the *Ring* cycle today must necessarily be seen from a modern viewpoint. Wagner was unable to escape the limitations of his view because his consciousness, like that of his hero Siegfried, was constituted, not from instinctive and natural processes, but by his own historical and social background. For Hegel, this constitution of the self is metaphorical: he posits an absolute spirit that develops itself as self and as society. Feuerbach substitutes for this spirit human feeling and implies that the self is constituted by feeling. To some extent Wagner follows him in this, but the large degree of Hegelianism in the *Ring* negates Feuerbach to some extent; Wagner sometimes seems to think of love as a metaphysical rather than a material force.

Wagner was very much a child of his times not only in the concerns and ideas he developed in his plot but also in his concept of his own role as artist and composer and in the position of music in his drama. It is clear from his writings that Wagner thought of music as a direct, instinctive expression of the self, and in spite of his constituting a social origin for Siegfried (although he is ambiguous on this point), he seems to retain a sense of music as natural or instinctive.

But I would like to argue that music does not express the self in any intuitive way. The problem of the relationship between the subject (the thinking individual) and the object (physical reality) that has occupied philosophy and forms the basis for the plot of the *Ring* is also important in the music. Wagner emphasizes this; he imagines a subject-object relationship between music and poetry. He sees the text as man, music as woman—they find themselves, like Siegmund and Sieglinde, in each other. Thus he affirms the musicality of language (especially in his theories of the origin of language) and the linguistic nature of music (in the leitmotif). He posits music as expression not only of the composer but of the text.

What Wagner fails to notice, however, is that the expressivity of music is, like the self, socially determined. Rather, he imagines that the music expresses *nature*—a human nature that exists prior to and apart from society—just as he sometimes posits such a nature for Siegfried. So for Wagner music takes the part of the hero: it expresses the advanced consciousness of Siegfried as well as of Wagner himself. But because musical meaning is conventionally determined does not mean it can express only conventional notions. Wagner's music is a dialogue between the social expectations of music and his own efforts to transcend or violate these; he creates music that not only speaks to the conventional expectations of his audience but goes beyond these expectations to create new conventions.

Wagner's real contribution lies in the considerable extent to which he was able, in spite of everything, to acknowledge the domination of music by the conventional, especially in linguistic terms. His power lies in his making explicit and exploring the linguistic origin of musical meaning. This acknowledgment tended to free him from musical rules—when he represents Siegfried and Brünnhilde in the last act of *Siegfried* with two different tonalities that reflect each other, he opens the way for the breakdown of tonality itself. And many of his other innovations in harmony and structure stem from his efforts to increase the dramatic function of music *for* the text. The result is a powerful musical language that was enormously influential.

This book examines the *Ring* cycle in light of the historical concerns that Wagner's study of Hegel and Feuerbach brought to his work and simultaneously considers the *Ring* in light of more recent theory. In chapter 1 I discuss Wagner's relation to the thought of his day, attempting to ascertain the extent of Wagner's reading and knowledge of the thought of Hegel and Feuerbach. This chapter also examines the concept of love as Wagner uses it. In chapter 2 I explore the relationship of language to music in the *Ring,* examining music as a form of communication, particularly as used by Wagner in the leitmotif and other forms of musical development peculiar to him. The remaining chapters cover the four operas of the *Ring* cycle itself, arguing that the Feuerbachian I-Thou relationship is the organizing principle of the *Ring* cycle and that the concept of love on which the cycle is based is far more than a sentimental celebration of human passion but is instead derived from specific Hegelian notions of mutual recognition.

Finally, in the conclusion I argue that Wagner's concept of love is inherently flawed. He himself identified with Siegfried and later with Wotan (when he began to see Wotan's renunciation as a heroic gesture) rather than with Brünnhilde, who, as woman, he saw as *in essence* self-sacrificing. In his efforts to define a new concept of the self and open the possibility for a new society, Wagner could not escape the limitations of patriarchal traditions of domination in his own thinking. Thus the *Ring* stands as a moment of reified thought rather than as a revolutionary force.

1

WAGNER, HEGEL, AND FEUERBACH

Wagner is usually considered a disciple of Schopenhauer and Feuerbach rather than Hegel. He expressed his enthusiasm for Feuerbach in letters and conversations and even dedicated his essay "The Art-Work of the Future" (obviously modeled on Feuerbach's *Philosophy of the Future*) to him. After his discovery of the writings of Schopenhauer in 1854, Wagner's philosophical models changed radically; he abandoned the essentially optimistic materialism of Feuerbach for the metaphysical pessimism of Schopenhauer. But before discovering Schopenhauer, Wagner read and studied Hegel, and internal evidence in the *Ring* cycle and *Oper und Drama* shows the influence of Hegel. The issues treated in the *Ring* and in Wagner's contemporary critical writings show that the ideas expressed by Hegel (though in many cases as modified by Feuerbach) had deeply permeated Wagner's consciousness. Although it is likely that many of these ideas came directly from his reading of Hegel as well as Feuerbach, one must not discount the enormous indirect influence Hegelian ideas may have had. During the period of the gestation and writing of the text of the *Ring* cycle, Hegel's dialectical historicism was the predominant mode of thinking in Germany, especially among the group of revolutionaries with whom Wagner was friendly in Dresden.[1] Bakunin, for example, who was interested in the *Ring* and talked with Wagner about it in 1848, was an avid student of Hegel.[2] And no less a figure than Engels gives eloquent testimony to the fact that Hegel's ideas were extremely influential at the time. Hegelian thought, he says, was

> a triumphal procession which lasted for decades and which by no means came to a standstill on the death of Hegel. On the contrary, from 1830–1840 Hegelianism reigned most exclusively, and to a greater or less extent infected even its opponents. It was precisely in this period that Hegelian views, consciously or unconsciously, most

16

extensively permeated the most diversified sciences and saturated even popular literature and the daily press from which the average "educated consciousness" derived its pabulum.[3]

Wagner was certainly part of that educated public. Even Feuerbach's repudiation of Hegel did not counteract Hegel's influence on Wagner. Engels points out that "a philosophy is not disposed of by the mere assertion that it is false"; he argues that such a powerful work as Hegel's would continue to have an enormous influence even though some of its details might be rejected.[4]

That Hegel's influence on Wagner was considerable was suggested by Nietzsche, who should had been in a position to know. Writing after Wagner's death in *The Case of Wagner,* he described him as *"Hegel's* heir. . . . Music as 'idea.' "[5] Additionally, in *The Gay Science* Nietzsche wrote that "until the middle of his life, Richard Wagner allowed himself to be led astray by Hegel,"[6] and in a letter written in 1888 Nietzsche said that now "all Wagnerians are followers of Schopenhauer. This was different when I was young. Then it was the last Hegelians who held onto Wagner, and 'Wagner and Hegel' was still the watchword of the fifties."[7]

Nietzsche seems to be right. The only philosophical work of a modern writer in Wagner's Dresden Library was Hegel's *Introduction to the Philosophy of History.*[8] And a friend of Wagner's Paris days, Friedrich Pecht, mentions in his memoirs that he once visited Wagner in Dresden and found him reading the *Phenomenology of Mind* (although Pecht reports that in spite of his enthusiasm Wagner could not explain the passage he read aloud to his visitor).[9] In *Mein Leben* Wagner gives his own version of reading Hegel, corroborating the enthusiasm and the confusion Pecht recalls:

> For my introduction to the philosophy of Hegel I chose his *Philosophy of History.* Much of this impressed me, and it appeared as if I would gain admittance to the inner sanctum by this route. The more incomprehensible I found many of the most sweeping and speculative sentences of this tremendously famous intellect, who had been commended to me as the keystone of philosophic understanding, the more I felt impelled to get to the bottom of what was termed "the absolute" and everything connected with it.[10]

The revolution, he goes on, interrupted his studies, and he next turned to Feuerbach (to whom he dedicated "The Art-Work of the Future," completed in 1849).[11]

However, by the time he wrote *Mein Leben,* Wagner had lost

some of his earlier enthusiasm not only for Hegel but also for Feuerbach. In the autobiography he finds Feuerbach's work rather thin and says he could not ignore "the sprawl and rather unhelpful prolixity in the development of the simple basic idea, the interpretation of religion from a purely psychological standpoint."[12] Nevertheless, he says that his reading of Feuerbach was most important to him as "the proponent of the ruthlessly radical liberation" from authority. He testifies that he found in Feuerbach the courage to renounce philosophy altogether and to go his own way; Feuerbach's conclusion that "the best philosophy is to have no philosophy at all" was important to him because, he says, it made the study of philosophy "immeasurably easier." Also, he says that he liked Feuerbach's idea that "spirit" lies in the "aesthetic perceptions of the tangible world"[13] (in opposition to Hegel's abstract reason as spirit). He goes on to say that he had already studied Schelling and Hegel but that Feuerbach's criticism of Hegel affirmed an opinion he had drawn independently: "As a matter of fact, I had already been struck by the verdict of an English critic, who had candidly confessed that his obscure but unconvinced respect for German philosophy had been attributable to its utter incomprehensibility, as represented most recently by the works of Hegel."[14]

To some extent, then, Wagner was merely following a trend in criticizing Hegel, who had fallen into general disfavor in the German reading public by the time Wagner published *Mein Leben* in the 1870s. Engels, in his book on Feuerbach, notes that earlier the metaphysical questions that interested Hegel, such as those concerning the contradiction between subject and object, between nature and mind, were much in discussion, and the influence of the Hegelian system was all-important. "Then came Feuerbach's *Essence of Christianity*," says Engels, describing it as a book that did away with the contradiction between subject and object and put materialism on the throne again: "The spell was broken. The 'system' was exploded and cast aside. And the contradiction, shown to exist only in our imagination, was dissolved. One must himself have experienced the liberating effect of this book to get an idea of it. Enthusiasm was general; we all became at once Feuerbachians."[15] Like Wagner, Engels goes on to criticize Feuerbach's writing, decrying his "literary, sometimes even highflown, style," which he says made the book more popular than perhaps it deserved, but he says that it was "at any rate refreshing after long years of abstract and abstruse Hegelianizing. The same is true of its extravagant deification of love, which, coming after the intolerable rule of 'pure reason,' had its excuse, if not justification" (pp. 18–19). What Feuerbach showed about Hegel, says Engels, was that the idea of the absolute spirit as a force that exists before and apart from material reality was nothing but a "fantastic survival" of the belief in God. Feuerbach argued, in contradistinction to Hegel, that "matter is not a product of mind, but mind itself is merely the highest product of matter. This is, of course, pure materialism" (pp. 24–25). Feuerbach's rejection of metaphysics and celebration of sensuous reality, which Engels describes as important to the development of Marxism, also influenced Wagner's ideas deeply.

However, we should not take Wagner's disavowal of Hegelian idealism too seriously. Wagner did, as he testifies in *Mein Leben,* attempt to come to an understanding of Hegel's metaphysics, the metaphysics that was the subject of discussion among the educated Germans at the time. In the Hegelian scheme presented in the *Phenomenology,* a book that Wagner studied carefully, the world is ultimately a rational place. Hegel postulated that a metaphysical force (the exact status of which depends on the interpreter) exists as absolute spirit. This spirit Hegel postulates as necessary, because the things of this world cannot exist alone since they are contradictory: they can only be understood as parts of the whole. Thus this metaphysical reality, or spirit, must be the explanation that unites the contradictions of the world—and spirit is, according to Hegel, reason. Further, Hegel says, a philosophical argument must start from finite reality—from matter itself—and progress to spirit. In the *Phenomenology,* he felt that he must show that finite reality has to exist; it has to exist in order to realize spirit. Thus for Hegel God or *Geist* (spirit) is grounded in necessity and in physical reality.[16]

Wagner repeats this notion of necessity in "The Art-Work of the Future":

> Nature engenders her myriad forms without caprice or arbitrary aim *("absichtlos und unwillkürlich"),* according to her need *("Bedürfniss"),* and therefore of Necessity *(Notwendigkeit).* This same Necessity is the generative and formative force of human life. Only that which is uncapricious and un-arbitrary can spring from a real need, but on Need alone is based the very principle of Life.[17]

The idea that Wagner takes from Hegel here is that the material forms of nature are necessary because the spirit must create them in order to *be* spirit. These forms, as Wagner goes on, are the forms of human life also: this is the major thesis of the *Phe-*

nomenology in its explorations of the stages of human life and history. Wagner also suggests, a little later in "The Art-Work of the Future," that "the more truthful is Knowledge, the more frankly must it recognize that its whole existence hangs upon its own coherence with that which has come to actual, finished, and fulfilled manifestation to the senses, and thus admit its own possibility of existence as *a priori* conditioned by actuality" (p. 79). Thus Wagner makes a stand with Hegel for the importance of material existence, for starting with the natural world as it exists. But Wagner rejects spirit as the aim of knowledge (or consciousness) and substitutes physical reality itself, joining Feuerbach and others in judging Hegel not to have escaped idealism and to have created his philosophy as a disguised religion in which the term "absolute spirit" is merely substituted for the term "God."

If absolute spirit did not appeal to Wagner, however, many aspects of Hegel's thought did.[18] One of these was the dramatic, narrative outline Hegel suggests for history. As Charles Taylor describes the structure of the *Phenomenology,* Hegel has created a philosophical story that must have caught Wagner's imagination:

> Like the finite subject, the absolute subject must go through a cycle, a drama, in which it suffers division in order to return to unity. It undergoes inner opposition, in order to overcome it, and rise through its vehicles to a consciousness of itself as rational necessity. And this drama is not another parallel story to the drama of opposition and reconciliation in man. It is the same one seen from a different and wider perspective. For man is the vehicle of *Geist's* spiritual life.[19]

This dramatic movement of necessity through division and opposition forms the basis of the plot not only of the *Phenomenology* but also of the *Ring.* The *Phenomenology* moves from the individual's simple apprehension of reality, of *things,* to his awareness that he must know himself if he is to know the world. So he seeks knowledge of what humanity itself is, a knowledge that usually eludes him. Hegel outlined various stages of individual and social life, as well as the failures of societies and institutions that have blocked self-awareness, in the belief that the failures themselves are instructive.[20] These stages are repeated at various levels in the *Phenomenology,* a repetition that also occurs in the *Ring* cycle, where each opera, each character, and each new situation suggests many parallels with what has gone before. But the repetitions are always with a difference; the movement of the *Ring,* like that of the *Phenomenology,* is a spiral, not a circle.

Wagner, like many of his contemporaries, took to heart Hegel's notion of history. It is, as Gadamer suggests, a vision of the world that is quite different from the Enlightenment vision that preceded it: for Hegel, "the real world exists precisely as continual change, *constant* change."[21] Similarly, Engels pays tribute to Hegel's concept of history, in which

> all successive historical situations are only transitory stages in the endless course of development of human society from the lower to the higher. Each state is necessary, therefore justified for the time and conditions to which it owes its origin. But in the newer and higher conditions which gradually develop in its own bosom, each loses its validity and justification. It must give way to a higher form which will also in its turn decay and perish.[22]

Along the same lines, Richard Rorty, evaluating Hegel in light of his critique of philosophical foundationalism, writes that

> Hegel made unforgettably clear the deep self-certainty given by each achievement of a new vocabulary, each new genre, each new style, each new dialectical synthesis—the sense that now, at least, for the first time, we have grasped things as they truly are. He also made unforgettably clear why such certainty lasts but a moment. He showed how the passion which sweeps through each generation serves the cunning of reason, providing the impulse which drives that generation to self-immolation and transformation.[23]

Wagner too valued the Hegelian notion that self-certainty is open to attack (though he perhaps limited this attack in ways with which neither Hegel nor Rorty would agree). Wagner's Hegelian notion of the stages of history being inevitably transformed and destroyed by the very forces that make them for a time seem so right and complete is reflected in the stages that he develops in the *Ring* cycle, where history is seen as a dialectic of the progress, not of Hegelian spirit but of Wagnerian love.

This vision of the individual as part of a general process of becoming was Hegel's view of history, a vision in which individuals create a history of consciousness that spirals ever upward toward more complete self-realization. Hegel found this self-realization in absolute spirit, in rationality. But Wagner read Hegel selectively; what Wagner rejected in Hegel was what Feuerbach and other critics rejected, the overall metaphysical system that Hegel sees as driving history. Wagner replaces metaphysical spirit with love (whereas Marx rejects spirit entirely and concentrates on the Hegelian dialectic of history). Wagner refrains for the most part from turning love into a synonym for Hegel's spirit, keeping it in the material realm, although the exact status of love as a concept is sometimes unclear in the *Ring*. However, Wagner's adaptation of Hegel's dialectic is somewhat more complex than his use of Hegel's vision of history: it is clear that Wagner understood Hegel's contention that every stage of consciousness contains its own negativity, which will eventually destroy it. Wagner constructed the *Ring* on a general principle of negativity—the ring itself represents the absence or negativity of love, its antithesis.

One aspect of Hegel's thought that Wagner usually seems to accept is the notion of the hero and of his place in history. Wagner's heroes reflect this Hegelian concept rather than a notion more common to romanticism, which suggests that the hero, the strong individual, opposes (rather than epitomizes) the general trend of history. For Hegel, the individual is both subject and object of history. That is, as object he is created by social forces and merely acts out an inevitable role, while as subject he is a free, self-determining individual. For other romantic writers, however, the individual frequently stands independent of social forces except in a superficial way. Nevertheless, Wagner was not always clear on this point and vacillates between these two definitions of the hero. Wagner sometimes, in Hegelian fashion, sees the hero as instrument rather than instigator of history. Only such a concept can make sense of Siegfried, who is victim as much as hero. In many ways, however, Siegfried is pictured as independent of his society, as the romantic hero who opposes history.

World history, then, for Hegel is often worked out by these heroes, who are simply people who possess a better understanding of the movement of spirit than their fellows and who are the instruments of that spirit in reshaping the world.[24] Wagner's conception of the artist and artistic genius seems derived from this notion. He seems to have pictured himself, like Siegfried, as the Hegelian world-historic figure and tended to see himself as the hero of his own works. In "A Communication to My Friends" he describes the process of creation in Hegelian terms, noting that in choosing Siegfried "I had entered a new and most decisive period of my evolution, both as artist and as man: the period of *conscious artistic will* to continue on an altogether novel path, which I had struck with unconscious necessity, and whereon I now, as man and artist, press on to meet a newer world."[25] Here Wagner sees himself as part of the stages of consciousness that are, in the Hegelian scheme, constantly forging newer and better ways of being. Wagner goes on in the "Communication" to say that only the person who has come to possess a *"reasonable Will* (ver-nünftigen Willen)" which he defines as "the willing of the recognized Spontaneous and Natural,"—only such a person can foresee a better future or even understand the past or the present (p. 279). Wagner evidently sees himself as the possessor of Hegelian spirit or superior consciousness; however, he goes on in the "Communication" to say that he is not claiming the title of genius for himself. Rather, he says, genius is the ability of the individual to be receptive to the impressions and perceptions of present life ("the force of the receptive faculty").[26] The artist is the person who "gives himself up without reserve to the impressions which move his emotional being *(Empfindungswesen)* to sympathy." A little later, he says that what brings this force to "full productiveness . . . is the Art already evolved outside that separate force, the Art which from the artworks of the ancient and the modern world has shaped itself into a universal Substance, and hand in hand with actual Life, reacts upon the individual with the character of the force that I have elsewhere named the *communistic*" (pp. 286–88). This argues for a modern view of the artistic work as an amalgam between the traditional forces of genre and history and the individual energy and circumstance of the artist and is in line with Wagner's view of operatic development in *Oper und Drama,* in which the history of opera is presented as a dialectic with his own works the culmination of the process.

In *Oper und Drama,* then, Wagner pictures himself as the artist-hero of a historic process in which the music drama emerges as the superior form of expression, the "art-work of the future." *Oper und Drama* is a dialectical history in which both absolute music and poetry are shown to be inadequate for various reasons—music because it is too vague, poetry and drama because they are too specific, too entangled in history, and too devoid of feeling or instinct. Finally, in the third part of the essay, Wagner analyzes the contributions each artistic form can make to the other, postulating a synthesis that will be so successful in raising the listeners' consciousness to new levels that the new art form will actually "anull the State."[27] In this work, Wagner explores speech and music from an initial unity through historic separation to a new, more conscious unity (pp. 224–350), following the Hegelian model for history. He analyzes each previous type of opera as lacking something, and even holds that Shakespeare is deficient in that his dramas are strong on poetic realization of ideas but cramped in limitations of time and space; time and space, argues Wagner, were opened out in Racinian drama, but in Racine the real physical world was slighted. The music drama, he suggests, can resolve all these difficulties; he sees the music drama as a culmination of the separated and incomplete developments of poetry, music, and theater in the past (p. 127). And he evidently intended, in the *Ring*, to create a music drama that would culminate this historical process.

The *Ring*, then, would on one level form a synthesis of dialectical processes inherent in the history of art and on another explore equivalent processes in the individual and society. In *Oper und Drama* he wrote about the "march of this evolution" of the individual, which is "a progress to the winning of the highest human faculty; and it is travelled, not merely by Mankind in general, but substantially by every social Individual" (p. 224). In the character of Siegfried, he said in a letter to Röckel, "I have sought to portray my ideal of the perfect human being, whose highest consciousness manifests itself in the fact that all consciousness can find expression only in living and acting in the present."[28] Siegfried was intended to embody Hegel's notion of consciousness at its highest individual stage.

The Hegelian idea of the hero, exemplified in Siegfried, as one who expresses spirit better than his contemporaries and therefore is the object of history, is related to the Hegelian notion of fate. From the standpoint of the individual, the events that happen to him are his fate, different from the events he participates in himself; he is instrument of a force greater than himself. From this point of view, the injunction to reconcile oneself with fate can only be seen as a call for submission or surrender. But in Hegel's view, the call of fate should be seen instead as the demand felt by the individual to reach a greater understanding of the rationality and rightness of the cosmic movement: "To be united to infinite spirit, even more to see oneself as its vehicle, would be to recognize in one's fate an expresion of a reality from which one could not dissociate oneself."[29] Thus in the *Ring* Siegmund is the first of the human characters called to a fate that is represented as a reality greater than himself but serves to forward the progress of spirit in the world. Wagner associates a particular melodic fragment with this notion, and wherever this "fate" motive reappears, it is meant to remind us not of the tragic destiny of the characters involved but of their role as instruments of the force of love making its way in the world.

In Hegel, then, the individual, caught in this history of the changing forms of spirit, is also caught in the dialectic process that spirit creates. The result is a series of stages of consciousness, stages that individual persons and groups of people must go through in order to achieve the next higher state. The *Phenomenology*, according to Shklar, is really "an historical psychology of the conscious mind, and also a justification of such a science."[30] This historical psychology is what Wagner tried to develop in his own way in the *Ring*.

Domination and Mutual Recognition

The Hegelian concept of history that Wagner at least partly espoused differed from the prevailing notion of revolution common to the romantics. Hegel's stages of consciousness, which he felt that every individual, every society, and finally humankind itself must go through, presented a new idea of the revolution that his romantic contemporaries felt so important. But earlier romantics were unable to grasp that real freedom is impossible without the development of a new mode of consciousness: "independence and dependence are indissolubly linked parts of a single, self-divided consciousness, a continuation of the see-saw of dominion and bondage. These are not really alternatives. The one cannot and does not overcome the other. Freedom must be found in a far more radical change of human self-consciousness, in a genuine 'recognition' among egos."[31] Thus for Hegel, and for Wagner, simply revolting against the status quo, simply reverting to a natural sense of identity and freedom, is not adequate. Instead, the individual must go through the various stages of consciousness in order to achieve a higher concept of freedom and individuality itself. Wagner borrowed not only Hegel's idea of the stages of consciousness but his grasp of the importance of patterns of domination in history; and in the *Ring* cycle Wagner chose to concentrate on two distinctive social relationships that Hegel discussed: that between the master and slave and that between two individuals who mutually recognize themselves in each other. Wagner adopts Hegel's idea of mutual recognition as an important part of his definition of love and the domination of the master-slave relationship as an important preliminary stage. Thus his two pairs of lovers, Siegmund/Sieglinde and Siegfried/Brünnhilde, achieve mutual recognition; Siegfried, to some extent, goes even further and attempts to make mutual recognition, as Hegel felt it must be made, the basis of all social relationships.[32]

Mutual recognition is one of the most important concepts in Wagner's model for the *Ring*, Hegel's *Phenomenology*. In it, according to Shklar's summary, there are five complete cycles of human relationships.[33] In the first, the unsocialized individual depends on sense impressions. Although the natural mind finally comes to understand these, it begins the progress toward self-understanding as a social being only when it sees that understanding depends ultimately on its own mind. The second cycle, Hegel's cycle of self-consciousness, begins when the individual ego recognizes in itself desire both for self-sufficiency and social interaction. There is, however, always the possibility of a split between these two aims, and Hegel shows a series of historical experiences to demonstrate how this split works and how independent, asocial men cannot close the contradictions of their lives by themselves. He begins with separation of men into masters and servants. Then a new cycle begins, one in which the individual learns to use natural reason—that is, he observes nature and learns from it. However, this kind of reason is destined to fail, according to Hegel, because it moves from observing nature to looking at other humans as if they also were physical objects—self-sufficient reason, for Hegel, cannot help but see humans as *things*. Then begins a new cycle of reason, this time of moral reason or subjectivity. But individuals who practice moral reason also fail because they find that they cannot exist without society; moral reason is too self-centered for success.

Of course it would be a mistake to attempt to hold the *Ring* cycle too closely to this model. I have already mentioned and will explore in more detail later how Wagner rejected Hegel's central concept—reason—and replaced it with love. But he did use much of the structure and thought of the *Phenomenology*. Hegel's first stage of consciousness is represented in various ways by most of the characters in *Das Rheingold*. The gods hold sense impressions to be most important—they cannot imagine, as Wotan later tells Fricka, a world that does not actually exist. But in some ways the world of *Das Rheingold* reflects the second stage also, particularly in Loge, who is similar to Hegel's skeptic, and in Wotan, who at the end of this opera and in *Die Walküre* begins to emerge into the second stage, realizing that his own view of reality depends on his own perceptions (though he is rather slow to come to this realization and attempts to maintain a relationship of dominance with Brünnhilde). Mutual recognition, and with it a real understanding of consciousness, appears first with Siegmund and Sieglinde, only to be destroyed. But their relationship produces Siegfried, who represents the new self-consciousness, informed by love and learning from nature; he is the hope for the new movement of spirit in the world. However, he too is doomed to failure because the society into which he is thrust in *Götterdämmerung* is not ready: it seems difficult to understand this last opera and its place in the cycle without Hegel's idea that the hero, the individual best embodying the new self-consciousness of spirit, cannot exist alone. Rather, a new society of such individuals must be formed. This is the realization that Brünnhilde comes to at the end, and the point at which the *Ring* breaks off, leaving open the question of whether such a society can become reality.

For Hegel, the individual subject only comes to understand itself and its place in the world through understanding the object—physical reality. Real understanding, however, comes only from the recognition that other humans are both objects—they exist as things independent of the observer—and other subjects—they exist as autonomous consciousness. In a state of self-certainty the individual subject is convinced of the nothingness of the object (that is, a person becomes convinced that nothing exists outside one's own consciousness); however, in such a state of mind it is inevitable that the subject will eventually experience the object in some way that causes a sudden realization that the object has an independent existence of its own.[34] This will occur only when the object is in fact another human. That is, in order to break out of this cycle of self-sufficiency that blocks further growth of consciousness, the individual must come to know the other as a person, as something more than a thing. And this happens, according to Hegel, at the risk of losing his or her life. True freedom from solipsistic subjectivity, according to Hegel, depends on this point, because until individual self-consciousness is willing to lose itself (by risking death) it cannot really come to know itself as an independent self-consciousness. Without this risk, the person sees him or herself as alive but fails to grasp that true human essence is to be a free and independent agent (p. 233).

Such recognition of the object as another person, and hence the subject as autonomous, is for Wagner a love relationship. Wagner, in a letter to Röckel, repeats the Hegelian notion of the relationship of the subject to the object exactly: "Egoism comes to an end only in the merging of the 'I' ('Ich') with the 'thou' ('Du'), but the 'thou' does not present itself at once when I place myself in conjunction with the whole world: 'I' and 'the world' is nothing more than 'I' alone; the world becomes fully actual for me only when it has become for me a 'thou,' and thus it becomes only in the presence of a beloved individual."[35] For Wagner, as for Hegel, the other must be seen as an autonomous subject in order to bring "egoism" to an end, but for Wagner that other autonomous subject is not just anyone, but the "beloved."

In explaining Hegelian ideas to Röckel, Wagner fails to credit Hegel, perhaps because, as Engels said, such ideas were simply "in the air" or because his terminology also comes from Feuerbach here. But the extent to which Wagner has absorbed Hegel is clear. For example, he demonstrates the importance of Hegel's idea of mutual recognition in *Oper und Drama* when he argues that "the Feeling stays cold amid the reflections of Understanding: only the reality of an object kindred to itself can warm it into interest. This object must be the sympathetic image of the instinctive doer's own nature" (p. 207). In that essay, Wagner also applies the Hegelian idea of mutual recognition to the function of art itself: "Art, by the very meaning of the term, is nothing but the fulfillment of a longing to know oneself in the likeness of an object of one's love or adoration, to find oneself again in the things of the outer world, thus conquered by their representment" (p. 155).

Much of Wagner's development of the ideas of freedom and love in the *Ring* cycle comes not only from Hegel's concept of mutual recognition but also from the famous master-slave passage in the *Phenomenology*. This section, though it consists of only a few pages, was enormously influential in Marx's development of his ideas of the importance of labor. In Hegel's overall scheme, this passage is less important than it is for Marx, but it has a drama and interest to which Wagner must have responded. In Hegel, the master-slave relationship is seen as the first step from a state of nature to a stage of social life prior to mutual recognition. The human individual, as a natural being equipped with sense-certainty but not self-consciousness, encounters other humans, whom he at first assumes to be natural objects. He therefore treats them as objects, using and enslaving them. The master-slave relationship develops when two humans meet in the first, Ur-social contact. Each individual consciousness attempts to treat the other as a natural object; the other naturally resists, and a battle ensues. The result of this battle is either that one of the two is killed or that one of the two is enslaved. If one is killed, of course, society and consciousness have not progressed. However, if one is enslaved, the ensuing social relationship gives rise eventually to a further development of consciousness. Therefore, for Hegel the master-slave relationship is a necessary step in the development of society.

The master-slave relationship is extremely important because in the *Phenomenology* "the master is the consciousness that exists *for itself;* but no longer merely the general notion of existence for self." That is, the individual no longer exists as a being unaware of itself. Rather, its existence is mediated through that of another person (pp. 234–35); the individual achieves a degree of self-knowledge through this relationship. Thus the master obtains recognition for his or her consciousness from the slave; however, there is no growth because as master he or she becomes simply a consumer, passively content with life. The master-slave relationship is flawed for the master because the master does not learn to recognize the existence of the slave as an autonomous agent (continuing to see him or her as a *thing*), though the master feels autonomous because of the way the slave reacts to the master's own consciousness.

Hegel's interpretation of the consciousness of the master, then, pictures the person who practices domination over others as incompletely human. Slavery, according to Hegel, does not work because it is antithetical to reason. The person who feels like the master of others suffers from a flawed self-awareness and misunderstands the situation. For while the master feels autonomous, he or she actually depends upon the slave not only as a servant but for his or her very identity, since without a slave there can be no master. The loss of slaves for such an individual would mean a loss of identity because of this self-definition in terms of the 'thing' owned. In addition, by allowing the slave to work with physical reality and in separating himself, as lord, from labor, the master has reduced his or her own sphere of activity merely to thinking rather than acting. Now a passive consumer rather than an active creator, the master has lost the ability to attain true human fulfillment.[36]

Wagner pictures the master most clearly in the character of Wotan, who moves from this role in the first two operas of the *Ring* to being a purely passive observer in the last two. However, for Wagner as for Hegel, the slave, not the master, is the real instrument of a new consciousness. The experience of slavery is essential for Hegel, who argues that the progress toward self-realization cannot be forwarded by the master because this lack of self-identity and passivity is a trap. Instead, the slave is the individual who gains new insights from the master-slave relationship. Hegel suggests that the experience of slavery forces the slave into a reversal of consciousness: "being a consciousness pressed within itself, it will enter into itself, and change round into real and true independence" (p. 237). That is, paradoxically, independence and freedom for Hegel were possible only for those individuals who have developed their consciousness in the experience of bondage.

For Wagner, who always converts Hegelian thought from a goal of reason to one of love, the servant is not the proletariat, as for Marx, but woman in her traditional roles of wife and lover. Hegel's description of the necessary psychology of the slave sounds something like the necessary psychology of woman as Wagner uses it. For Hegel, the slave is the candidate for the new consciousness because he or she has known fear: the slave's consciousness

> has been in that experience melted to its inmost soul, has trembled throughout its every fibre, and all that was fixed and steadfast has quaked within it. This complete perturbation of its entire substance, this absolute dissolution of all its stability into fluent continuity, is, however, the simple, ultimate nature of self-consciousness, absolute negativity, pure self-referent existence, which consequently is involved in this type of consciousness. (P. 237)

This is what happens to Brünnhilde, and to love in general, in moving from Freia's capture to Brünnhilde's immolation. Women in the *Ring* are the natural subjects of domination and fear. Brünnhilde truly quakes and fears for her life under Wotan's wrath, but she conquers this negativity of being (symbolized by her long sleep), rising to a new self-consciousness that her own fear has taught her. However, fear, a necessary part of the slave psychology, is exactly what Wagner removed from his Hegelian concept of the hero as it appears in Siegfried; instead, Brünnhilde learns fear *for* Siegfried and passes her "wisdom," the knowledge she has gained through fear, to him.

The master-slave relationship also emphasizes the slave as the one who has a new relationship with nature or physical reality. While the master, whose physical needs are met by the slave, becomes more and more remote from reality, the slave learns the resistant objectivity of things and comes to have respect and love for physical reality. He or she learns to shape things into new forms, and in dealing with reality learns something about his or her own consciousness: "in fashioning the thing, self-existence comes to be felt explicitly as his own proper being, and he attains the consciousness that he himself exists in its own right and on its own account *(an und für sich)*" (p. 239). Through labor the slave comes to an awareness of his or her own independence. Labor, though not so important in Wagner as in Marx, is a recurring theme in the *Ring* cycle. The relationship with objects describes, among other things, the relationship of Alberich and Mime—

Mime as slave forms the tarnhelm and develops the independence from Alberich he needs to carry on in later stages (though he later fails to form the sword). And Siegfried represents a higher stage of development than Siegmund in part because he recreates the sword rather than simply claiming it.

The emphasis on physical reality in the master-slave relationship is related to Hegel's concept of nature itself. Physical reality, or nature, is transformed by the slave's labor into objects that reflect human consciousness. It is important to realize that Wagner was following a Hegelian notion of nature. The natural world at the beginning of *Das Rheingold* and as it appears at various other points in the cycle is usually taken as a simple, romantic image of nature as something separate from and independent of human lives. But in fact, nature is represented in the *Ring* cycle not by the image of the Rhine, the forest, and the various storms alone, but also by the nature goddesses: Erda, the Norns, and the Rhinedaughters (Brünnhilde belongs to this group too). These women represent a natural world that has already been radically transformed by human consciousness; the natural world into which Alberich steps in the first scene of *Das Rheingold* is already a social world with a human history, and the long-held E-flat chord represents a negative, not a positive force. For Wagner as for Hegel, there is no simple relationship between humans and nature. Hegel argues, for example, in the *Phenomenology* that people do not interact with reality (nature) in a unitary moment-to-moment fashion, but that "we have to put the *whole* of sense-certainty as its essential reality, and no longer merely one of its moments" (p. 155). Nature is treated in the *Ring* cycle as a whole, and to accept one of its moments, as at the beginning of *Das Rheingold,* as the definition of nature in the entire work is to underestimate Wagner's plan. The ring is the symbol of this wholeness of nature in man's experience: as gold, it has the immediate sense-certainty of a momentary experience, but as ring, it exists as world-power because it suggests transformed nature that models an inadequate human consciousness and is already, even before the second scene, opposed to love and the new consciousness. But by the end of *Götterdämmerung* it has been transformed, as symbol, still further, and has moved into harmony with love.

The key to the human relation to nature and to physical reality for Hegel is desire: the unself-conscious natural mind is satisfied with the reality of natural things, but the developing mind experiences desire. This occurs because the subject experiences desire for the object: the individual can only progress in growth and self-realization by interacting with the other, either as a physical thing or as another consciousness (p. 159). Desire in the *Ring* cycle comes into the world with Alberich; the natural world represented by the unshaped gold in the Rhine river is an object of desire for him. He however attempts to consume it by reshaping it (a figure repeated on a higher level when Siegfried reshapes the sword fragments). Desire is transformed through Brünnhilde's experience as slave in a master-slave relationship with Wotan and through the mutual recognition of the separated twins into sexual desire, something Hegel never envisioned as central to human progress in the world, but which Wagner of course does.

Society and the New Consciousness

The voyage of the desiring ego in the *Ring* cycle follows a clear movement from the allegorical exploration of the relationship of desire, nature, and domination in *Das Rheingold* through the development of love and the new consciousness in *Die Walküre* and *Siegfried*. In *Götterdämmerung*, however, the progress becomes less clear. In order to understand exactly what Wagner attempted in *Götterdämmerung*, we need to understand a little of Hegel's concept of society and social behavior. His scheme is essentially one of social progress in history; the stages of individual consciousness outlined in the first part of the *Phenomenology* are an abstraction, a symbol of the historical progress of which they are a part. For Hegel, the individual does not progress outside of society, except perhaps at the most primitive levels; to be human for Hegel is to be social. Social behavior, which constitutes history, consists of the customs of people built up from their intuitive realization of spirit at whatever stage they find themselves; Hegel saw *Geist* as the spirit of a people, and Wagner reflected this idea in his dedication of the *Ring* to the spirit of the German people. However, for Hegel this social law, reflected in ethics, was always flawed, because the people's grasp of spirit at any one stage in history was incomplete. Hegel suggested that the hero or world-historic figure, entering into a flawed society, provides the impetus to move society to the next stage. Thus in the *Phenomenology* self-realization becomes not an individual project but a social one.

The goal of the mutual recognition of one free and autonomous agent with another is then for Hegel the development of a society of such individuals. Hegel does not stop with individual

development but emphasizes that individuals live as parts of societies and that the role of the individual is both determined and
limited by the society he or she lives in. Wagner adopted this idea;
the *Ring* cycle is about the movement from the arrogance of
Alberich and Wotan, in their different ways, through the struggle
for mutual self-recognition in love with Siegmund and Sieglinde,
toward a world in which this mutual recognition could become the
norm, the social reality—suggested at least by Brünnhilde and
Siegfried. One of the most difficult things about the *Ring* cycle is
to understand the role that *Götterdämmerung* plays in the totality;
many people more or less agree with Shaw in his opinion that the
philosophical issues become less important in this opera, which is
more like a usual operatic story of love and betrayal.[37] To some it
would have seemed more logical for Siegfried and Brünnhilde to
continue their love relationship, to enjoy the triumph of mutual
recognition and love, and to overcome somehow, in their heroic
status, the temptations and machinations of evil in *Götterdämmerung,* an ending that Wagner considered using. Indeed, Wagner
began his *Ring* project with this opera, called *Siegfrieds Tod;* the
image of individual heroism betrayed and destroyed was his original idea and remains central to the concepts of the *Ring* cycle.

To some extent the difficulty in understanding *Götterdämmerung*
is a result of Wagner's lack of clarity. Certainly presenting his
philosophical ideas in allegorical form in *Das Rheingold* and the
other operas was somewhat easier than working them out in the
more realistic setting of the last opera. Thus *Götterdämmerung* may
reflect Wagner's unwillingness to choose between the romantic
concept of the hero as one who changes history and the Hegelian
concept in which the hero is an instrument of history. Yet Hegel
was not deterministic; he did not deny all autonomy to the individual. He felt that the working out of absolute spirit was syn-
onymous with autonomy, a concept that Feuerbach, characterizing
it as religious, rejected. Wagner in his prose commentary sometimes seems to retain the Hegelian concept of the importance of
history and the spirit of a people, with the hero as one who is the
advance guard of that spirit. At other times, however, he seems to
opt for a romantic notion of the hero as separate from society,
characterizing the state, by which he means institutionalized
power, rather than society as that against which the hero must
struggle. This ambivalence toward the role of the hero is reflected
in Siegfried and his history.

Wagner attempts to suggest in Siegfried an individual who is
created in natural law, outside of society, and who is betrayed

when he attempts to bring that natural law into a social setting. Wagner suggested in *Oper und Drama* that the position of the hero in society is much less clear than the position of the hero in nature:

> The Nature-necessity utters itself the strongest and the most invincibly in the physical life-bent *(Lebenstrieb)* of the *Individual,*—less understandably, however, and more open to arbitrary interpretings, in the *ethical view of society* by which the instinctive impulse of the State-included Individual is finally influenced or judged. The life-bent of the Individual utters itself forever *newly* and *directly,* but the essence of Society is *use and wont* and its "view" a *mediated* one. Wherefore the "view" of Society, so long as it does not fully comprehend the essence of the Individual and its own genesis there from, is a hindering and a shackling one; and it becomes ever more tyrannical, in exact degree as the quickening and innovating essence of the Individual brings its instinctive thrust to battle against habit. (P. 179)

A society ruled by convention hinders and shackles not only Siegfried but, earlier, Siegmund and even Wotan.

However, Hegel criticizes the natural intuitive goodness on which morality is commonly supposed to be based and that Wagner assumes of Siegfried. Hegel refuses to acknowledge the adequacy of spontaneous goodness, for if the individual believes in his own intuitive goodness, he will not really be motivated by universal good but only by his own notion of it.[38] This is a criticism of a basic Enlightenment idea that humans are naturally good. A society based on mutual recognition then would, for Hegel, not be identical with one based on law derived from intuitive goodness. Yet this is exactly the type of society Wagner seems to advocate at the end of *Götterdämmerang*.

Hegel calls sentimentality of the type Siegfried exhibits the "law of the heart." This is a form of self-consciousness that thinks that it has moral right on its side but cannot finally deal with reality. Hegel suggests in the *Phenomenology* that this sentimental, emotional goodness must always fail when placed in opposition to social reality, because the society of which it is a part must necessarily be built on a false concept of law: "This reality is thus on the one hand a law by which the particular individuality is crushed and oppressed, a violent ordinance of the world that contradicts the law of the heart, and, on the other hand, a humanity suffering under that ordinance—a humanity that does not follow the law of the heart, but is subjected to an alien necessity" (p. 391). The law of the heart fails because it is not a universal social law, because the two realms, individual feeling and social reality, have not yet come together. Thus in an imperfect society, the good-hearted person, even when acting according to an individual understanding of ethical behavior, "brings about, not *his* law, but—since the realization is inherently and implicitly his own, but explicitly alien and external—merely this: he gets involved and entangled in the actual ordinance, and, indeed, entangled in it, not merely as something alien to himself but as a hostile, overpowering dominion" (p. 393). That is, the individual, though motivated to act by his or her own realization of goodness, is still acting individually: Hegel's ethics must be realized in a social scheme in which *all* individuals act according to self-realization. Goodness must be external, not internal.

The reason the individual law of the heart fails is that it is met by other laws of hearts, other individuals, each of whom, instead of existing for the good of all, assumes that what is good for the self *is* the good of all (pp. 395–96). Hegel goes on to say that when the individual realizes that the law of the heart must be overthrown, he or she rages and puts the blame on others. Wagner suggests that Hegel's law of the heart exists as love: not love as mutual recognition (which Siegfried abandons when he takes Hagen's potion), but love as the individual good feeling and intuitive goodness Siegfried also embodies. When Brünnhilde sees that this kind of love is not enough (because of Siegfried's betrayal) she rages indeed. But she finally comes to the realization that the whole thing—the ring, power, property, masters and slaves, the gods themselves—must be overthrown so that other people can follow Siegfried's path. Though Siegfried and Brünnhilde perish, the love they represent will, presumably, find its way into the world. Thus Wagner seems to suggest in Siegfried both the law of the heart—intuitive goodness—and the advanced consciousness created by mutual recognition—the wisdom and love Siegfried learns from Brünnhilde.

Wagner, however, is not always clear about the problem of love in society. He sometimes seems to believe, with Hegel, that the individual must exist and develop within society and must fail when attempting to act alone. In *Oper und Drama* he stresses what he calls "a *conscious* individuality—i.e., an individuality which determines us in this one particular case, to act *so* and not otherwise"; that is, an individuality that reflects the lessons learned from mutual recognition, an individuality that is more than simple good-heartedness. This kind of individuality, he says, is developed only in society, not in nature: this individuality "we win alone within society, which brings us first the case in which we have to form decisions. The Individual without Society is completely unthinkable by us, *as* an individuality; for first in intercourse with other individuals, is shewn the thing wherein we differ from them, wherein we are peculiar to ourselves" (pp. 195–96). Yet when he goes on, he seems to opt after all for a possibility in which the individual is developed outside society:

> No one can depict an individuality, without the surrounding which conditions *(bedingt)* it as such: if this Surrounding was a natural one, giving ample breathing-space to the development of the individuality, and freely, elastically, and instinctively shaping *itself* anew by contact with that individuality—then this Surrounding could be truly and strikingly denoted in the simplest of outlines; for only through an exhibition of the Individuality had the Surrounding, itself, to gain its characteristic idiosyncrasy. The State, however, is no such flexible, elastic Surrounding, but a stiff, dogmatic, fettering and domineering might; which lays down for the individual in advance, "So shalt thou think and deal!" The State has assumed the education of the individual's character: it takes possession of him already in the mother's womb, through foreordaining him an unequal share in the means toward social self-dependence; by forcing its *morale* upon him, it takes away the instinctiveness of his viewing; and it appoints to him, as *its* property, the standing he is to take toward his surrounding. (P. 196)

Thus he seems to suggest that the hero can come into society from a place outside it—a very un-Hegelian notion—and attempts to show Siegfried's early life as occurring outside the state.

To some extent the confusion lies in the distinction Wagner draws between *society,* by which he means a small fellowship of humans, and the *state,* by which he means all political and religious institutions (later in *Oper und Drama,* he argues that a true individuality formed away from the influence of the State might be indeed be imagined by the poet but could not be presented in conventional drama). Implicit in Hegel's concept of the individual as being dependent on the state is a critique of individualism. The individual cannot exist alone; he or she is determined by society. Thus for Hegel those heroes who lead society are also determined by it; they are simply more responsive to the negative elements in their own societies than others. Wagner sometimes also sees the individual as determined by his society. In *Oper und Drama* he writes:

> The soil of history is *man's social nature:* from the individual's need to unite himself with the essence of his species, in order in Society

(Gesellschaft) to bring his faculties into highest play, arises the whole movement of history. The historic phenomena are the outward man- ifestments of an inner movement, whose core is the Social Nature of man. But the prime motor of this nature is the *Individual,* who only in the satisfaction of his instinctive longing for Love *(Liebesverlangen)* can appease his bent-to-happiness. Now, to argue from this nature's man- ifestments to its core,—from the dead body of the completed Fact to go back upon the inner life of man's social bent, from which that fact had issued as a ready, ripe, and dying fruit,—in *this* was evinced the evolutionary march of modern times. (P. 175)

Thus Wagner replaces the Hegelian movement of reason in the world with the instinctive longing for love as the motivating force of social progress, and in the movement from *Siegfrieds Tod* (later renamed *Götterdämmerung*) backward in the *Ring* retraces what he feels is the modern revolutionary movement from the corrupt state backward in search of a more natural social reality.

This sacrifice of individuality was an idea that already interested Wagner (reflected in the sacrifices of the loving women characters in his earlier operas), and that later fueled his interest in Schopenhauer's extreme rejection of individuality. In *Oper und Drama,* Wagner makes clear that he sees the individual as counting less than the society as a whole, in a paraphrase of Hegel:

Man can only be comprehended in conjunction with men in general, with his Surrounding: man divorced from this, above all *the modern man,* must appear *of all things the most incomprehensible.* The restless inner discord of this Man . . . was not so much to be explained, as Christianity had sought to do, from the nature of the Individual-man himself, as from the confusion wrought on this nature by an unin- telligent view of the essence of Society. (PP. 168–69)

Humans, then, for Wagner as for Hegel, are only truly human in society. But for Wagner, an imagined society based on love can only be hinted at through art; in reality, society is corrupted into the state.

The possibility for redemption of the state, for the acknowledg- ment of a more "intelligent view" of society, lies for Wagner in self- sacrificing love. He finds his model for Brünnhilde's sacrifice in Antigone. In *Oper und Drama,* he takes *Oedipus* as a story about the war between the individual and the state. He describes Oedipus as a heroic individual who understood the true ethical nature of man and Creon as one who, attempting to maintain the habitual ways of the society, opposed change (p. 186). He suggests that the usual, uninspired thinking of the mass of individuals when concerned with morality becomes religion and when concerned with society becomes the state. Hidden in Laius's decision to destroy his child, according to Wagner, is the assumption that the good of the state comes before the good of the individual.[39] Wagner saw the force necessary to overcome this false ethics not in Oedipus, however, but in Antigone. Her rebellion against Creon resulted in the overthrow of the corrupt state: "But to bring *the unconscious part* of human nature to *consciousness within Society,* and in this consciousness to know nothing other than *the necessity common to every member of Society,* namely of *the Individual's own free self-determining,*—this is as good as to say, *annul the State;* for through Society has the State marched on to a denial of the free self-determining of the Individual,—upon the death of *that,* has it lived" (pp. 193– 94). The self-determining individual, then, must act to destroy the state that would prevent self-realization. Both Antigone and Brünnhilde do this. Thus the ending of the *Ring* means that Brünnhilde has made a mark for self-determination for herself and for Siegfried and has brought to the consciousness of society the need for love. Brünnhilde must destroy the state, represented both by Wotan and Alberich, in order to create new conditions of freedom. And freedom works best in the service of self-recognition achieved through love.[40]

Love

Wagner derives his all-important concept of love from the subject-object relationship explored by Hegel. He did not, at least in the *Ring* cycle, simply postulate love as physical, emotional, and irrational. Rather, he saw it as the fundamental human relationship and while obviously exploiting its emotional possibilities also stressed its rational basis in mutual recognition. Wagner's model in transforming mutual recognition through feeling is Feuerbach, who suggests in *The Principles of the Philosophy of the Future* that "love is the true ontological proof of the existence of an object apart from our mind; there is no other proof of being but love and feeling in general."[41] Wagner explored all aspects of feeling as ontology in the *Ring,* from what Feuerbach calls "the simple, natural self-love which is innate in all things,"[42] to the mature relationship of Brünnhilde and Siegfried. The simple love Feuerbach refers to is shown in the *Ring* to be inadequate; society destroys this self-love in individuals, and Wagner ultimately calls for self-sacrifice that must replace self-love.

For Wagner, then, love is not always the conventional emotion expressed in much romantic literature. Rather, by love Wagner means a specific thing, drawn from his reading of Hegel and Feuerbach. He saw love as a basic psychological need both for the individual and society itself and not just a luxury. In "A Communication to My Friends," Wagner discusses Zeus's need for love in the myth of Zeus and Semele (relating this to *Lohengrin*):

> What then is the inmost essence of this Human Nature, whereto the desire which reaches forth to farthest distance turns back at last, for its only possible appeasement? It is the *Necessity of Love;* and the essence of this love, in its truest utterance, is the *longing for utmost physical reality,* for fruition in an object that can be grasped by all the senses, held fast with all the force of actual being. (P. 335)

Thus he thinks love is an intuitive psychological need but bases it, following Feuerbach, in the realm of material reality; love is based in sexual attraction between individuals. However, Wagner occasionally seems to want to substitute his concept of love for that of Hegel's spirit. Individual, sexual love often becomes for him an expression both of mutual recognition and the force that guides human history as Hegel saw spirit (as reason) guiding it. In "A Communication to My Friends" he relates discovering this love as spirit in the character of Elsa, who he says "made me a Revolutionary at one blow. She was the Spirit of the Folk, for whose redeeming hand I too, as artist-man, was longing" (pp. 347–48).

For Wagner love is, as *Götterdämmerung* demonstrates, intimately bound up with society. Love is necessarily an outgrowth of freedom: in "the Art-Work of the Future" he says that "it is a sorry misconception of Freedom—that of the being who would fain be free in loneliness. The impulse to loose one's self from commonality, to be free and independent for individual self alone, can only lead to the direct antithesis of the state so arbitrarily striven after: namely to utmost lack of self-dependence" (p. 98). Freedom and love are combined in the allegorical figure of Freia; the implications of her name and being are worked out throughout the cycle, culminating in *Götterdämmerung,* where Brünnhilde and Siegfried reach the highest level of self-realization and individual freedom only through giving up selfish interests in a relationship of love.

But love for Wagner, no matter how much he tried to see it as a philosophical concept as well as a material basis for human life, nevertheless remained a relationship of domination. He was trapped in his patriarchal understanding of the role of women; he could not see beyond the society in which he lived to a radically different form of society in which women would be truly equal. Even though the interrelation in mutual recognition that Hegel stresses implies a relationship of absolute equality, none of the love relationships in the *Ring* are equal—Wotan seduces Erda, Alberich seduces Hagen's mother, and even for Brünnhilde love is a relation of domination, for she must finally give up her wisdom, her immortality, and her autonomy.

Love then for Wagner does not always, in spite of his intentions, mean granting autonomy to the other person. Granting autonomy to another is potentially self-destructive, or as Wagner sees it, perhaps always self-destructive. However, he argues in *Oper und Drama* that equality is not destructive, that in earlier societies the assertion of one person's individuality was often suppressed because it was seen as an infringement on the individuality of others. But the new individuality he espouses is, he says, expressed in love, not self-restricting will, and so can result in a society in which self-assertion and equality can exist simultaneously (p. 353). Yet Wagner could not really conceive of love as equality because he thought women were by nature different from men. In spite of the fact that he evidently sees Brünnhilde as an example, like Siegfried, of the new, higher self-consciousness, he sees self-sacrifice as the essential way in which women express love.[43] And expressing love is, for Wagner, the essential—indeed the only— way women express the self. He sees woman as *in essence* passive, a receptacle, not a creator of individuality. In *Oper und Drama* Wagner is very clear about his concept of love as it relates to women:

> The nature of Woman is *love:* but this love is a *receiving (empfangende),* and in receival *(Empfängniss)* an unreservedly *surrendering,* love. Woman first gains her full individuality in the moment of surrender. She is the Undine who glides soulless through the waves of her native element, till she receives her soul through love of a man. The look of innocence in a woman's eye is the endlessly pellucid mirror in which the man can only see the general faculty for love, till he is able to see in it the likeness of himself. When he has recognized himself therein, then also is the woman's all-faculty condensed into one strenuous necessity, to love him with the all-dominant fervour of full surrender. (P. 111)

He goes on to say that woman only attains her individuality, her will, when she loves, by taking into herself the individuality of the beloved object. In this passage it is clear that the idea of mutual recognition that he got from Hegel does not really extend to women—the man sees, when he perceives woman, not another autonomous agent but simply a reflection of himself.

Furthermore, for Wagner women not only express love by reflecting men but also by bearing them. Part of the ideology of self-sacrifice he postulates for woman includes her sacrificing herself to motherhood:

> A woman *who really loves*, who sets her virtue in her *pride*, her pride, however, in her *sacrifice;* that sacrifice whereby she surrenders, not *one portion* of her being, but *her whole being* in the amplest fullness of its faculty—when she *conceives*. But in joy and gladness to *bear* the thing conceived, this is *the deed* of Woman—and to work deeds the woman only needs *to be entirely what she is*, but in no way to will something: for she can will but one thing—*to be a woman!* To man, therefore, woman is the ever clear and cognisable measure of natural infallibility *(Untrüglichkeit)*, for she is at her perfectest when she never quits the sphere of beautiful Instinctiveness *(Unwillkürlichkeit)*, to which she is banned by that which alone can bless her being—by the Necessity of Love. (Pp. 114–15)

This seems to describe Sieglinde, for whom Brünnhilde's announcement of Siegfried's conception is a moment of great emotional intensity, of self-realization. That Wagner suspects, perhaps unconsciously, that something is wrong with this ideology is suggested by his language: woman is *banned* to this passivity, and he emphasizes, because he seems to feel it needs emphasis, that she must not *will* anything.

Love, then, for Wagner is a complex notion drawn from a number of sources. Although to some extent he sees love as a conventional romantic glorification of private emotional experience, his concept of love extends far beyond the conventional. Love in Wagner is related to the Feuerbachian emphasis on sensuous reality. This sensuousness is for Feuerbach a replacement of religious feeling, and for Wagner it becomes a replacement for Hegelian spirit or reason as expressed in mutual recognition. Love also sometimes takes on, as reason does for Hegel, a metaphysical force and becomes the necessity that fuels inevitable changes in human consciousness and human society. Yet Wagner insists on seeing love as embodied in woman, and he has a conventional, patriarchal view of woman's role and her essence. Thus love becomes in the *Ring,* in spite of Wagner's ideas to the contrary, the emblem and instrument of domination.

2
LANGUAGE AND MUSIC IN THE *RING*

Wagner's ideology of love, which for all its derivation from theories of equality and freedom is based on the domination of women, extends in his theoretical writings to music. Wagner frequently presents the relationship between music and text metaphorically as a love relationship, imaging the text as masculine and the music as feminine. This relationship, like his image of relationships between real men and women and between his men and women characters, is ostensibly one of equality, each part contributing to make a whole, the music drama. Yet, like his notion of love between men and women, his idea of the relationship between text and music has elements that are antithetical to equality; furthermore, his practice does not always follow his theory. For although Wagner evidently believed in equality between music and text, he actually emphasized to a much greater extent than any composer before him the infusion of language *into* music, and if the resulting relationship is not always one in which language dominates music, it is only because the musical tradition in which Wagner worked was so strong. In fact, Wagner based much of his theory and to some extent his practice on exploiting the linguistic elements of music.

Wagner's concept of love, so important in his theoretical writings as well as in the *Ring*, is extended in *Oper und Drama* to art itself. He asserts metaphorically that love is the relationship between music and drama, arguing that art itself (the art of the future, that is) is a result of a mutual recognition between opposite but equal human faculties. He suggests that imagination is the mediator between a masculine understanding and a feminine feeling, which meet in the new, complete human: "In this Purely-human are nurtured both the Manly and the Womanly, which only *by their union through Love become first the Human Being.*"

Therefore, he argues, the necessary impetus to art, which he calls "the poetic intellect," is love, and especially "the love *of man to woman.*" But he emphasizes that this love is more than just feeling or appetite. Rather, it is "the deep yearning to know himself redeemed from his egoism through his sharing in the rapture of the loving woman; and *this yearning* is *the creative moment (das dichtende Moment)* of the Understanding" (p. 236). Thus artistic creativity itself is a function of mutual recognition between understanding (intellect or reason) and feeling. And this act of creating results in the new, more perfect form of art, the music drama.

In his attempts, before reading Schopenhauer, to develop a metaphysical meaning for music that would fit with his understanding of history and human existence, Wagner describes in "A Communication to My Friends" the essence of music as being identical with the essence of love. He says that he himself came to recognize that the "Need of Love" was the primary need in everything, including art and all of human society. The prevailing lack of love in his culture, which he felt impelled to attempt to overcome, was manifested in art and music by formalism; he thus implies that formalism in music excludes emotion (p. 306). He develops this idea further in *Oper und Drama,* where he says that "*every musical organism is by its nature—a womanly;* it is merely a *bearing,* and not a *begetting* factor; the begetting-force lies clean *outside it,* and without fecundation by this force it positively cannot bear" (p. 109). His argument has now shifted (like his understanding of love) from a relationship of mutual equality between music and text to one in which music is subordinate. The role of music, like that of woman, is of passive receptacle for the new life, which is actually created by the man or the poet. Thus music, like a woman without a man, is uncreative and incomplete without text. Further, just as he believes that women are naturally ecstatic about their subordinate role, so he believes that music fulfills its highest destiny as the servant and bearer of the text.

He even extends the joyful subordination he assumes natural to women and music to the performers. Heinrich Porges, observing rehearsals for the first *Ring* at Bayreuth, states that Wagner demanded nothing less than self-effacing love from his performers. Singers and actors, Wagner insisted, can only achieve artistic "freedom" by agreeing from the outset to "subordinate themselves without reservation to the creator of the work, and thereby acquire that gift of self-abandonment *(Selbstentäusserung)*" that he discussed in his essay "On Actors and Singers."[1] Obviously,

Wagner's ideal of equality did not extend to performers; although equality was a mental concept for Wagner, it was not always a practice.

The type of love that demands complete subordination by one partner also plays a part in Wagner's relationship with his own audiences, from whom he attempted to obtain complete, self-effacing devotion. Thomas Mann, taking his cue from Nietzsche, discusses this aspect of Wagner's artistic personality, suggesting that Wagner always employed what Nietzsche called a "double focus"; he had a propensity for concentrating on the one hand on the highest artistic goals and at the same time doing whatever was necessary to appeal to his bourgeois audience. This propensity revealed an instinct, according to Mann, "for satisfying sophisticated needs *and* more cheerfully commonplace ones, for winning over the select few *and* capturing the masses—an instinct that relates, in my own view, to Wagner's appetite for conquest, his thirst for this world, his 'sinfulness' in an ascetic sense: to what the Buddha calls 'attachment' or 'craving', his desire, his sensual-metaphysical longing for love."[2]

This "sensual-metaphysical longing for love" is in some ways, as Mann implies, related to Wagner's need for domination. In his theoretical efforts to justify his musical practice, he extends this domination disguised as love to the relationship between language and music. In *Oper und Drama* he outlined the history of opera as a dialectic between these two elements, words and music, now one and now the other being in the ascendant. He argued for the music drama (and implicitly for the *Ring*) as the place where music and text finally become equal. To some extent he was right: the *Ring* is remarkable for the extent to which it incorporates linguistic meanings into musical ones, yet Wagner's theory emphasizes, in spite of himself, language *over* music. Wagner evidently preferred to picture himself as a poet or dramatist first and a composer second, and implicitly, by connecting music with the female and poetry with the male, he demonstrated his belief that language has a rightful place of eminence over music.

Semiosis of Language and Melody

But to say that Wagner felt music was subordinate to text is not at all to argue that the music of a work like the *Ring* cycle is reducible to the allegorical implications of a few repeated motives. In actuality, Wagner's theory of music and poetry and his exploitation in the *Ring* of the linguistic tendencies inherent in music are much more subtle than critics usually admit. In *Oper und Drama* Wagner attempted to create a theory that continued and extended the ideas of Hegel and Feuerbach; in the *Ring* he sought to produce the realization of philosophy that the romantics had long sought.[3] Wagner saw in the music drama an art form that could potentially draw on the resources of both music and poetry to create a new type of semiotic system that would synthesize music and language while overcoming the limitations of both. He predicted that this new semiotic system would become the medium of the artwork of the future, an artwork that would have the potential to communicate with an audience in a way never possible before. This he confidently expected to occur in the *Ring*, which would draw not only on this new means of communication but also on myth, which he, like his fellow romantics, saw as a body of stories and concepts that already encapsulated in codified form the spirit of the people during a particular historical period. Thus the *Ring* would be the instrument of revolution because it would, with its culmination of new artistic means and old myth, bring to consciousness in profound ways the long-buried will of the German people.

This new artistic means described in *Oper und Drama* was the combination of language and music possible only in the music drama. In particular, Wagner developed a theory describing how a musical entity, a melody, can become meaningful within a linguistic structure, the drama. These melodies, of course, are now usually called leitmotifs, although Wagner himself did not apply that name—or any other—to the theory of repeated melody he developed in *Oper und Drama*. Melody, he argues in that work, is the element in which meaning resides; although harmony and rhythm are the "blood, flesh, and nerves" of music, melody is the outward shape by which we read, as we read the eyes of a person, the inward Soul of the music (p. 104). Thus later in *Oper und Drama* he can argue that a melody, rather than any other aspect of music, can be used to present the remembrance of an emotion experienced previously, a "merely-thought-of emotion *in all its pure-melodic record*" (p. 328).

These repeated melodies, or leitmotifs, are perhaps the aspect of the Wagnerian theory of meaning and music that have gotten the most attention from commentators. Indeed, many musical analysts feel that the leitmotif has perhaps received too much attention, being neither the most important nor the most interesting element of Wagner's music. Nevertheless, the leitmotif may be the most important aspect of Wagner as the artist who sought more than any other to create new ways to express meaning, and it constitutes his unique contribution to the relationship between music and words. Wagner, of course, intended the leitmotifs not as allegory but as musical moments that would fill two important functions in the drama: reminiscence and foreshadowing. He discusses both these functions in *Oper und Drama*, arguing that the repeated melody makes present—objectifies—the emotional content of a dramatic situation by tying it to previous events in the drama. Similarly, Wagner argues that melody can also create a sense of expectation: what he calls "Instrumental-speech" employed by the orchestra (in the form of a repeated melody) can create a sense of need or longing for the specific object of thought to which it will become attached (p. 331).

Thus clearly Wagner thought of repeated melodies as objectified feeling/thought, as devices that extend both the referential quality of language and the emotional function of music. Wagner did not think of leitmotifs as substitutes for single words or phrases, as they have frequently been taken. That Wagner did sometimes attach words—names—to the leitmotifs does not necessarily disprove this (Westernhagen notes that the motives are sometimes labeled in the sketches),[4] but simply shows that Wagner used words as shorthand musical notation to help him remember which theme to use where. While it also indicates that he had a definite meaning in mind for any leitmotif so named, we need not assume he intended it to be reductive and strictly referential. Rather, he intended a motive to imply a meaning and an emotion or to recall a previous situation so as to enlarge the emotional impact of the present moment.

The objectified emotion represented by the leitmotif is more, however, than just feeling. Rather, as Wagner discusses the repeated motive, it is a complex combination of emotion and thought. He defines a thought as an "image" in the mind, an image of something real but absent. It is present as memory in the mind, however, only because it has made a "definite impression" on us at another place and time. This impression, he goes on, "has lain ahold of our feeling" (p. 326), a feeling that we communicate as expression (he also notes that the "power of combination" of abstract thought, the medium of philosophy, does not enter into this discussion—thought as *sensual*, not abstract, is the medium of art). A thought, then, for Wagner is really a *memory* of a sensual experience:

A thing which has not made an impression on our feelings *(Empfin-dung)* at the first, neither can we *think* it; and the antecedent emotional-phase *(Empfindungserscheinung)* is the conditioner of the shape in which the thought shall be enounced. So that even Thought is roused by the emotion, and must necessarily flow back again into Emotion; for *a thought is the bond between an absent and a present emotion, each struggling for enouncement.* (P. 327)

This thought, a midpoint, a yielding of one emotion into another, is the kind of thought expressed by the poetry of drama. So the "Verse-Melody" of the music drama "materializes the thought—i.e., the non-present emotion recalled by memory,—converting it into a present, an actually observable emotion" (p. 327). But the emotion is also conditioned by the music itself; a repeated melody is a feeling that comes back to us as a thought. Music then becomes not pure feeling but thought itself. This thought or remembered emotion embodied in the music is the impetus for a new emotion, now presented in the drama: "Such a melody, once imparted to us by the actor as the outpour of an emotion, and now expressively delivered by the orchestra at an instant when the person represented merely nurses that emotion in his memory,—such a melody materialises for us this personage's Thought." What is expressed by the leitmotif, then, is more than emotion and more than thought—it is "the thought's *Emotional-content brought to presence.*" Wagner goes on to argue that "music cannot think." However, he says, music "can materialise thoughts, i.e., she can give forth their emotional contents as no longer merely recollected, but made present" (pp. 328–29).

Some critics have suggested, however, in spite of Wagner's contention that the repeated melodies embody thought, that the leitmotifs are not to be confused with language but are suggestive of emotion only. Raymond Furness calls them "musical ideas, or 'carriers of feeling'" and suggests that "no intellectual description could do justice to their high emotional pressure."[5] Deryck Cooke, too, argues that the association of the leitmotif with the word is only on the story level. Wagner's musical reminiscences, he says, "go far beyond the mere business of preserving the coherence of the plot. They are powerfully emotive . . . and they normally establish profound emotional and psychological connections between events and characters."[6] Wagner, Cooke insists, "never intended his music to convey the conceptual ideas of the drama—the drama itself was there for just that purpose; the music was intended to express the profound emotional and psychological realities behind the concepts."[7]

These critics want to suggest that the leitmotif is strictly emotional because they are uncomfortable with Wagner's efforts to make musical meaning more exact. Music is usually thought of as the most abstract art, but Wagner attempted to refute this. He wanted to obtain for the music drama the explicitness of meaning available to poetry—exploiting not only the referential and contextual meanings of words but their emotive content, and at the same time exploiting not only the emotive content of music but making that content more exact by connecting it to words and contexts. Wagner argued in *Oper und Drama* that while music by itself must remain vague, when coupled with speech or specific dramatic events it takes on a very precise character that contributes to the overall meaning of the drama (p. 330).

This goes contrary to the general understanding of musical meaning—Julia Kristeva, for example, argues that "musicality" in language is equivalent to the erupting of vaguely determined psychological drives into the logical and specific cultural contexts of ordinary language.[8] The symbolist poets, as another example, attempted to appropriate for poetry what they considered to be the vague, suggestive meanings of music. These poets could be considered among the earliest examples of modernism, which, Raymond Furness argues, could be defined in all the arts as the use of private images and autonomous metaphors abstracted from their context (or the increase of abstraction in painting). This abstraction demonstrates, he says, that specific experience becomes, in modernism, less important than broadly symbolic or emotive effects: "it is true to say that the adoption of the principles of musical composition by the other arts is the most dominant characteristic of modernism."[9]

While Wagner would perhaps agree in theory with the notion that music by itself is inherently vague and emotional, his whole effort in the *Ring* was to replace this vagueness with specificity, to replace abstract emotion with contextualized feeling/thought. Music may be vague as it is usually used—as language can also be vague—but Wagner sought to prove that music can take on more explicitness when its inherent linguistic elements are exploited.

Wagner's real intent, then, for what is now called the leitmotif was to show how a present thought or emotion is conditioned by previous ones. The repeated melody mediates between past and present. In theory, Wagner sought to develop a philosophy of music based on this mediation. If in practice the repeated motives

sometimes seem more like mechanical devices than true mediation, this is due to the difficulty of putting the theory into practice
and sometimes to the listeners' failure to grasp the complexity of
the interplay of music and language in the music drama.

Because he saw the leitmotif as mediating between past and
present, Wagner could employ it as a structuring device. Certainly
one of his purposes in creating the leitmotif system was to create
unity by establishing a series of reminiscences that would form a
network of meaning within the drama. He may have depended in
part on Hegel for his ideas about the importance of the reminiscence, for Hegel includes reminiscence as part of his theory of the
movement of spirit in the world. Each individual, Hegel says in
the *Phenomenology,* seeks insight as to what knowledge is. But the
general mind has already gone through a number of stages. The
new individual, in order to progress, has to go through these
stages too, but the task, once accomplished by some, is simplified
for others. For each new thinking individual, then, the task has
been made simpler because the mind in general has already gone
through the necessary steps to reach that point. These steps are
codified in the *concept,* which Hegel explains as a kind of mental
shorthand that images previous processes of thought without
requiring the individual to repeat them himself (pp. 90–91). Thus
Wagner may have intended the reminiscent leitmotifs to represent events made into memories and available for the minds of the
characters on stage. These events are immediately presented on
stage in the action and mediately presented in the music later;
subsequent characters can mentally reenact, through the use of
repeated motives, what their predecessors have already experienced. Perhaps the most significant example of this aspect of the
leitmotif is the motive associated with Sieglinde when "remembered" by Siegfried—Siegfried does not really remember, of
course, but imagines and goes through in imagination the stages
of consciousness that his parents have already gone through. In
his imagining of mother-love, he is preparing his own mind for
the experience of love.

To some extent, Wagner drew his ideas on memory, which he
applied to the repeated motive, from Feuerbach. For Feuerbach,
Hegelian self-realization through mutual recognition occurs in
human love. In *Thoughts on Death and Immortality* Feuerbach had
argued that Hegelian spirit actualizes itself as the image one
person develops of another: the person is actualized by the Other
in a love relationship, and this actualization is not complete until
the individual is held in memory by another—a process not com-

plete until after the individual's death. For Feuerbach, an individual is never completely autonomous; the life story of any individual progresses by becoming entwined with the consciousness that others have of that person. That is, any individual grows throughout his or her life in the ability to share his or her own consciousness, and this sharing is a relationship based on love. As the individual grows older, the shared consciousness, in the form of the memory he or she has of others and that others have of him, becomes more prominent than the original self-consciousness until it becomes, after death, the essence of the individual. So the physical act of death is the expression of the ultimate shared consciousness, in which the boundary between one individual and the next is obliterated, and the individual is totally engulfed in the consciousness of others.[10]

This profound use of recollection as the realization of Hegelian spirit evidently lies behind the emphasis on memory (and loss of memory) in *Götterdämmerung*. This use of recollection may have been what Wagner had in mind as he described the relationship between memory, thought, and feeling in *Oper und Drama*. If so, then the repeated motive was a part of the process that is the subject of the *Ring*—the process of constituting the new consciousness. Musically, Wagner may have come much closer to realizing his ideas about memory in the long passage just before Siegfried dies in which he recalls, in a great musical recapitulation, Brünnhilde's awakening in act 3 of *Siegfried* than he does in the use of the repeated motive in the earlier music of the cycle.

The leitmotif, then, is in many ways simply an extension of Wagner's theory of memory and self. Many commentators, however, unaware of Wagner's theory of repeated verse-melody and the theoretical background in Hegel and Feuerbach, assume that the leitmotif is in fact simply a substitution of a melody for a word (such as fate), a character (such as Siegfried), or physical object (such as gold). Furthermore, commentators also talk of the leitmotif as if it were a separate issue from other types of music that Wagner employed to create meaning.

Wagner also argues in *Oper und Drama* that the structure of the *Ring* cycle depends on this interrelationship between music and language, and that the music alone could not create a comprehensible structure in a long work. He says that the orchestral motive is not absolute music, and it extends the space and time of the drama backward and forward. In fact, he suggests, the use of purely musical structures in a work as long as the *Ring* cycle would be confusing and impossible, and he derived the repeated motive as a method of creating unity over long stretches of composition from the model of Greek tragedy (pp. 363–64). Wagner felt that the motives allowed him to create a new, literary mode of developing music in the *Ring:* after finishing the composition sketch of *Das Rheingold* he wrote to August Röckel (25 January 1854) that it had "turned out to be a firmly entwined unity" and "there is scarcely a bar in the orchestral writing that does not develop out of preceding motives."[11] Further, he argues in "On the Application of Music to the Drama" that the motives represented a new way of developing music through dramatic meaning. Thus the way the motives are transformed throughout the work is an important principle of the music, though development depends on the drama rather than purely musical events.[12] This use of the repeated motive as a method of achieving literary rather than musical structure has attracted many writers to Wagner: Thomas Mann, for example, says he was interested in the leitmotifs because they add strength to Wagner's music drama by making the music itself a great narrative voice, almost as if Wagner were writing novels rather than dramas: "The recurrent motif, the self-quotation, the symbolic phrase, the verbal and thematic reminiscence across long stretches of text—these were narrative devices after my own heart, and for that very reason full of enchantment for me."[13]

Language, then, is an inevitable part of music for Wagner, both for conveying the emotional impact of a moment in the drama and for creating a coherent structure over a large work. In both cases, Wagner usurps for language a function traditionally carried by music alone. Indeed, Dalhouse believes that the "central maxim" of Wagner's esthetic is that music needs a "formal" motive, a reason for existing that has its origin outside of purely musical structures, and the formal motive of a melodic element is either speech or physical action.[14] Many critics decry this attitude on Wagner's part, refusing to accept that language ever can be a part of music. Theodor Adorno, for example, says that the leitmotifs fail; Wagner intended them to create subtle relationships among textual elements and supposed emotional responses to them. Instead, he says, even in Wagner's own day audiences tended to make "a crude link" between the leitmotifs and the things they were supposed to represent; Adorno suggests that the listeners missed the effect that Wagner was trying to achieve, an immediacy with which emotions and meanings could be grasped in the music drama. The necessity for commentaries describing the provenance of each leitmotif reveals, he says, the "bankruptcy" of this "aesthetics of immediate unity."[15]

Some critics feel that the leitmotif has come to mean something Wagner did not foresee at all, arguing that while Wagner himself did use the term *Hauptmotive* (principal motives) for certain musical ideas in *Tristan,* he did not do so for the *Ring.* Deryck Cooke argues on technical grounds that *motive* is not really the right word; it means, he says, "the shortest significant thematic idea," and very few ideas in the *Ring* are that short (the Nibelung motive is an exception). Most motives, he says, are full symphonic themes (such as the song of the Rhinedaughters), thematic phrases (such as the ring motive), chord sequences (such as those associated with the Wanderer), or cadences (such as the phrase that first appears on the words "Weibes Wonne und Werth").[16] Cook denigrates the reductive uses to which commentators have put these motives. Indeed, the music as objectified feeling that Wagner attempted to produce in the *Ring* demonstrates that he never intended the leitmotif to be regarded in the reductive way it frequently has. The repeated melody was for Wagner an expressive semiotic system that synthesized and transcended—in true dialectical fashion—both absolute music and language alone. Thus feeling/thought in the music drama takes the place of language alone in the spoken drama.

Theories of Language

Wagner attempted, then, to develop this new semiotic system because he felt language alone to be reductive and limited. However, he argued that language had not always been so limited. He outlined his own history of language in *Oper und Drama,* derived primarily from Schlegel and Herder, who believed that the first efforts of early humans to express themselves were poetic and musical in nature.[17] For Wagner, as for Herder, music and speech derive from the same source in human prehistory; early speech was rather like singing, concentrating on sound rather than meaning. That is, Wagner believed that speech arose first from a primitive human interest in sounds, and early peoples repeated and structured speech based on how it sounded. Reference in language, he thought, came as an outgrowth of this interest in sound rather than the other way around. This primary unity of speech and sound Wagner analyzes as going through a dialectical process of separation into language and music and final reunion in a higher form, verse-melody.

Wagner, following Herder, also argued in *Oper und Drama* that because a language belongs to a group of people as well as to individuals, it constitutes not only a set of signs but a way of thinking. In Herder's theory, words are not only tools for the use of humans; they are the means by which human consciousness comes into being. They are also, of course, the expression of that consciousness. So, for Herder, "a people's language is the privileged mirror or expression of its humanity."[18] Wagner similarly argues that language comes from the poetic, naturally expressive attitudes of a people, and in his insistence in *Oper und Drama* on the importance of the German language for opera and dedication of the *Ring* to the spirit of the German people, he attempts to present this work as a reflection of the spirit of the Germans as he felt it was reflected in their ancient language.

The German spirit Wagner attempted to evoke in the *Ring* cycle was the motivation for his adaptation of the early German verse-form, *Stabreim*. German is, Wagner says in *Oper und Drama*, the only possible language for music drama because it is the only modern language in which words are accented consistently on the root syllable (p. 358). *Stabreim* employs this quality to structure poetry. The usefulness of *Stabreim*, he feels, is that it allows the poet to establish relationships between particular words and concepts simply through the way the words sound. Verse written in *Stabreim* is thus similar to music in that it emphasizes the place of a word in the overall phonetic pattern, something like the way a musical note derives meaning from its place in a tonal pattern.[19]

However, Wagner takes a more Hegelian stand when he argues that language cannot or does not keep up with the new consciousness. In a letter to Röckel Wagner wrote that "suddenly language itself fails us for intelligible communication, since our language was formed in the service of a kind of condition very different from that which we have newly gained. The difficulty now is to communicate in that atrociously limited language of pictures without arousing misunderstandings at every turn."[20] Thus another reason he turned to the outdated *Stabreim* was that he wanted to create a distance from everyday language and consciousness for the *Ring*, a work in which he sought to express a new consciousness.

Wagner depends more on Herder's view of language than on Hegel's as it appears in the *Phenomenology* (though Hegel is influenced by Herder also). Unlike Wagner, Hegel argues that language (the modern language Wagner despaired of) is necessary to the development of a new consciousness because it is necessary to be able to describe, even if very stumblingly, what is experienced in order to rise to self-awareness and knowledge.[21] This Hegelian idea is clear in Siegfried's awakening into self-consciousness; part of his new consciousness is the new knowledge of meaning he gains in his dialogues with the woodbird and Mime (these occur only after he has risked his life in slaying the dragon, even though he did not fear for his life in so doing). Hegel also emphasizes that language is abstract rather than concrete; language moves us instantly from the specific, from hereness and nowness, to the general. Words make the world into things, as symbols for use. Animals, Hegel argues, use things too: they eat them. But people turn things into signs just as they turn bread and wine into religious symbols.[22]

Hegel's idea that words are abstract rather than concrete, even a word such as "this" or "here," is confirmed by the twentieth-century theorist of language and language development, L. S. Vygotsky. He argues that a word does not refer to a single object but to a group or type of objects—a word is already a generalization, and a generalization is a "verbal act of thought" that reflects reality in a quite different way from sensation or perception. Drawing from Hegel, Vygotsky affirms a "dialectic leap" not only between inanimate nature and sensation but also between sensation and language. The difference between sensation and thought is the presence in the latter of the generalized perception of reality—what Vygotsky sees as the essence of language. Consequently meaning is an act of thought. But at the same time, meaning is the essence of language. Thus meaning is a function both of thought and language, not one or the other.[23] The essential point in Vygotsky's theory is that language and thought develop at the same time in the child and that they are interdependent. So Herder's and Wagner's assumption that a language equals a mode of thinking peculiar to a particular group of people may be confirmed in his work. That meaning is inseparable from language suggests that meanings even when constituted by musical materials rather than speech are related to language; modern linguistic theories corroborate the dependence of music on language that Wagner emphasized in his exaggeratedly metaphorical way.

Vygotsky's theory provides a link between Herder and Hegel and another twentieth-century theorist, M. M. Bakhtin.[24] His work can help us understand the place of musical meanings in the *Ring* because much of what he notes about language can be applied to musical meaning, especially in the linguistic uses to which Wagner put music. Bakhtin's theory of language deemphasizes the word and the speaker more than most such explanations. He refutes the black-box theory of communication in which one soul sends a message to another soul in a predetermined and natural language. Rather, he emphasizes the role of society in creating language itself and the role of dialogue in creating meaning. He argues that theme (the overall meaning of a particular utterance in its context) and evaluative stance are inherent in words and are more important than their specific reference. He suggests that inner speech, and eventually consciousness itself, is a product of society and impossible without it, rather than the other way around. Thus what Wagner asserts about ancient language, the essence of which he attempted to revive in the *Ring,* Bakhtin asserts is true about all language. Where Wagner sees a modern, limited language Bakhtin sees merely a superficial understanding of language. Bakhtin sees as implicit in all communicative systems what Wagner thought he was recreating—in a new and powerful form—in his combination of ancient verse forms and music.

Bakhtin's theories of the relationship of language to meaning seem particularly appropriate to Wagner because Bakhtin, like Wagner, derives his theory of meaning from not only Herder and Hegel but also Feuerbach (Bakhtin owes a further debt to Marx that Wagner does not, there being no evidence that Wagner was familiar with any of Marx's work). Bakhtin applies Hegel's notion of mutual recognition to the specific social interaction between individuals, arguing that the fundamental social interaction that Hegel sees is in fact the point at which meaning and language arise (Hegel places the derivation of language earlier, in the confrontation between the unself-conscious mind and nature). The I-Thou relationship that Feuerbach and Wagner derive from Hegel's mutual recognition and interpret as a love relationship is interpreted by Bakhtin as a linguistic and social relationship. Where Wagner moves into music and the repeated motive, Bakhtin moves into a theory of meaning based almost completely on language.

Just as Feuerbach asserts that an individual is created by the consciousness that others have of him or her, Bakhtin argues that humans understand each other—and hence themselves—through language and that the I-Thou relationship of Feuerbach is embedded in language itself. Bakhtin emphasizes that all human utterances are dependent on a particular social situation and always aimed at an addressee, even if that addressee is imagined (p. 85). All utterances, he says, including written utterances and pieces of literature, are in response to something—another utterance, an action, a situation—and are designed to be responded to in turn. Thus any speech act, any word or sentence or other linguistic entity, is but a link in a chain of utterances in which everyone is constantly engaged (pp. 72–73). He places a great deal of emphasis on his idea that words and language do not come from the speaker alone but depend on the social situation and on the fact that language itself is determined by the social world in which it exists. Words, he says, are oriented toward the listener; a word is "a two-sided act." What word the speaker chooses to use in a particular situation is determined as much by the person it is addressed to as by the person speaking. While this point is perhaps obvious, Bakhtin intends more than simply word choice. Rather, he argues, implicit relations among speakers are part of the creation of a word and of language itself: "A word is a bridge thrown between myself and another. If one end of the bridge depends on me, then the other depends on my addressee. A word is a territory shared by both addresser and addressee, by the speaker and his interlocutor" (p. 86). Thus for him understanding, not just speaking, is part of a dialogue, and to understand an utterance is, in a sense, to enter into a dialogue with it. Understanding is not passive, then, but a part of this dialogic process, and to understand another person's utterance means to orient oneself with respect to it and to see how to fit it into the context of action and speech in which both speaker and listener find themselves (p. 102). Mutual recognition for Bakhtin is a process not just of recognizing the existence of another consciousness, as Hegel would have it, or of incorporating the other through memory and intertwined consciousness, as Feuerbach would have it, but of sharing another's consciousness through language (and to some extent other sign systems). This sharing of another's consciousness was what Wagner attempted to do with his repeated motives, which he said objectified for us (the audience) the unconscious motivations of the characters on stage.

The most obvious example of our tendency to incorporate the consciousness of another occurs when we quote the words of others. The long narratives in the *Ring* cycle are examples of such reported speech. In reported speech, Bakhtin says, a speaker not only quotes the words of another but he or she implies something about the speech being quoted and reveals respect or its lack for the speaker (p. 113). Reported speech occurs frequently in the *Ring* cycle, not only in the form of embedded narratives but musically as well in the repeated or quoted motives. Bakhtin points out that reported speech is only partially incorporated into that of the speaker—it retains at least some elements of the original presentation. Thus it represents an objectified form of the basic unit of meaning in speech, that is, dialogue (pp. 115–17). Reported speech (or reported music) in the *Ring* cycle frequently indicates the speaker's attitude toward the authority of the person being quoted—Wotan, for example, quotes both Erda's words and her music in his dialogue with Alberich in act 2 of *Siegfried*. But his failure to acknowledge the source of his newfound wisdom (he allows Alberich to believe that the ideas are his own) suggests his basic contempt for Erda; he feels free to appropriate her words and music and make them sound as if they are his.

The Word and the Leitmotif

That the leitmotif is often seen as a replacement for a single word is one reason many musicians decry the study of leitmotifs, feeling that it is reductive to suggest that a musical entity is the equivalent of a word. Certainly most explanations of the leitmotif are reductive. However, they are based on a reductive understanding of language. The word, in Bakhtin's theory, is an essential element in all thinking and all human consciousness, and he also argues that the word is essential to all forms of meaning, including music. All music, he argues, like other nonverbal sign systems, is necessarily interpreted by words in the form of inner speech. He states that the word is "the medium of consciousness" that "accompanies and comments on each and every ideological act. The processes of understanding any ideological phenomenon at all (be it a picture, a piece of music, a ritual, or an act of human conduct) cannot operate without the participation of inner speech. All manifestations of ideological creativity—all other nonverbal signs—are bathed by, suspended in, and cannot be entirely segregated or divorced from the element of speech" (p. 15). Thus he would argue that any musical meaning is associated with the word or with language. Bakhtin does not suggest, of course, that sign systems such as music do not have meaning all of their own (p. 15). Rather, what he insists on is that all human activity is accompanied by inner speech—that is, we transform all meaning that we meet in the outer world into our own inner world, and that inner world is necessarily composed of words and patterned on speech:

> In fact, not even the simplest, dimmest apprehension of a feeling—
> say, the feeling of hunger not outwardly expressed—can dispense with
> some kind of ideological form. Any apprehension, after all, must have

inner speech, inner intonation and the rudiments of inner style: one can apprehend one's hunger apologetically, irritably, angrily, indignantly, etc. We have indicated, of course, only the grosser, more egregious directions that inner intonation may take; actually, there is an extremely subtle and complex set of possibilities for intoning an experience. Outward expression in most cases only continues and makes more distinct the direction already taken by inner speech and the intonation already embedded in it. (p. 87)

Thus for Bakhtin, any musical entity is necessarily accompanied by an inner ideological comment, an interpretation—an interpretation that occurs in language as inner speech. But such interpretation is infinitely more complex and subtle than simply assigning a word to a melody. A Bach fugue may be described as stately or lighthearted, a Schubert melody as nostalgic or tragic, but this reflects a perhaps mistaken attempt to express in single words a whole complex of ideas that appear as inner speech. Even if one insists that melodies are neutral in their emotional content, that very neutrality is an ideological commentary, an inner stance taken toward the music. Or if one tends to think structurally rather than in impressionistic terms and takes delight in Mozart's balance, symmetry, or contrast, or Beethoven's exploitation of thematic elements, one is still applying an inner ideological stance toward the music. In the leitmotif, Wagner takes advantage of this aspect of music as interpreted by inner speech: the motives associated with the gold, the sword, or Siegfried, for example, rely on the audience's inner ideological association of trumpet calls with such concepts as honor, strength, or integrity. Thus Wagner, when he specifically associates a motive with language, with the words sung with it, or the dramatic context in which it appears, is not really creating, in spite of his theories, a new type of semiotic system. Instead he is accentuating a tendency already important in music.

The parallels between the leitmotif and the word are further clarified when one realizes that words are often used, in ordinary speech, in a manner very much like music, expressively rather than referentially. Bakhtin argues that some brief expressions, which seem almost like words because they are so often used together, serve two purposes: to inform about experiences (his example is "I feel joy") or to express experiences directly (as in a phrase such as "Great!"). Transitional forms (such as "I'm so happy!"—spoken with intonations suggesting joy) are also frequently used. In the first case (informing about experience), the inner sign—the expression of emotion—has been completely changed to outer, objective language. It is a *result* of introspection.

In the second case, however, introspection about inner experience (emotion) has erupted to the surface without being converted to explanation; the inner experience is displayed as it were for external observation, although of course it has been altered somewhat in the very process of expression. In the transitional case, the result of introspection is expressed objectively but highly colored by the initial introspection (p. 36). This may explain the differences between the leitmotif and other aspects of music in Wagner; in the leitmotif feeling is objectivized or commented upon, whereas other aspects of the music are used in an attempt to express inner experience spontaneously. But these feelings, always, are socially created (and ideologically loaded), or else they could not be expressed at all: the emotions Wagner assumes his music to express, mediately in the leitmotif and immediately in the general musical ground, are actually available for him to express as music and for us to understand only because our culture in general conceives of and expresses emotion in these or similar forms. Wagner's music, that is, does not spring from or speak to a deep intuitive inner human essence, but from the habits of thought, feeling, and expression that Western culture has encoded in its music.

Wagner often exploited these habits of thought and feeling, which were already encoded in nineteenth-century music, by associating them with the drama in a specific way that suggests an expression of the inner speech of an individual character. However, this does not necessarily suggest a more specific meaning for the leitmotif than for other types of music. Words are no more specific than leitmotifs. A word, in Vygotsky's description, in fact, strongly resembles a leitmotif: "The primary word is not a straightforward symbol for a concept but rather an image, a picture, a mental sketch of a concept, a short tale about it—indeed, a small work of art."[25] However, defining leitmotifs as if they were words often causes a problem because it creates the impression that the leitmotif carries a single, unitary meaning. But this idea is an error arising from an unthinking attitude toward language. Bakhtin argues that a word does not carry such a single meaning. On the contrary, he says, *"Multiplicity of meanings is the constitutive feature of word"* (p. 101). When words seem to have a single meaning, he says, it is because the meaning lies in the context. Speakers learn to use words in a multiplicity of contexts, so the speaker can choose to emphasize some of the implications of a word through inserting it into a particular context and can ignore others. Similarly, the leitmotif, which shares multiplicity of meaning with the word, can help to illuminate subtleties of meaning in different contexts; for example, the melodically descending scale passage associated with Wotan's spear is used in such a way that its connection with contracts is sometimes emphasized (and some contexts suggest a more pejorative meaning than others) while at other times its connection with physical force is the important issue.

It is usually assumed that leitmotifs, like words, get their meaning from their association with certain characters, things, or actions. That is, as Vygotsky suggests about language, it is usually assumed that a sign is associated with a meaning by proximity—that an event occurs or object appears to the child at the same time the sound of the word is made, and that he or she associates the one with the other and so learns to use the sign. But Vygotsky argues that the thought (that is, the generalization) must come before the sign. The world of experience must be greatly simplified and divided into categories before it can be dealt with by memory or by language. So the child learns categories from parents and adults and the word or words that go with them. In order for a word to carry meaning, it must be included in a certain context that, according to a convention that the child has already learned, society sees as a category. Thus words do not receive their meaning from association with things, but from prior association with categories.[26] Similarly, the leitmotifs receive their meaning not from association with specific words but with the "thought" these words represent, categories that are assumed to be operable in the contexts in which they appear. For example, the so-called renunciation motive is often assumed to mean a single, unitary thing—renunciation—because it is first heard in proximity with the statement by Woglinde that a person must renounce love before he can forge the ring. Yet a careful examination of all its appearances in the *Ring* suggests that a category is operating that is somewhat larger than renunciation. This rule of association, however, leads Deryck Cooke to spend a great deal of time in his study of the *Ring* analyzing why Siegmund sings this theme as he pulls the sword from the tree just at the moment when he is coming into rather than renouncing love. But in fact, as Cooke argues, Wagner never intended any of the leitmotifs to exist as substitutes for words.[27] Instead, such repeated melodies form part of a contextual meaning relating, like words and actions on stage, to generalizations that are already in effect.

Another aspect in which the leitmotif is like the word when the word is properly understood becomes clear when one realizes that words, as already mentioned, take an evaluative stance that is most easily discernible in spoken intonation, an aspect of language readily imitated by music. For Bakhtin, any word as it appears in speech has not only meaning but also always implies a value judgment; there is no such thing, he says, as a word without an "evaluative accent" (p. 103). Bakhtin's point is that no use of language is ever possible in which an evaluative stance is absent. That this evaluation is presented most clearly in the intonation of spoken utterances (whether a given utterance is spoken fast, slow, slurred, high in the voice, etc.) demonstrates how easily evaluation is moved to music. Wagner's music often forms an evaluation of the text in exactly the way spoken intonation does—through tempo, pitch, or articulation. Wagner also presents evaluative judgments of the text in ways that do not strictly imitate speech—in his use of orchestration (Siegfried's horn call has a different evaluative force when it is played by the strings, for example) or through conventional concepts of beauty in music (the differences between the Rhinedaughters' greeting to the gold in *Das Rheingold* and its variant, with different harmonization and orchestration, as it appears associated with Hagen in *Götterdämmerung*). Wagner gives his leitmotifs an evaluative stance in the way he creates them from the general musical ground—the motives associated with Siegfried, for example, suggest a quite different evaluative stance than those associated with Alberich. What the leitmotif does, however, more than the general music of the *Ring* or any other opera, is to extend this sort of meaning outside of the context, to give it continuity, in order greatly to enhance the ability of music to express meaning beyond the here-and-now.

The evaluative stance of language is less obvious in the individual word than in overall groups of words in context, what Bakhtin calls an utterance. In fact, he says we do not hear or respond to individual words but to their ideological content, and this content comes not from reference but human behavior, from the social ideology into which the utterance is inserted. "That is the way we understand words," he argues, "and we can respond only to words that engage us behaviorally or ideologically" (p. 70). Thus what a composer does in setting words is to try to set the whole, the flavor, of the content, not the meaning of the individual words. Also, seeing meaning in language as a product of groups of words in context, rather than as belonging to individual words, emphasizes how musical meaning, which does without words entirely, is similar to linguistic meaning. Musical meaning, except for Wagner's sometimes specialized use of the leitmotif, lies in its general context—how tonalities, tempos, or even whole structures contrast with or fit into the general musical context and the musical tradition in which they are formed. So to argue that Wagner emphasized linguistic meaning in music is not to suggest that musical entities have reference (though sometimes they do, being potentially the same as words or any other sign system), but that language itself gains meaning from its position in a social context, and that music does too.

Not everyone, of course, believes that Wagner's infusion of language into music was successful. Adorno, for example, suggests that the Wagnerian leitmotif is intrinsically flawed because the very insistence on repetition of the leitmotif makes it suspect—a leitmotif loses the innocence it would need in order to be used, as Wagner frequently attempts to use it, to characterize the persons on stage as innocent or noble. The act of repeating something causes it to be a comment on itself. This is because, in Adorno's terms, Wagner's music does not master time, as Beethoven's does, but negates it; he sees the repeated gesture of the leitmotif as inherently static. Thus, for Adorno, the leitmotif is an expression of Wagner's compulsive nature; Wagner, he says, makes a theory of a fault, creating the leitmotif because he could not create and develop motives in a genuinely musical way, as Beethoven did. Adorno further refutes Wagner's idea that the leitmotifs allow music to develop linguistically rather than as in a symphony, arguing that the leitmotifs are used allegorically and do not, contrary to Wagner's contention, develop psychologically, thus contributing to the generally static quality of Wagner's work. And the changes of instrumentation that go with the various appearances of some of the leitmotifs, he adds, do not help—they simply disguise the fact that there is no development. He argues that among the functions of the leitmotif can be found, "alongside the aesthetic one, a commodity-function, rather like that of an advertisement: anticipating the universal practice of mass culture later on, the music is designed to be remembered, it is intended for the forgetful."[28]

Language, Tonality, and Orchestration

An important aspect of Wagner's general use of music organized to serve the text is his use of tonality. He is well known for what Adorno calls his "emancipation of the dissonance from its various resolutions." However, Adorno argues that Wagner has an "undialectical" view of harmony, that his harmonic progressions are essentially static, and that the overall keyplans of the operas, in spite of Lorenz, have little overall effect on the organization of the works.[29] Robert Bailey tends to agree with him, saying that it is "unthinkable" that the movement from the Valhalla music in D-flat at the end of *Das Rheingold* (which he argues is musically, as well as textually, a prelude to the cycle) to the Valhalla music at the end of *Götterdämmerung*, also in D-flat, constitutes a movement away from and back to a tonic.[30]

This undialectical process of harmonization, which Adorno contrasts to Beethoven's building of structural tensions out of harmonic contrast, is in Wagner "the incarnation of the processes of exchange in society as a whole"; that is, for Adorno, Wagner's music creates an absolute equivalence of all elements, and tension and resolution of tension become the same. Adorno also relates this to what he sees as Wagner's authoritarianism, suggesting that his use of harmony implies the right of a social authority to make the rules.[31] Yet recent research points out some things about the tonality that Adorno may have missed. Patrick McCreless, for example, feels that in some Wagner works the contrast of tonality so important to the classical style, rather than being abandoned, is developed one step further: whereas Beethoven sometimes substituted a contrast between two conflicting keys—a tonic and non-dominant tonal center (that is, the dominant tonal center that traditionally contrasts with the tonic is replaced by some other contrasting key center), Wagner goes a bit further and sometimes allows the contrasting tonality to take over the tonic and become a new stable tonal center itself.[32]

This movement of tonal centers in a nontraditional form is in some instances derived from Wagner's inclination to structure music according to linguistically determined criteria. Robert Bailey points out two types of nonconventional uses of tonality in Wagner, both related to language. The first of these, which he calls the "expressive" use of tonality, is derived from sequential melodic construction. That is, the repetition of a theme or passage one half step or one step higher serves to "underscore intensification." Or moving a melody down one step or one half step indicates relaxation. Similarly, tonal centers can be sequentially related: for example, the beginning of *Die Walküre* is one half step higher than the end of *Das Rheingold*.[33] This use of tonality is derived from the sense that higher equals better, an ideology embedded in linguistic practice. That is, while one normally thinks of a higher pitch as incorporating more tension than a lower one, this is strictly conventional. While it is true that singing high in one's voice or playing very high within the compass of some instruments produces a feeling of tension derived from the extreme effort required to produce the sound, in fact the same effort is often required to produce a sound very low in a range. The tension inherent in low sound, however, is less often exploited by composers (Wagner, in fact, was a pioneer in the use of very low orchestral instruments), and the convention is not nearly so strong.

More important than the relative pitch of keys, however, is what Bailey calls the "associative" tonalities Wagner employs. That is, in the *Ring* certain keys are associated with certain characters or ideas, or, alternatively, specific melodies are associated with a specific tonality throughout. Some examples Bailey gives are the onstage instruments, which have their own tonalities: Siegfried's horn call when played from the stage is always in F major, though when played from the pit it is sometimes in other keys. In addition, some themes have their own tonality: the Valkyries' theme, for example, is always in B minor, the Nibelungs' theme in B-flat minor, the curse motive and the tarnhelm theme in B minor, Valhalla in D-flat major (later also E major) and the sword theme in C major (later also D major).[34] When these themes are used in such a way that the musical structure is built around their predetermined key relationships, linguistic considerations rather than traditional rules of harmony have again dominated the musical structure of the *Ring*.

These associative key relationships, ruled by their relationship to the text, are in part responsible for Wagner's emancipation of dissonance. For in putting linguistic meaning before rules of music, he was bound to break the rules of music sometimes. At first in the *Ring* cycle he did so hesitantly, but the freedom from music traditions implicit in its connection with language become more and more important to him, especially as he began to adapt a Schopenhauerian view of music and its meaning. So he began to feel free to abandon the developmental processes of Beethoven for the freer linguistic processes he had already attempted to exploit with the leitmotif. The importance of language in music moves in his later work from being associated largely with the leitmotif to a wider association with tonality and dissonance. For example, because Brünnhilde is frequently (though not always) associated with E-flat (the key of her being confined to sleep at the end of *Die Walküre*) and Siegfried frequently with C (the key of the sword and heroism in general), they come together in the last act of *Siegfried* as a mutual recognition not only of two characters but also as two keys that eventually resolve to one, but not before the two keys assert themselves in new ways together.[35]

Another way in which linguistic meanings find their way into Wagner's music is in the orchestration. Wagner's use of orchestral instruments to provide meaning in the *Ring* cycle was unique at the time: even Adorno agrees that Wagner's use of color as a part of the musical process "in such a way that colour itself becomes action" did not exist before. For example, for Wagner the horn goes beyond its traditional use as something for flourishes and assumes an expressive function; he replaces the natural horn with the valved horn (on which a chromatic scale could be played).[36] Wagner used such innovations in orchestration in order to strengthen the linguistic meanings of his music and connect the music more strongly to the text: the expressive use of the horn provides an added dimension to the heroic figures associated with it, and the doubling in unison that Wagner frequently employs adds a feeling of depth, sometimes even suggesting an other-worldly dimension, for the passages presented in that fashion.

Music, Language, and the Self

The complex interrelations Wagner develops between language and music are also related to his concept of the individual's relationship to society. Bakhtin (whose theory of language, because it is partially derived from Hegel, often helps explain Wagner) extends the Hegelian notion of the individual created by society to language. All meaning, in language and in other sign systems, is, in Bakhtin's theory, social in origin. He argues that the idea that the individual stands in opposition to society is false. Rather, he says, the individual consciousness is literally created by its interaction with society:

> The individual, as possessor of the contents of his own consciousness, as author of his own thoughts, as the personality responsible for his thoughts and feelings,—such an individual is a purely socioideological phenomenon. Therefore, the content of the "individual" psyche is by its very nature just as social as is ideology and the very degree of consciousness of one's individuality and its inner rights and privileges is ideological, historical, and wholly conditioned by sociological factors. (P. 34)

This is the radical version of Hegel's view of the dependence of the individual on the society that he or she is nurtured in, and is a view that, as we have seen, Wagner sometimes, though incompletely, endorses in his prose writings and in the fates of his characters in the *Ring* cycle.

Bakhtin, however, goes further than either Hegel or Wagner with this idea. In fact, for Bakhtin, language creates the self:

> Language lights up the inner personality and its consciousness; language creates them and endows them with intricacy and profundity—

and it does not work the other way. Personality is itself generated through language, not so much, to be sure, in the abstract forms of language, but rather in the ideological themes of language. Personality, from the standpoint of its inner, subjective content, is a theme of language, and this theme undergoes development and variation within the channel of the more stable constructions of language. Consequently, *a word is not an expression of inner personality; rather, inner personality is an expressed or inwardly impelled word.* And the word is an expression of social intercourse, of the social interaction of material personalities, of producers. The conditions of that thoroughly material intercourse are what determine and condition the kind of thematic and structural shape that the inner personality will receive at any given time and in any given environment; the ways in which it will come to self-awareness; the degree of richness and surety this self-awareness will achieve; and how it will motivate and evaluate its actions. (P. 153)

Siegfried's learning of language after he has risked his life and *not* experienced fear is one step in his restructuring of his own personality, his own self-awareness. For Wagner understood the implications of the Hegelian stand on language and society in something of the same way Bakhtin does, although he was not so articulate about it. The importance he places on Siegfried's learning the true meaning of words from the bird rather than from Mime is clearly in line with this mode of thought about language. Siegfried must *not* learn language from Mime (Siegfried says he has had to force Mime to teach him to speak, but speaking turns out not to be an adequate understanding of language, since real understanding comes from the woodbird). To learn language from Mime would be to structure Siegfried's personality in the ideological image that Mime's language is capable of creating. Instead, in learning or relearning language from the bird, Siegfried creates himself in the image of nature rather than Mime's corrupt society. (Siegfried's stance as a child of nature is exceedingly problematic, however.)

Bakhtin takes Hegel's idea that the individual consciousness is only possible in society to its logical conclusion, arguing that the inner being, the "soul" of the individual is not in fact located within the individual but is an external process located entirely in sign systems such as language, gesture, and action. Thus after these sign systems are employed, there is nothing left over, nothing left unexpressed, nothing hidden (p. 19). The inner self, the psyche, is entirely a product of these material sign systems, created by social conditions. Bakhtin argues that the reality of the inner psyche is actually the reality of the sign itself. He does not argue, of course, that inner psychological or physiological forces are not present, but rather that their organization into the self, their meaning for the individual as well as for the group, is entirely a product of that society as it is objectified in the sign systems it creates. But he emphasizes the creative nature of the constitution of the psyche by the society, not endorsing a scientific determinism but arguing instead that the self exists at a place on the border between the inner psyche and the outer social world. Here, he says, the inner psyche and the outer world meet, not in a physical encounter but in the sign itself. "Psychic experience," he says, "is the semiotic expression of the contact between the organism and the outside environment. That is why *the inner psyche is not analyzable as a thing but can only be understood and interpreted as a sign*" (p. 26). Wagner, in his (partial) espousal of the idea that the individual self is determined by society and in his romantic notion that music reflects emotional meanings (which of course implies that he pictures an active emotional life *within* the psyche), ends in effect at the same position about music that Bakhtin takes concerning language. Wagner created the music of the *Ring* to stand as an objectification, a socially determined and socially readable sign, of the inner world of individuals who are products of their society. That he was successful is clear in the popularity and influence his music and his musical idiom retain even today. For in creating music that seems to express the inner emotional life of his characters, Wagner was giving form to the consciousness of his period. Passion, desire, reverence, joy—whatever emotional response an audience may be likely to associate with a particular moment in the drama, he was able to give musical shape by using his enormous command of the resources of meaning embedded in Western musical practice.

For Wagner, the musical voice embodied in the orchestra is an expression of inner speech, sometimes that of the characters, sometimes that of the narrator. And this inner speech is entirely created from conventional musical materials—not only the tendencies of harmony and musical structure that Wagner followed but also the implicit ideologies of music he employed. This is not to deny Wagner's great creativity, however. His unique awareness of the interaction between speech and music, his understanding, however partial, of the modern concept of self, combined to allow him to extend the borders of convention in musical meaning.

Theodor Adorno, Wagner's most perceptive neo-Marxist critic, suggests that although Wagner frequently failed in his attempts to create a believable inner life for his characters, this very failure "reveals traces of a political awareness of the way the individual is determined by material reality." He goes on to suggest that

Wagner belongs to "the first generation" to realize that the individual in such a society is doomed to failure, that "it is not possible for an individual to alter something that is determined over the heads of men." However, Adorno feels that Wagner did not go far enough in this recognition and that he tried to suppress this knowledge: in the music drama, "the opacity and omnipotence of the social process is then celebrated as a metaphysical mystery by the individual who becomes conscious of it and yet ranges himself on the side of its dominant forces."[37] Adorno, as always, is concerned with the extent of oppression in Western culture; he recognizes the extent of domination in Wagner's ideology. Yet his insistence that Wagner retreated from his radical sense of the individual's inability to separate himself from historical patterns of domination applies more to *Parsifal* or *Meistersinger* than to the *Ring.* The ending of *Götterdämmerung* demonstrates, not the glorification of social forces of domination but the destruction of the greatest hopes of the individual to separate himself from these (even though Wagner does embed a certain ambiguity in the ending).

In the *Ring,* Wagner used his extensive musical means to suggest a psychological reality for the inner self that seems to contradict his theoretical investment in Hegelian and Feuerbachian notions of historical reality. The musical means Wagner used were often necessarily conventional, but always with his own uniquely intensified adaptation of the conventions. The intensity of the music is one thing audiences often respond to—Adorno, not surprisingly perhaps, found this intensity a fault in Wagner, but others find it compelling and interesting. In the first act of *Die Walküre,* suggests Bryan Magee, intensity reaches a new level: "Here, for the first time in his work, Wagner hit the gusher to the unconscious, and out poured a flow of molten material from the innermost core of the world of human feeling, from that buried, remote and dangerous interior to which he ws to retain access ever after."[38] This is a common reaction to Wagner, but this "core" of meaning does not come, as Magee implies, from human essence but, as Bakhtin argues, from human cultural practice. This is not of course to denigrate Wagner's achievement; one of his major accomplishments was that he was especially sensitive to social expressions of emotion and able far more than other composers of his time to place this common core of emotional or inner experience into objective form.

Wagner's music does not, however, encode some mysterious inner human essence. Bakhtin argues strenuously against the idea of the sacredness of the individual self, the soul, as a mysterious entity that is naturally or magically formed, separate from and independent of other humans around us. That is not to say, of course, that individuals do not have inner experience that is usually called consciousness. Rather, Bakhtin argues that individual consciousness, because it is constituted of inner speech, of signs, and because signs are material things created by social interaction, exists only as language or inner speech:

> The individual consciousness is nurtured on signs; it derives its growth from them; it reflects their logic and laws. The logic of consciousness is the logic of ideological communication, of the semiotic interaction of a social group. If we deprive consciousness of its semiotic, ideological content, it would have absolutely nothing left. Consciousness can harbor only in the image, the word, the meaningful gesture, and so forth. Outside such material, there remains the sheer physiological act unilluminated by consciousness, i.e., without having light shed on it, without having meaning given to it, by signs. (P. 13)

Thus Wagner's music, rather than reflecting an inner, intuitive life of the emotions for the characters (and for the audience), is actually creating, in objectified form, the signs by which members of Western culture denote inner experience. Music does not actually express an inner happening; rather, the signs of music are the social, outer materials into which has traditionally been invested a sense of what constitutes inner, emotional experience. Musical signs may very well embody other meanings than emotion, but Wagner was particularly interested in this aspect of the traditional Western conception of music. Thus the music of the *Ring* is an immense and complex statement of musical signs of emotional meanings, but these are traditional, conventional meanings, not individual, inner ones.

Wagner's contributions to the changes in musical structure—in his innovations in tonality and orchestration—are, like his use of the leitmotif, related to language and his argument that music should always serve the drama. In characterizing music as feminine and poetry as masculine, he implied, no matter what he may have thought about equality in other contexts, a relation of dominance of music by language. To some extent this domination is characteristic of the music in the *Ring* cycle. Yet in his most influential approaches to musical composition, language was always exploited as a part of music rather than as something external to it. Composers who followed Wagner in his approach to harmony, orchestration, or even the repeated motive, frequently did so in contexts in which the linguistic origins of his techniques were inconsequential. Thus Wagner's musical innovations quickly freed themselves from the text and returned to absolute music.

3

DAS RHEINGOLD

Although the text of *Das Rheingold* was written after those of the other operas, almost as if it were an afterthought, it was neverthe-less designated as a prelude to the three other operas of the *Ring* cycle. Perhaps Wagner called *Das Rheingold* a prelude to underline its character: the opera's relation to its own story is quite different from that of the other works in the *Ring*, which become in-creasingly more realistic as they move from the world of gods to that of humans. In *Das Rheingold*, however, the audience is clearly expected to read the gods and their doings as a Feuerbachian religious allegory. As allegory, *Das Rheingold* sets up the situation that allows for the later development of self-consciousness Wagner explored in his history of the world.

In some ways *Das Rheingold* parallels the early parts of Hegel's *Phenomenology*, in which the individual's relations to unmediated physical reality are examined. The prelude especially has been taken to suggest something about nature and the human response to it; although Wagner may have meant to suggest unmediated reality, untouched nature, in the opening, many critics have sug-gested that the attempt is naive and doomed to failure. Peter Ackermann, for example, criticizes the composer's efforts to es-tablish a mythical primacy for nature here.[1] His critique is drawn from the general criticism of Western culture in Max Horkheimer and Theodor Adorno's *Dialectic of Enlightenment*, where the au-thors deplore the tendency of reason to make things into con-ceptual relations of time and space or into mathematical relationships, a tendency that they see as a fundamental move-ment toward domination. The domination of nature reflected in modern technology, they feel, has its origin in habits of thought that derive from the Enlightenment effort to include physical reality as a part of the mental: "The task of cognition does not consist in mere apprehension, classification, and calculation," but attempts to negate reality itself (by reducing it to a function of thought). But reality remains, and in attempting to deal with it

Enlightenment thought returns in spite of itself to myth, which it cannot escape, because reason sees myth as the unchangeable status quo of reality; myth is "cycle, fate, and domination of the world reflected as the truth and deprived of hope." What is missing for most persons wrapped up in this habit of thought is a dialectical, historical concept of reality, and the effort of thought needed to place real things into a historical and social meaning: "In both the pregnancy of the mythical image and the clarity of the scientific formula, the everlastingness of the factual is confirmed and mere existence pure and simple expressed as the meaning which it forbids."[2] Thus for Horkheimer and Adorno neither myth nor reason can cope with reality as historically derived, but both must fail because they interpret the world as static.

According to Ackermann, then, Wagner was unable to escape this impasse between reason and myth. The return to myth in *Das Rheingold* is the means by which Wagner attempts to release himself from the rational problem of Hegelian self-consciousness that he set up for Siegfried. After writing the texts for *Siegfrieds Tod* and *Der junge Siegfried* (which later became *Götterdämmerung* and *Siegfried*), Wagner realized that this nature hero and Hegelian hero all wrapped into one simply did not work. Unable to resolve contradictions in his own thinking concerning the relationship between Siegfried and Brünnhilde, he retreated further and further into myth in an attempt to explain, even conceptualize, the reality that he hoped the *Ring* cycle would reflect. And finally, in so doing, he composed the prelude to *Das Rheingold*, the place where myth attempts to escape language and reason altogether and lose itself in wordless sound, in a chaos of physical reality. Thomas Mann, catching this quality in the prelude, suggests that Wagner mythologizes music itself:

> For the bottom of the Rhine, with the shimmering hoard of gold where the Rhinemaidens delight to sport and play, was none other than the world's original state of innocence, untouched as yet by greed and evil curse—and by the same token it was *the beginning of music itself.* And it was not just the music of myth that he, the poet-composer, would give us, but the very myth of music itself, a mythical philosophy and a musical poem of Creation, the story of its growth from the E flat major triad of the deep-flowing Rhine into a richly structured world of symbols.[3]

As Mann says, the prelude constitutes a history of music.[4] It begins with a single note, the famous E-flat, with no harmony and no rhythm. The lack of rhythm is particularly remarkable, since rhythm is so important in the first scene. The music gradually adds the fifth, then the third to constitute a major triad, and rhythm is introduced: at first simple, then becoming more complex. Passing tones from the dominant seventh are added, and then finally a whole scale appears. The prelude thus is an allegory of the process of individuation, the Hegelian theme of the *Ring*. The cycle will move in fact from the faceless void of the prelude, in which everything is potential but undifferentiated, to the strong individualism of the hero Siegfried.

The prelude is also a clear example of the ideology of authenticity that Wagner is working with. The persistent 6/8 and 9/8 rhythms, which continue into the first scene, are meant to suggest the flowing of water. These rhythms, as well as the melodically presented triads and chords, remain so important that they control the structure of such themes as the Ring motive throughout the cycle. The orchestration is also suggestive: the pedal point E-flat is played by the double basses, the spatial relations of up and down already being important textually as well as in musical traditions. The "melody" is on the horns in E-flat—in the *Ring*, horns are frequently associated with authenticity (as when a horn becomes Siegfried's instrument). The instruments throughout the prelude, however, are not differentiated much in sound, suggesting a unity of nature, and the total effect is almost that of a great Rossini crescendo.

The idea that the prelude to *Das Rheingold* constitutes a mysterious, mythic force comes from Wagner himself, from his well-known story of how the idea of the prelude came to him in a vision. He describes in *Mein Leben* an experience he had while at La Spezia, where the music appeared to him in a vision of mythic proportions in which the self is dissolved into eternity: in this vision "the E flat major triad never changed, and seemed by its continuance to impart infinite significance to the element in which I was sinking."[5] Wagner explained this prelude in similar mythic terms, according to Porges, at the rehearsals for the *Ring*: "Regarding the orchestral prelude as a whole, built on a single E flat major triad, Wagner insisted that its huge crescendo should throughout create the impression of a phenomenon of nature developing quite of its own accord—so to say, an impersonal impression."[6] And Bailey agrees that the prelude, as well as the entire first scene, represents unconsciousness—only in scene 2, he says, do we get the coming of consciousness (he goes on to argue that because the text of the first scene of *Das Rheingold* constitutes a prelude, the musical structure is also that of a prelude, at least in its relation to other scenes and operas; the structure of a prelude and three scenes, he says, repeated in *Götterdämmerung,* is also the structure of the cycle as a whole.)[7] Peter Ackermann argues that the *Rheingold* prelude postulates the transcendentalism of music itself.[8] In fact, however, this transcendental claim for music is negative. Hegel claims that whatever reality we start with will be shown to contain an inner necessity for contradiction and self-destruction. Wagner seems to have understood this inherent negativity in all being; the music of the prelude shows that tone, music, and harmony demonstrate this inherent negativity. The long-held single chord of the prelude *must* develop; its length alone creates the need for change.

Some have challenged Wagner's famous story of the inception of the prelude in a dream. Westernhagen argues that the music for this prelude derives from a much earlier sketch Wagner made of the Norns' scene for *Siegfrieds Tod* and predates the vision at La Spezia. However, Westernhagen holds that even if Wagner had the motive itself ready before the vision, what presented itself to him in the dream were the specific details of composition (although the key and the orchestration [horns] were already present in the earlier sketch): "What 'came upon' Wagner in La Spezia was the outcome of that rising tension, not a careful motivic development, but an irresistible natural event."[9] John Deathridge more cynically suggests that Wagner may have found his vision after reading Schopenhauer's *Parerga and Paralipomena,* which discusses dreams and visions.[10]

The view of the prelude as a musical presentation of mythic creation and a metaphor for nature because it is in some way itself natural has been challenged in other ways as well. Peter Ackermann, for example, analyzes the prelude as a set of variations—a very conventional and therefore "unnatural" form. He argues that although the prelude is usually assumed to suggest chaos, nature in an undifferentiated, unconscious existence, the music is actually divided into very regular periods, and he finds a logical break between the characterless single-note theme and the variation form to which it leads.[11] Ackermann argues that the beginning of *Das Rheingold* is already the moment of the dialectic of Enlightenment, that Wagner's compliance in his culture's attempt to dominate nature is clear from the beginning. History, in the *Ring,* begins with the destruction of nature.

The creation myth that Wagner attempts to invoke musically here is perhaps related to his reading of Hegel's discussion of the rise of consciousness out of unconsciousness. "Consciousness," says Hegel, *"distinguishes* from itself something, to which at the same time it relates itself; or, to use the current expression, there is something *for* consciousness; and the determinate form of this process of relating, or of there being something for a consciousness, is knowledge" (p. 139). That is, consciousness and knowledge arise when the subject begins to distinguish itself from the world as object. This basic human experience is what Hegel describes in the history of consciousness in general, and what Wagner creates in his prelude in terms of music being distinguished from simple sound (though of course his simple sound, the E-flat chord, is already music and already meaningful). Melody distinguishes itself from harmony and becomes a thing. And it is through melody, as we have seen, that Wagner felt music expressed itself most concretely.

Thus for Wagner this prelude does not represent the ultimate reality, the good from which all evil is differentiated (in the form of Alberich and his ring) and to which the world must return at the end. Although the ring does revert to the Rhinedaughters at the end, the world is a far different place. Self-knowledge, which is Wagner's ultimate good (when it is based on material and self-sacrificing love), has entered the world and made it better. Wagner did not, then, postulate this natural world of the prelude as an idealized nature that is unequivocally good. Hegel points out again and again that the initial stage of unity of spirit with nature is not true oneness—it is an error to consider this unity the most excellent mode of consciousness.[12] For Hegel, a new unity must develop through human consciousness. Thus the primal unity of *Das Rheingold* is a negative, and the cycle creates a progression, not a meaningless circle; the return of the gold to the river at the end of *Götterdämmerung* is just a way of getting rid of something that is no longer significant (let the children have the thing, as Loge says). What is real at the end is the development of consciousness into love.

Scene 1

The first scene of *Das Rheingold* is sometimes interpreted as an allegory of the rape of nature by industrialized man and the loss of love that the power and domination of capitalist societies require. Significantly, nature here is represented by women—the three women who echo not only the Lorelei of German myth but also the witches of Macbeth and the fates of Greek mythology. Yet the three Rhinedaughters are stripped of the abilities of these other women to foresee the future or control the present; they are instead innocent victims of Alberich's cunning. Porges was one of the first to suggest this interpretation: he says that the Rhinedaughters reflect a "naive gaiety," in contrast to Alberich.[13] However, as Horkheimer and Adorno point out, the historic casting of women in the role of creatures somehow more natural than males is a move of dominance, and the figure of woman as a "natural being" is a "product of history, which denaturizes her."[14] That is, the impulse to treat women as more natural creatures than men is also an impulse to dominate them by depriving them of the power of intellect, an impulse that Wagner, in spite of his glorification of such women as Brünnhilde, could not escape.[15]

Place is also important in *Das Rheingold*. The setting, as described at the beginning of the first scene, suggests the values inherent in the spatial scheme of the *Ring*. The scene is typically romantic, a place wild and craggy (also suggesting the standard romantic notion that nature allows man access to the wild and primitive in his own nature). It is darker in the lower part of the stage, brighter above; the simple ideology of higher being equated with good and lower with evil is called into play. In this scene and throughout *Das Rheingold,* characters enter from below, rising from an inferior place or a place of unconsciousness (Alberich comes up into the Rhine from below, just as Erda comes up from the earth onto the mountain home of the gods; Loge too enters from below, climbing up from the valley, and even Wotan rises from sleep). The text at the beginning makes this emphasis on place very clear: Alberich climbs up a rock from a chasm below, and he addresses the Rhinedaughters as "Ihr, da oben!" ("You, there above").[16] Part of the characterization of Alberich as evil depends on the values usually assigned to below (inferior) and black (evil). The light and dark imagery here is also connected with the sun, for the space in this scene is dark at first, then brightly lighted when the rising sun is reflected off the gold. This light imagery is important for Siegfried later in the cycle, but it becomes somewhat less clear in this scene when, after the gold is stolen, the Rhine loses its light and becomes, like Nibelheim, a place of darkness.

Woglinde's entrance at the beginning of the first scene introduces a new chord (the subdominant, A-flat) for the first time—it comes as a welcome relief, the unrelenting E-flat having produced a negative tension that demands change. Melodically, her appoggiatura (F–E-flat) is the germ for the theme of the greeting to the

gold later so important. Her first words are nonsense syllables—
the emphasis on nonsense words throughout this scene constantly
reminds us that the Rhinedaughters are of nature. If the opening
music suggests the beginning of music, the first words suggest the
development of language from natural sounds, uttered as an
expression of enthusiasm and joy, and illustrate Wagner's theory
of the origin of language explained in *Oper und Drama:*

> Weia! Waga!
> Woge, du Welle!
> Walle zur Wiege!
> Wagalaweia!
> Wallala weiala weia!
>
> Weia! Waga!
> Wandering waters,
> Lulling our cradle!
> Wagalaweia!
> Wallala weiala weia!

(P. 4)

In line with his theory, here Wagner makes words clearly secondary to music and suggests a primitive innocence for language.
However, Bakhtin argues that only the inarticulate animal cry is
without an ideological, socially-created grounding; when humans
communicate, even in the most primitive circumstances, they do
so in a world in which meaning is already social and ideological (p.
93). The "natural" world of this first scene is already political and
cultural, a world in which women's roles are already tied to nature
and purity, and racism (in the form of Alberich—he is described
as a toad, black, and pictured as insensitive) has already emerged.
Wagner implies that these conditions always existed, instead of
positioning them as part of culture (Wotan's world) where they
would be open to change.

But Wagner does not allow his moment of pure expression to
last long. The first dialogue of the cycle, between Woglinde and
Wellgunde, already shows that language implies value. Wellgunde
asks if Woglinde is "watching alone." Although no mention is
made at this point why they must watch or what they must watch
for, the point is clear that value and danger reside within their
purview. The point is even stronger when Flosshilde, the advocate
of morality in this scene, appears for the first time and reminds
her sisters they must get back to their duty:

Des Goldes Schlaf
hütet ihr schlecht;
besser bewacht
des Schlummernden Bett,
sonst büßt ihr beide Spiel!

The sleeping gold
calls for your care!
Back to your task
of guarding its bed,
or else you'll pay for your games!

(P. 4)

The contrast between the opposing elements of sleep and consciousness will be important throughout the cycle; sleep suggests a lack of Hegelian self-awareness. The gold itself sleeps; its awakening will set off the rise of self-consciousness in the world.

The greatest contrast with the E-flat comes, of course, at Alberich's entrance; he enters in G minor, the first real key change of the opera. Major-minor symbolism is used here quite conventionally; Alberich's music is frequently in the minor to suggest his evil nature. The conventional contrast between chromatic and diatonic music is also important, Alberich's music being comparatively chromatic; in this scene he is characteristically accompanied by chromatic scales to demonstrate his artificiality. Yet such conventional musical symbolism must frequently be subordinated to normal musical development. Several motives are associated with Alberich; the first has a limping rhythm played by the orchestra. These give some relief from the persistent water rhythms of the scene, yet they owe much to the prevailing music, and in general the value of musical unity wins over that of dramatic contrast. In addition, Alberich's entrance provides not only a musical difference but he signals the existence of a political world. At the beginning of the scene, the Rhinedaughters, although they do have an ideology, exhibit no hierarchy and hence no social structure (even though they do have distinct personalities); hierarchy, and consequently the question of power, enters only with Alberich.

Alberich is usually considered the villain of the *Ring* cycle. Fredric Jameson defines the villain of melodrama as one who on the one hand reinforces "our essentially ideological conception of evil" and on the other seems to explain "the existence of social disorder."[17] Alberich fits this description: he explains the presence of social disorder in the plot by stealing the gold and thus, in a sense, inventing greed, and he reinforces Wagner's ideology of the hero: Alberich appears inherently evil when Flosshilde describes him as being shaped like and sounding like a toad. Cooke, however, sees Alberich less as villain than as a victim who is forced by the behavior of the Rhinedaughters into renouncing love, arguing that because Alberich's love for the Rhinedaughters has an idealizing quality, their rejection is a genuine humiliation for him: "The idealization vanishes, leaving only his inflamed desire for physical sex, now turned sadistic, as he vainly chases them with the aim of raping them."[18] Alberich is filled with rage and frustration by their teasing and determines to take one (or more) of the women by force, although of course they are far too agile for him. Wagner implies that Alberich does not really need to forswear love; he already has no capability for the relationship between equals that love demands. However, he has been humiliated, as Freia will be later; humiliation or shame is the recognition of the self as unworthy because it has been seen as unworthy by others. It is a powerful psychological force, and Wagner places it here as the opposite of the mutual recognition he defines as love. He makes humiliation the initial motivation for the power that will oppose love.

Cooke is not the only viewer who tends to see Alberich as victim. In spite of everything, Alberich is often regarded as a sympathetic character. This is perhaps because, musically, his entrance relieves somewhat the relentless E-flat as well as because of his treatment by the Rhinedaughters. For these viewers, the ideology represented by the Rhinedaughters is not presented strongly enough, as if Wagner unconsciously had doubts about who could win a confrontation between man and woman. Thus the Rhinedaughters appear not only natural and simple but cruel.

Flosshilde's song to Alberich parodies an operatic love scene, she singing a lyrical time while Alberich inserts comments. Only the context suggests to the audience, if not to Alberich, that she is faking emotion. The entrance of the harp as Flosshilde speaks strikes us as ironic; it lightens the texture and suggests a delicacy of touch that neither Alberich nor Flosshilde has. Flosshilde's wooing of Alberich is accompanied by a solo violin (presented as a lyric instrument associated with love at various points throughout the cycle). This love scene is carried out on two levels; we have to believe Alberich is serious, even though he is not very convincing. The girls, on the other hand, even the seemingly serious Flosshilde, are playing at their parts as lovers, teasing Alberich

Example 3.1

with no real awareness that he offers a threat. It is difficult, however, to see them as the dangerous seductresses that Fricka does later.[19] Still, the Rhinedaughters represent women who are willing to sell love and as such are a parody of what Wagner felt was the true nature of women. They tell Alberich that he should look for a lover who is like himself, thus introducing the concept of mutual recognition to be important later, though they do not now understand it and are not capable of such understanding. The Rhinedaughters also sing about the free one they will be true too—freedom and love are already firmly intertwined. They mock Alberich because he wants to possess rather than love and does not understand the difference.

During this scene, a short theme, which although it grows out of the Rhine music is associated with Alberich's rage, evolves into a new theme (the intervals are widened from thirds to fourths and fifths to establish the differences between the chromaticism of Alberich's music and the triads and fifths of the Rhine music)— the first statement of the motive associated with the gold (example 3-1). Although this development of the gold theme from Alberich's music is effective, it seems to make little sense dramatically, showing that at this stage of his compositional development Wagner often maintained, in spite of his theory, an independence between music and text.

A sense of breathlessness and awe arises from conventional musical means as the Rhinedaughters watch the light developing from the gold; the harps provide arpeggios while the horns play the gold theme very softly and the strings supply tremolo harmony. The Rhinedaughters greet the gold with an ecstatic cry, reverting to their nonsense language, and they sing its praises in a chorus that emphasizes joy, play, dancing, and singing. They express a precapitalist joy of possession; they view the gold as beautiful and valuable in itself, not as a medium of exchange. They are like children, living in a state close to unconsciousness; like Hegel's description of children, they are "rich in sense-perceptions but poor in thoughts" (*Lectures,* p. 81). Wagner in presenting them obviously had in mind a primitive society in which all needs are met by nature and the false desires of consumerism have not

yet been aroused. Nevertheless, the Rhinedaughters are not completely naive; they tell Alberich how the ring can win for him the
world's wealth, and they are aware of the danger that it might be
stolen by the greedy. Their implication in the cultural world is
suggested musically; Dalhouse notes that the first note of their
song, already presented several times in this scene, is an appoggiatura that suggests in its dissonance "a characteristic divergence"
from the simplicity of the elemental. This appoggiatura now
appears, extended, as a ninth in the first chord of the greeting to
the gold, of which a chromatically darkened variant later becomes
associated with the bondage of the Nibelungen.[20]

Woglinde, in one of the most important passages in this scene,
tells Alberich that only the person who renounces love can forge
the ring and so gain world power. Woglinde not only mentions
love but also power:

> Nur wer der Minne
> Mach versagt,
> nur wer der Liebe
> Lust verjagt,
> nur der erzielt sich den Zauber,
> zum Reif zu zwingen das Gold.

> Only he who renounces
> love's power
> Only he who renounces
> love's joy
> Only he can master the magic
> to forge a ring from the gold.

(P. 15)

The "renunciation" theme to which Woglinde sings these words
seems misnamed (example 3-2). A notion that applies better to all
its appearances in the *Ring* is that it suggests the need for love, a
need even Alberich feels, though on a primitive level. Thus the
theme usually labeled renunciation really suggests love's necessity
(as Siegmund says when he sings the theme while he withdraws
the sword in *Die Walküre*), a substitute for Hegelian necessity as
reason.[21] The need for love appears over and over again as the
motivating force behind the movement of the plot throughout the
Ring and represents Wagner's adjustment of Hegel and Feuerbach to his own ideology. The text here suggests that it is not so
much love itself that the ring's maker must forgo, but the power
and joy love brings. The ultimate aim of love, for Wagner, is for

Nur wer der Min-ne Macht ver - sagt, nur wer der Lie -be Lust ver -jagt

Example 3.2

the individual to surrender completely to it, as Brünnhilde does, so that the only power the person subscribes to is love (this is the conscious ideology of the text, as opposed to the unconscious one in which the power of love becomes male domination). So by adopting the ring and the political and economic power it symbolizes, Alberich in fact is giving up real power as Wagner sees it, the power to change the world through self-sacrificing love. Here the renunciation of love is the negative; the positive, love itself, appears gradually throughout the cycle. Wagner reverses the Hegelian dialectic, presenting the negative first. But a more conscious creature than Alberich (that is, Wotan), must emerge to weigh the relative merits of love (as he sees it) and power in order for the dialectic to begin to change things.[22]

As Alberich decides to renounce love for gold, the theme already associated with the gold (example 3-1) is stated in the orchestra first in the minor then in a diminished form (this theme is presented in C major, an ideologically loaded "natural" key). Thus spatial imagery is used even in the music, the diminution of the major triad representing a negative value. The spatial diminution is also clear in the other important theme associated with Alberich in this scene, the so-called ring theme, constituted as it is of minor triads. This theme, however, is explicitly labeled by Wagner in the composition sketch as the "world inheritance" motive.[23] Although throughout the cycle this motive frequently appears when the ring is mentioned by characters on stage, in fact Wagner evidently wanted it to indicate a larger notion, the feeling/thought aroused in a character like Alberich by the notion of political power. The words Wellgunde sings, in fact, when this motive first appears emphasize the world power inherent in the ring that is to be fashioned from the gold.

Scene 2

The prevailing rhythmic intensity of scene 1 and its harmonic homogeneity provide an impetus into history as we seek a relief

Example 3.3

from timelessness. The interlude to scene 2 is structured partly from a two-note theme related both to Alberich's lament over being denied love and the melody with which the Rhinedaughters greet the gold. The motive associated with the need for love (renunciation theme), having here a dark but high coloring (horn and English horn) is also prominent, and the trumpet presents a reveille-type figure as the second scene opens. Like many themes of the *Ring* cycle, this one (which is really a developmental motive rather than a theme) suggests the ideology of honor and militarism associated with the trumpet call. The motive associated with world power (the ring motive), very prominent in this interlude, gradually is transformed at the end of the interlude into the motive usually called the Valhalla theme (example 3-3). Westernhagen, citing this example, notes that many themes show up first in embryonic form in sketches as well as in the score, a fact that, he argues, shows that the musical development of the leitmotif is a spontaneous process, not a deliberated one.[24] However, the linguistic connection Wagner attempts to draw in this manner between the ring as a symbol of political power and the world of Wotan is obvious. In fact, the Valhalla motive is simply a variant of the ring or world power motive.[25] The contrast between the two variants, the Valhalla motive being very diatonic while the ring motive is built on minor and diminished triads, spells out in simple musical terms the ideologies suggested. Yet the development of one theme out of the other undercuts this seeming simplicity. Wagner attempted to encapsulate in musical form his ideas about political power explained in *Oper und Drama* (and derived from Hegel) where he argued that the political power of the state, no matter how well-intentioned, is still tyrannical and destroys individuality. Thus the two variants of the power motive, the one associated with Alberich and the other with Wotan, are intended to suggest that all forms of power are repressive; in the end, both forms of power must be destroyed by Siegfried's goodness and Brünnhilde's sacrifice.

These two themes illustrate that the musical associations with the principle symbols of power in this opera are iconic (that is, the themes in some way sound like what they represent). The Valhalla motive is impressive and regular, and the ring motive is indecisive and circular (while the later spear motive is emphatic and linear).[26] The frequent recurrence of these themes is also a paradigm of their meaning; according to Horkheimer and Adorno, the symbols of domination are frequently repetitive ones, heralding the relation to nature and the forces that tie the subjugated to it: "For the vanquished (whether by alien tribes or by their own cliques), the recurrent, eternally similar natural processes become the rhythm of labor according to the beat of cudgel and whip which resounds in every barbaric drum and every monotonous ritual. The symbols undertake a fetishistic function."[27] Wagner recognizes the relationship of this unyielding repetition to domination in the repeated rhythmic motive associated with the Nibelungen. In a less obvious form, however, the ring or world power theme, particularly repeated as it is in almost unchanging form throughout the cycle, becomes a fetish of domination that reminds us, in its obvious musical derivation from the water music of the first scene, of the domination of nature.

The world power motive, in its ring and Valhalla variants, suggests a more complex view of domination, however. The domination of nature involves the transformation of nature into a commodity, symbolized by the transformation of the gold into the ring. Wagner was perhaps influenced by Proudhon's slogan, "Property is robbery," which he called the "signal of revolutions."[28] The ring obviously symbolizes property as theft—Alberich steals the gold from the Rhinedaughters and Wotan steals it in turn from Alberich. But the musical connection between the ring and Valhalla reminds us that Valhalla too is property—and Wotan intends, in fact, to steal it from the giants by robbing them of payment for their labor.

The beginning of the second scene moves us into a world of law and contracts. According to Adorno, in Wagner's works law viewed as myth is deficient; it is "unmasked as the equivalent of lawlessness."[29] That is, the laws by which Wotan rules are in this scene shown to be inadequate to a complex social reality, and Wotan must fall back on the violence implied by the spear to enforce them. The violence on which Wotan depends for his power is connected both with his status as god and his spear; Adorno argues that in the *Ring* "mythic violence and legal contract are confounded" because Wagner intuits the origin of law in violence and also expresses the experience of his own society that the protection of property is regarded as the highest good.[30]

The position of Wotan in the ideology of the cycle is already complex at the beginning of this scene. Scene 2 opens on a mountain top, height representing positive value; it is described as a free, open space ("Freie Gegend auf Bergeshöhen"). As the scene opens, the gods apparently live in this open space, which they are about to give up for the castle Valhalla, an enclosed space designed for protection, that is, designed out of fear of loss of power. Wotan's waking words emphasize this:

> Der Wonne seligen Saal
> bewachen mir Tür und Tor:
>   Mannes Ehre,
>   ewige Macht
> ragen endlosem Ruhm!

> The sacred hall of the gods
> is guarded by gate and door:
>   manhood's honor
>   unending power,
> rise now to endless renown.

(P. 19)

Wotan's words here, like the conversation between Hagen and Gunther at the beginning of *Götterdämmerung*, suggest a human society based on hierarchy and domination rather than on mutual recognition. Wotan's ideology of power and honor seems moral (suggested by the conventionally grandiose elements of the Valhalla music), but this ideology is finally proven false, the state power that Brünnhilde must destroy as Antigone, the example Wagner cites in *Oper und Drama*, destroys Creon's power. That the castle is a symbol of honor and power is clear, and Wotan's world is already political and ideological. But Valhalla needs gates and doors (later supplemented by the heroes) for protection. Although the threat against which it is to be guarded is vague at the beginning of scene 2, these lines show how Wotan is thinking, and the equation of power and fear that later becomes much clearer to him is here foreshadowed. Wotan goes on to indicate that the castle, conceived in dreams, is a product of his will, and he predicts that it is eternal.

Wotan of course is wrong. Wagner perhaps originally conceived this character as a benevolent ruler, who although corrupted by the culture in which he is entangled is still able to set in motion the process of rising self-consciousness embodied in Siegfried and by which Brünnhilde and Siegfried are to save the world. But as is well known, Wagner changed the ending he originally intended, in which Brünnhilde and Siegfried were to be taken into Valhalla and the gods were not destroyed, and with it the function of Wotan. Now throughout the cycle Wotan seems to ask for our respect, then our disapprobation. In this scene he is to some extent opposed by Fricka, who contrasts his masculine values based on domination to feminine values based on cooperation. But even her values turn out to be inadequate; by the end of *Das Rheingold* Wotan has conceived his great idea, imaged by the sword theme and later by the sword itself. He has, in other words, discovered the inadequacy of his own mindset and begun the process that will lead (though not of course by the paths he thinks or plans) to a higher one.

To some extent Wotan embodies Hegel's man of common sense, the thinking educated person in a culture who despite his accomplishments has not come to self-consciousness, or not to any self-consciousness that could matter, partly because common sense, in its self-reliance and faith in self-made ideas, shows no understanding of the role played by culture.[31] Adorno and Horkheimer go even further than Hegel in criticizing common sense, suggesting that it is characteristic of bourgeois society, which insists on "sobriety and common sense. . . . The wish must not be father to the thought."[32] Wotan embodies both this bourgeois denial of pleasure and the moral uprightness encoded in this attitude. He forbids Donner to use force on the giants to rescue Freia, insisting on the use of subtler and less instinctive methods of domination. Similarly, he rejects the possibility of pleasure in marriage or at home, yet seeks but does not find pleasure in his travels. He knows his own wishes to be dangerous and destructive, and he attempts to find ways to comply with them without destroying the contracts on his spear. If Hegel's political philosophy begins with a restatement of Rousseau's claim that man everywhere thinks he is free but is really in chains,[33] then Wagner places Wotan in this position at the beginning of *Das Rheingold*. In the course of the remaining scenes of this opera, Wotan gradually comes to realize that he is indeed in chains, even though he did not know it at first, and at the end of *Das Rheingold* he determines to do something about it.

Wotan, along with the other gods, also embodies a Feuerbachian allegory of the failure of religious faith. "Only an impoverished humanity has a rich God," according to Feuerbach, and as humanity is impoverished, especially without love, so it creates a god rich in these qualities.[34] This is Feuerbach's explanation of Christianity with its emphasis on love and sacrifice. Wotan's society has not created a god rich in love—love is a new element trying to find its way in the world of the *Ring*—but it has created a god rich in dignity, control, and power, qualities the ancient society of the *Ring,* as we see it exemplified in Hunding or Gunther, lacks.

Many of Wotan's problems stem from the inadequacy of his conception of law. The only way Wotan can deal with Freia, the embodiment of woman, is as property, even though he has a vague idea that such behavior is not helpful. According to Adorno, contracts are essential throughout the *Ring.* The contrasts so important in the cycle (he believes Wagner is following Schopenhauer) are predicated on anarchy, and everything threatens to break into violence, destruction, and total war unless specifically restrained by contracts; he argues that Wotan readily agrees to violence in situations in which he is not specifically bound by codified agreements.[35] Commentators, however do not always recognize the relation of law to domination that Adorno outlines. Cooke, for example, while noting that the "spear itself represents first and foremost Wotan's sheer will to dominate—the laws engraved on it are *his* laws, and everyone, including himself, obeys them only because he wills it so" nevertheless goes on to say that "the prime motive behind this is the building up of an ordered civilization."[36]

But Wotan cannot build an ordered civilization based on the contracts on his spear because they violate what Wagner sees as the essential force creating culture: love. According to Hegel, if certain things such as the sanctity of property or promises are presupposed, they carry with them certain practical principles—and these practical principles, not philosophic or ethical ones, are what is in force (this is part of his critique of Kantian ethics). Thus what is really at work in a given situation is the adherence to social custom, which Hegel sees as basic, rather than to a philosophic principle of ethics *(Phenomenology,* p. 80) that operates. Wagner embodies his own version of this argument in *Das Rheingold,* implying that Wotan's rules and Alberich's property are really the same thing. At the heart of contracts and laws, if they are to work, must lie not violence or greed but love. The *Ring* cycle works out the contradiction between holding property by force (theft) and the emptiness of rational laws—against these is placed the social reality based on mutual recognition developed through the human characters. Therefore both Alberich and Wotan, in spite of the ideological differences implied for them through music, set, and costuming, are to be regarded as failures: for both, says Cooke, who has examined in detail the parallels between these two characters, world dominance is gained from ravishing the raw material of the world (gold, the ash tree) and exploiting it (turning it into the ring or the spear), and in both cases the raw materials are ruled over by three women (the Rhinedaughters and Norns).[37]

Wotan's problem, as well as his might, is symbolized by the castle. He must, in the course of the next few scenes, come to a new consciousness of the inadequacy of his own life, and in that lies his superiority to Alberich, who never gains insight into the necessity for change. That Wotan will feel the need for a new consciousness is inevitable: an essential idea of Hegel's is that man struggles for an external embodiment that expresses him but is frustrated by the realities on which he depends.[38] Wotan is already involved when we first see him in a struggle to attain such a consciousness; he has created Valhalla as an external expression of man. When he sees the likelihood of this form of reality failing him, after Erda's visit, he conceives a new reality, symbolized by the sword. But this fails in an even more integral way. For Hegel, the fact that men have the wrong purposes in mind is what defeats them—their plans can only go awry because even though they may do all the right things to achieve their purposes, the purposes themselves are contradictory. Wotan's purpose is glory, as he reveals in his opening lines; clearly, for Wagner, this is a mistaken goal. But Wotan is not the only character with mistaken purposes—Alberich's goal is selfish pleasure, the Rhinedaughters' is play (another form of selfish pleasure), while Loge's is self-serving freedom. The contradictions of all these positions are built into their goals—they all have to fail. The only thing that will succeed, of course, is self-realization through love, but in scene 2 no one knows that yet.

Wotan's failure to see the necessity for love is reflected in his opening words, which suggest not only humankind's visions of glory but specifically patriarchal dreams. Fricka, with her concern about Friea's fate, attempts to suggest to him that his unyielding patriarchy has caused problems. His willingness to treat women as property is the cause of his present problems and, less directly (because this attitude toward women is based on a lack of recognition and equality), his future ones. However, Wagner does not allow Fricka credit for a higher consciousness either; she does not become a hero of the drama. She could form an alliance with Brünnhilde, but instead Brünnhilde wins her independence without ever realizing that she shares the problem of Wotan's dominance with Fricka, Freia, and other women (sisterhood is not in Wagner's vocabulary).

Example 3.4

Two motivic moments growing out of the music at the beginning of scene 2 play important roles in the drama to come. The germ of what is usually called the spear motive appears for the first time here, as Fricka urges Wotan to wake up and consider what the completion of the castle means (example 3-4). Though the motive is without its characteristic rhythm here, the descending scale is distinctive (and emphasized—it occurs in the cellos and basses alone in this recitative with very little other accompaniment). The germ is distinctive enough to connect it in the listener's mind with the completed theme as it later occurs (example 3-5). This motive is thus associated with contracts and law before it is associated with Wotan's spear.

Another important motive occurs at the end of the Valhalla music, at first in the orchestral ritornello (example 3-6), later under the voices, finally with an added vocal part that is also frequently repeated later (example 3-7). This cadence forms the conclusion of the Valhalla motive and is musically prominent throughout the cycle, either connected with or separated from the rest of the theme. Conceptually this cadence is very important: a heavily emphasized ending to the Valhalla theme, it signals the end of the reign of the gods. Although the inevitability of their death becomes ever clearer in the music throughout *Das Rheingold,* it is not really articulated in words until *Die Walküre.*

The first suggestion that Wotan is mistaken comes from Fricka. She is traditionally conceived as a small-minded person who hinders Wotan and fails to give him sexual satisfaction. Westernhagen, for example, notes that in the sketches Wagner broadened the melodic line somewhat in Fricka's part, because "Wagner took pains to avoid the intonations of a nagging wife."[39] To see her as a nagging wife would be to allow masculine prejudices to obscure her real place in the drama. She represents conventional morality, the idea of morality as an absolute that

Example 3.5

Example 3.6

Hegel criticized in Kant. And the morality she represents is associated with traditional values granting women the role of keepers of domestic harmony and order. (Wagner perhaps followed Shakespeare here, whose female characters frequently uphold the importance of vows and oaths in contradistinction to the men.) But Wagner implies that Fricka's moral values are just as reductive and doomed to failure as Wotan's values of law and violence. When Fricka notes that the agreement to exchange Freia for Valhalla was made by men, who excluded women from the decision, she asks what men will not harden their hearts to do where power is concerned (accompanied by the ring variant of the world-power motive). She does not value power as the men do; this is true of women throughout the cycle. Nevertheless, she has her own idea of power. She later becomes interested in the ring, asking Loge if it will give her power over her husband to keep him faithful. Similarly, when Wotan reminds her, as she complains about the promise to the giants, that she too wanted the castle, she counters that what she wanted was a place of peace and domesticity for her husband so he would stay at home. Although she sees the castle as a home rather than a fortress, her view is still too limited. She pictures domestic harmony and stable family life as the highest good. She lacks the imagination to picture the rapturous passion of mutual recognition; a Brünnhilde is required to redeem

heh – rer   herr – li – cher Bau!

Example 3.7

women. Fricka's conventional morality is perhaps Wagner's dramatization of what Hegel saw as an important problem in modern society; he felt that the task of his day was not to detach the individual from sensuous immediacy with a goal of achieving abstraction, as Enlightenment thought had suggested, but to force the individual to let go of his or her conventional habits of thought, "breaking down and superseding fixed and determinate thoughts" (*Phenomenology*, p. 94). Fricka's morality encapsulates the kind of thinking Hegel feared; her lack of imagination and inflexibility, however, become a catalyst for the events of *Die Walküre*.

Friea's entrance in scene 2 makes some of these problems even more clear. She is, as Deryck Cooke insists, associated with love. The first part of the motive accompanying her entrance, he says, is associated with her as a love goddess; but so is the second, although it is usually identified as a flight motive. The first part of Freia's theme returns later in the cycle in connection with Siegmund and Sieglinde and also when Siegfried climbs to the mountain top to find Brünnhilde. But the second half also develops, when Fasolt imagines Freia as his wife, as the main love theme of Siegmund and Sieglinde, and later it is associated with Brünnhilde and Siegfried. Cooke sees this second love theme as "one of the central and most fertile ideas in the *Ring:* it recurs as often as any, in more different forms than most, and undergoes a great deal of symphonic development."[40] This, he feels, is a musical acknowledgment of the importance of love in the *Ring*. However, he does not relate this theme to the ideas of Hegel or Feuerbach, and thus misses some of its importance. He does call attention to Wagner's "avowed conception, in his writings, of a universal love, rooted in family and sexual love, as the central force making for a regeneration of society,"[41] however.

Cooke also argues that Wagner intended for Freia to cut a weak figure as a goddess of love—she is called *die Schwache* (the weak one)—to suggest that love is helpless in a power-mad world.[42] In fact, however, Freia represents the potential for love rather than love itself: one of Hegel's important points is that the potential for something appears before the thing actually does. The potential new step in the development of consciousness is at first only an inner element; it then becomes clear to itself and moves outward[43] (this also suggests Wagner's theory of the repeated motive as a foreshadowing and his habit of presenting the germ of a motive before the fully-worked out motive appears.)

Freia, however, represents more than the potential for love. She is, as her name suggests, also a figure for freedom. That Freia represents freedom as well as love and youth is made clear in a number of ways in this scene. Her entrance is a cry for help, for Fasolt is attempting to take her prisoner, as she sees it (not, however, as he and Fafner see it). Fasolt, of course, is in love with her and treats her with consideration: he emphasizes, when they return with her in the evening, that they have treated her honorably. But for the giants as for Wotan, love is compatible with a lack of freedom; Fasolt joins Fafner in thinking that it is acceptable to force Freia to go with them. Their understanding of love is obviously inadequate.

Wagner borrows the equation between freedom and love represented in Freia in part from Hegel's description of the master-slave relationship. A person reaches self-knowledge, for Hegel, only by operating as an autonomous agent, by interacting freely with the things of the world. And true freedom is gained only by being willing to risk one's life, because that willingness demonstrates that the individual is not fettered by fear for his own life.[44] Thus overcoming fear is important to Hegel (although it is an idea Wagner specifically repudiates for Siegfried). But for Wagner, both freedom and love come to the person who knows no fear because he must be the one who never thinks of himself—self-preservation is not an ideal for Wagner. Freedom and love are equated because they both require complete loss of self-interest.

When the giants arrive on the scene, they are surprisingly different from what the audience has been led to expect. Wotan has presented them as violent (he had to overcome them with his spear) and deceitful (that is why he needs Loge). And Freia and Fricka view them as violent captors. However, text and music together suggest that the gods' view of them is not entirely just. Fasolt's first speech emphasizes how hard and skillfully they have worked to construct the castle (a point Loge verifies when he enters, implying at the same time how lazy the gods are). And Fasolt rebukes Wotan on moral grounds; he is in fact so taken aback when Wotan asks the giants what payment they are demanding that he is for a moment speechless. The question surprises the giants because they had assumed the contract was settled. But Fasolt regains his power of speech in order to deliver a powerful reprimand of Wotan on the subject of keeping his word. Fasolt is eloquent and right, articulating moral values that Wotan only pretends to hold. Wagner seems to suggest a kind of moral superiority for Fasolt (if not for Fafner) based on Hegel's master-slave relationship. The giants represent the laborer, the class that is assumed to be stupid and can be dominated through trickery rather than force. Wotan, as master, regresses, however, because he is the passive consumer of the castle who loses touch with reality. The giants on the other hand learn from their labor to enjoy physical reality; they are prepared to retire peacefully with Freia, the reward of their labors. Fafner, however, becomes corrupted by greed for the ring and brings about his brother's, and eventually his own, destruction.

Before the murder, however, Fafner explains to Fasolt that Friea is valuable as a commodity because she controls the golden apples that keep the gods young. The theme he sings sounds somewhat incongruous, for it is light and filled with grace notes, and Fasolt's is a deep and heavy voice. The theme has a family resemblance to the Valhalla motive, and the two motives represent two sides of the power of the gods: Valhalla, power by force, political and self-serving; the apples, the nutritive, loving power of woman (Freia is the one who nurtures the gods, literally keeping them alive). These two types of power are, in the ethos of the cycle, complementary, though for the moment they seem opposed. Wagner seeks to bring them together on another level later, in Siegfried and Brünnhilde.

Fasolt in this aria berates Wotan for not keeping his word, unaware, of course, that Wotan never intended to keep it. For Wotan never meant to honor a contract that was not made with equals—his earlier remark about having to subdue the giants with his spear still hangs in the air. Of course, the ethos of the opera will eventually suggest that contracts not bound by love are not valid. Here, though, the issue is trust: Fafner accuses Fasolt of being too trusting. Trust is also the issue in the exchange between Loge and Wotan on what to do about the contract with the giants. Loge denies having agreed to find a substitute for Freia, conceding only that he agreed to "look for" one. The point Loge so cleverly makes is that contracts depend on details of wording unless there is absolute trust and agreement—love—between the persons involved; therefore, for most purposes, contracts are suspect.

Loge's entrance has only complicated the issues with which Wotan must deal. According to Cooke, that Loge is unrelated to the other gods suggests that he represents not only Wotan's intellect but the power of thought itself, which is not connected to any one individual.[45] In some ways Loge suggests the Stoic as Hegel describes him in the *Phenomenology,* for the Stoic understands only abstract thought—when asked to give the content of the good and the true, the Stoic could only give the "abstract, contentless thought; the true and good are to consist in reasonableness." Stoicism, in the Hegelian scheme, is a form of freedom in thought that emerge only in a time of universal bondage and fear.[46] Loge, like the Stoic, is ever reasonable. Loge advocates the right thing—returning the ring to the Rhinedaughters—but only because it is reasonable, not because it is just or from any real understanding of the problem. Thus his freedom, based on superficial reason rather than equated with love, will evaporate before Wotan, who later enslaves him. That he has nothing to do with love is clear in his complaint that Freia has refused him the apples. Loge embodies a false kind of freedom—tending more toward destruction than redemption, more toward hate than toward love. Loge can also be interpreted in a Feuerbachian sense: he is not a god, or not fully a god, because man had not made a religion of reason (in spite of Hegel's attempt to conflate reason and God). However, in *Das Rheingold* Loge sets the example for searching for the truth and also sets an example for freedom; but he eventually fails when he is enslaved at Brünnhilde's rock because, in Hegelian terms, he is independent and makes his own way, refusing to participate in society. His kind of freedom cannot last because it insists on existing alone.

Loge's first speech emphasizes the values the castle stands for, and like Fricka he does so negatively, though more subtly. He describes the castle in terms that emphasize its strength and size and confesses to having inspected it himself, complimenting Fasolt and Fafner on their work. Loge deprecates the ideology that demands such an ostentatious castle, and the irony in his tone is reflected in the music here, which Cooke describes as "a brisk, flippant version of the solemn Valhalla theme."[47] Thus Loge implies the worthlessness of Valhalla, a realization Wotan comes to only much later.

Loge's narrative describing his search for a substitute for Freia is the first of many great narrative passages in the *Ring* and stands as an allegory for the inability of reason to comprehend love. On the level of the plot, part of what he says—how Alberich stole the gold from the Rhinedaughters—we already know from scene 1. The rest is telling us, as well as the characters on stage, what has happened since. In the course of this narrative, Loge reveals his own values to some extent, though his main value here is manipulation. He seems to echo the naive stance of the Rhinedaughters when he asserts that no one, "in Wasser, Erd, und Luft" (mention-

für   Wei - bes   Won - ne und   Werth!

Example 3.8

ing three elements—he himself constituting the fourth, fire), is
willing to forego love. Yet he immediately contradicts himself and
begins the story of Alberich, drawing it out for dramatic effect.
Indeed, Loge is sophisticated, and no doubt we are intended to
assume that he is well aware of the power of greed. Other values
that Loge represents here include the male view of woman as
Other—the repository of beauty and love separate from, no matter how important to, man, the real human. For Loge, as for
Wotan, woman is a thing to be talked about and used as barter.

Loge ends his narrative by telling Wotan of his promise to the
Rhinedaughters to tell their story and beg for the return of their
gold. It is the first of several times he will make this point to
Wotan, the multiple mentionings emphasizing its importance. In
doing so, he presents Wotan with an insoluble dilemma, the central problem of the plot. Wotan responds in anger, immediately
rcognizing the difficulty but not yet giving it the importance he
will later.

Wotan places value on the side of masculine power while Loge
represents another type of power—the deceit of reason. Both
suggest the importance of thinking (Wotan's bourgeois common
sense and Loge's reason) over feeling, and both ideas will be
shown to be wrong. Loge's rhetoric is often sophistic, illustrating
his role as representative of instrumental reason. He again indicates the values of the world of the gods when he suggests that
getting the ring will be child's play ("ohne Kunst wie im Kin-
derspiel!"). The way to get the ring is to steal it, he says, because
after all it was stolen: he advocates a kind of moral tit for tat, the
logical consequence of a morality based on property that Hegel
criticizes.

What Loge has been searching for is a thing more valuable than
love, something to offer the giants that will serve as a replacement
for woman's value, "Weibes Wonne und Werth" (example 3-8).
This phrase has already been hinted at by Fricka, when she berates Wotan for being willing to trade a woman for a castle. In

Fricka's version, the derivation of this phrase from the motive associated with the need for love (example 3-2) is somewhat clearer. Woman's value is that potential for love that Freia represents—the passive potential to reflect man's essence and to sacrifice herself completely for love that Wagner discussed in *Oper und Drama* and exemplified in Brünnhilde. In Loge's narrative the self-assertion represented by both Valhalla and the ring is opposed to the self-effacement required for the full development of human potential. Loge himself, as instrumental reason, is later transformed, indirectly, by Brünnhilde's love into the instrument (fire) for the destruction of selfishness and power.

While the narrative passages such as Loge's retelling of the story of the forging of the ring are an important part of the structuring of the *Ring,* the use of description is also important to the drama. Loge, near the end of scene 2, has several long passages of description, the first as he watches the giants bear Freia off to Riesenheim. He describes the offstage action with great force to the gods on stage, presenting an image of the giants as they take their prize off toward their homeland. This simple dramatic device creates a sense of large distances and epic action going far beyond the small confines of the stage. Then Loge turns to describing the action onstage—telling the gods how their appearance has changed as they grow old and gray. Again, this is a dramatic device necessary if the audience is to understand the full implications of losing Freia. In the course of this passage, Loge also describes the garden where Freia grows the apples that keep the gods young (all except him, of course). In this way, he fulfills one of the functions of the chorus in Greek drama, the practical function of informing the audience and reducing the necessity for enacting difficult scenes on stage.

The use of the apple theme and Freia's music in the orchestra as Loge describes the change in the gods and begins to figure out the connection with Freia's disappearance indicates the idea dawning on Loge. Here the leitmotifs are used as descriptions of consciousness—Loge begins to have an idea, and it is described in the music before he articulates it in words (the first appearance of the sword motive at the end of this opera is a famous example of this use of the leitmotif.) On a psychological level, Loge understands the motives of the participants in the drama better than the others—he tells the gods that the apples are the real reason the giants have taken Freia. It is a blow aimed, he says, at the very lives of the gods. He in effect prophesies the death of the gods, though of course it does not happen as he suggests it will here. At the end of the opera, he more accurately predicts how they will end—in his own fire.

Scene 3

Place is once again important as scene 3 opens: Alberich, the melodramatic villain, lives in a cave under the earth. The ideology of up-down is here explicitly related to that of freedom-slavery: the dark enclosed space contrasts as strongly as possible with the free open space of the gods' mountaintop. Yet in some respects the place is ambiguous: Mime describes the happy life the Nibelungen led here before Alberich gained the ring and enslaved them. To some extent, Nibelheim parodies Valhalla; it is the inversion of the mountaintop of the gods, yet Wagner's point is that neither place is adequate. The world into which Siegfried must go and from which Siegmund and Sieglinde must be drawn is seemingly the only adequate place, yet it finally proves its inadequacy too. Westernhagen points out that not only was Nibelheim an unusual setting for an opera scene at the time, but the "sound world" of this scene is quite unusual—two tenors and two basses, each treated in its own distinctive manner: "one might even say orchestrated: Wotan's bel canto; Alberich's declamatory delivery, often rhythmically unbridled and verging at one point on free recitative; Mime's wails, coloured by short sobbing accaciaturas; Loge's ironic hauteur, given a cold glitter by playfully interwoven coloratura—the whole spectrum of the possibilities of vocal expression" were already encoded in the sketch.[48]

The contrast between nature viewed in an esthetic sense and exploited as a commodity, so important in scene 1, reappears in Mime's telling Wotan and Loge about how Alberich has enslaved them—they were happy before, he says, forging trinkets for their wives as playthings. These women, like the Rhinedaughters, view gold and other objects as valuable for their beauty rather than as symbols of power. Mime also retells the story of Alberich's taking the gold and forging the ring, adding new elements, however, that neither the audience nor his listeners on stage (Wotan and Loge) know—what Alberich did with the gold when he returned with it to Nibelheim.

The morality of property and its effects on humans is reflected in the importance theft continues to play in this scene. Mime reveals that he has, as Alberich suspects, attempted to steal the

Example 3.9

tarnhelm he has been forced to fashion from the gold. The tarnhelm confers on its owner the ability to change forms or to disappear entirely. The tarnhelm is also closely tied with power in this scene—Alberich's power to disappear makes him into a nineteenth-century Big Brother who is, as he says, always watching Mime and the other Nibelungen from the vantage of his own invisibility. Invisibility is an emblem of the absolute corruption of power, suggesting the Hegelian master's inability to see his slave as a real person, and is placed in opposition to the exchange of glances that is developed later, especially in the first act of *Die Walküre*, as the emblem of mutual recognition.

Wotan, revealing his elitist tendencies, makes the same mistake in addressing Alberich he made to Fasolt; earlier he asked the giant what he could possibly want with Freia, and now he asks Alberich what he could possibly do with all that gold in Nibelheim. Fasolt responded with hurt but with great dignity, discussing the giants' desire to share in the beauty and love they felt the gods enjoyed. Alberich, likewise, shows more sense than Wotan in his reply, although in it he outlines his own reprehensible plan for world domination, saying that through the power of the ring he will enslave the gods themselves. The contrast in their replies shows the native worth of the giant as laborer and the villainy of Alberich as master.

The tarnhelm theme (example 3-9), with its ambiguous chromaticism, reflects the ideological implications of harmonization so important in this opera and throughout the cycle (though Wagner's uses of harmony changed during the long hiatus that occurred between the writing of acts 2 and 3 of *Siegfried*). The original major triad of the prelude to Rheingold suggests, as we have seen, the uncorrupted natural world; throughout the *Ring*, the more corrupt an idea, the more chromatic its music. This general tendency does not always apply, however: Loge, for instance, whose music is quite chromatic, is not unambiguously evil; nor, as we have seen, is he quite good (though his theme is as

Example 3.10

remote as possible from the simple trumpet calls of the "good" themes—of gold, sword, and that associated with Siegfried himself). However, the yoking of chromaticism with corruption holds for themes associated with the ring and tarnhelm, which are quite chromatic in relation to the gold and greeting to the gold themes from which they are derived (the tarnhelm theme is an inverted and darkened variant of the music sung in scene 1 by the Rhinedaughters when they first greet the appearance of the gold [example 3-10], suggesting a parallel between the transformation from gold to tarnhelm and the transformation of Alberich from a person to an invisible and corrupt master.) The tarnhelm is central to the action throughout the cycle, symbolizing not only invisibility but also confusion and hidden motives. According to Cooke, Wagner enlarged the symbolism of the tarnhelm in this scene through the transformations it engenders; the evil represented by the tarnhelm is represented as "monstrous and terrifying" when Alberich transforms himself into a serpent, and "contemptible and weak" when he takes the form of a toad—"this latter aspect providing not only the opportunity to stamp it out, but the impulse as well."[49]

Snatches of the love theme and Valhalla motives appear in Alberich's song in which he describes the ways the gods live and how he will change their lives. Since he was not on stage when these themes were first presented, his use of them shows that they represent ideas available to the entire culture, like language. These themes work like words; Alberich has absorbed their general significance even though he has not witnessed the specific events with which they are associated in the drama. But that they are associated with these specific events for the audience gives us insight into Alberich's mind; we know how he thinks because of *our* knowledge of the associations of these themes. The motives Alberich sings are the objectified feeling/thought originally associated with them and developed in their subsequent uses in the drama; as objects, they are present at this moment as semiotic material that allows us insight into the unknowable—Alberich's mind—as revealing as a person's choice of words in a conversation.

Wotan reacts badly to Alberich's discussion of what he will do when he gets power over the gods. Yet the issue here is pleasure— Alberich's point is that the gods already live in the pleasure that they deny other peoples. Wotan assumes, or tries to assume, a master-slave relationship with Alberich. The denial of pleasure to the lower classes, according to Horkheimer and Adorno, is one of the primary ways the ruling class establishes dominance: "The masters introduce the notion of enjoyment as something rational, as a tribute paid to a not yet wholly contained nature; at the same time they try to decontaminate it for their own use, to retain it in their higher form of culture; and administer it sparingly to their subjects where they cannot be wholly deprived of it. Enjoyment becomes the object of manipulation."[50] Pleasure, then, in this perverted way, becomes a symbol and an instrument of dominance. Wotan and the gods define pleasure for the other creatures of the world of the *Ring,* and Alberich, when he desires pleasure, can only desire it in the guise of their values and actions. Thus the very luxury in which the gods live becomes a tool by which they maintain control; Wotan can achieve dominance over Alberich and the giants, at least temporarily, because they can conceive of no use for their lives, no objects of pleasure, except those for which they must fight the gods.

Scene 4

In the transition to scene 4, the need for love theme is isolated repeatedly between passages of the Loge music. A motive derived from Freia's music is presented in heavy, accented notes (trumpet, bass trumpet, and trombone) interspersed between the motives earlier associated with the Nibelungen and Valhalla. Love is tragic, the music implies. Already the themes have a literary power in this music. The need theme itself has taken on a good deal of significance through its use by the Rhinedaughters and Alberich and later in the form of its variant in Loge's narrative as he recounts these developments. Giving it a darker, heavier orchestration and placing it between the other themes in this interlude adds linguistic meanings (the ideology of pain and unhappiness associated with music conceptualized as dark or heavy). In addition, the need for love motive has by now become one of the most frequently played themes; sheer numbers of recurrences draw our attention to it and suggest meaning for it.

Cooke notes that it was perhaps necessary to bring Alberich up into the mountain (rather than playing out Wotan's theft of the ring in Nibelheim) in order to set Alberich "firmly on a par with Wotan, as Wotan's opposite number and formidable rival." Nevertheless, Cooke goes on, his "savage delivery of the curse," not in the dark underground of Nibelheim but in the light of Wotan's mountaintop, "serves to remind us, and Wotan too, that the tyrannical power which lies latent in the ring is a terrible evil threatening the whole world."[51] But the curse also serves to place evil in the ring and in Alberich and to obscure it in other places. That is, the image of the ring as the symbol of power and of the curse as the instrument of death draws our attention away from the necessity for domination in Wotan's concept of honor and law and even from the horror of Wagner's ideology of self-sacrifice.

Wotan, however, is not above pointing out to Alberich that the ring does not really belong to him; when it suits him, Wotan cynically adopts Loge's position that all property is based on theft. Although Wotan does not come really to understand this idea until near the end of the cycle, he argues the point here, suggesting that Alberich cannot really claim the ring because he stole it from the Rhinedaughters. In the course of Wotan's and Alberich's argument over the ring and its ownership the word *Eigen* ("own") and the concept of ownership are heavily emphasized; here they are connected with power and tragically reiterated later by Sieglinde, when she asserts that she herself belongs, as property, to Hunding. As Wotan talks, the theme that occurred originally when the Rhinedaughters greeted the gold in scene 1 (example 3-10), reappears and seems to come from a distance—(three horns marked piano and *weich*), suggesting memory as a place, a removed or mediated consciousness perhaps related to dreams.

Wie durch Fluch er mir ge-rieth,   ver-flucht sei dieser Ring!

Example 3.11

The origin of the ring in the rape of nature is now only a memory, reified and denied by Alberich and Wotan (specifically rejected, of course, in the form of Wotan's responses to Loge's several pleas to return the gold to the Rhinedaughters). Further, the greeting to the gold is connected to Loge's calling Alberich's curse a "love greeting"; the Rhinedaughters' innocent attitude toward the gold has become corrupted in the curse.

As Loge releases his bonds after Wotan takes the ring from him, Alberich comments ironically on how free he really is. Like Wotan, and to some extent Loge, he does not take advantage of his own freedom. If he returned to Nibelheim at this point, forgot about the ring and domination, and learned to live again in the naive equality that Mime described earlier, he would be truly free. But human psychology will not allow him that; he has been infected by the desire for property and domination and is the first victim of his own curse, for although he does not actually die, he never achieves his goal and is superseded by his offspring Hagen as Wotan is superseded by his offspring.

Alberich's speech containing the curse is built of permutations of a single motive (example 3-11), which appears very prominently in the voice part and is played on the trombones, an instrument conventionally associated with the gods and fate. When he finishes, the comments of Loge and Wotan together almost constitute another statement of this motive, which shows how the motives penetrate the consciousness of the people hearing them; Loge and Wotan are using Alberich's music, as they are using his words and thoughts, when they respond to him and to the situation. The so-called curse motive, then, works just as Bakhtin argues language does: in his response to the situation, Alberich creates this new theme out of semiotic materials available to him, and his listeners meet him by appropriating it into their own response to the situation.

An important attribute of this curse motive, as Bailey points out, is that although it is always in B minor, it does not actually contain the B-minor triad—it needs something stronger (usually the motive earlier associated with the tarnhelm) to work with it in establishing this key.[52] The curse motive is, then, if not tonally ambiguous, at least tonally difficult, which emphasizes its position as an emblem of loss; it lacks the firm identity of a tonic chord. Furthermore, the curse motive is not easily transformed; in order to be recognizable, it has to be presented in the identical format each time, which also suggests its status as a motive of reification, of loss of flexibility. The text of the curse Alberich utters suggests a theory of property—property, he implies, causes only pain and envy and strife. Death is the payment of property, fear of death the result of property, and the owner of property becomes a slave to it. Later, Siegfried proves his superiority because he does not understand property, for he sets no importance on the hoard he wins from the dragon, and he also does not fear death. Wagner perhaps fails to notice that the sword is property too, and that it also brings death and destruction. Indeed, the sword seems to bring its own curse, that of the failure of pledges—Wotan's to Siegmund, Siegfried's to Brünnhilde.

The return of the giants with Friea allows the playing out of the exchange of love (or woman) for property (the gold). Throughout the *Ring* the exchange of glances suggests the possibility of mutual recognition. Fasolt, though since he is a giant is of a different kind than Freia and therefore, in Wagner's thought, incapable of entering a relationship of equality with her, is presented as a sensitive and loving individual. The giant demands that the others conceal Freia from his sight with the gold—he has some understanding of mutual recognition and knows that he must not *see* her, because to see her at all is to see her, not as property as the others do, but as an autonomous agent. Fasolt says he cannot give up Freia with her glance still in sight, and the ring, a symbol of the loss of love, is required to hide her eyes. According to Cooke, this is the "culminating image of the power-versus-love symbolism: the shining eyes of the goddess of love against the gleaming gold of the 'accursed ring' of tyrannical world-domination."[53] However, the eyes of love speak only to Fasolt, and the others, including Wotan, treat Freia as a commodity, concentrating on her exchange value.

Loge attempts to forestall the exchange of the ring for Friea, arguing that the giants cannot have the ring because it does not really belong to Wotan, picking up on Wotan's insincere argument to Alberich earlier. Loge typically attempts to manipulate others, as he did Alberich in scene 2, and here he is simply trying to confuse the giants. But Wotan misunderstands, thinking he is serious. Wotan cannot accept Loge's sophistry even when it could work for his own good. The disagreement between Loge and Wotan about returning the ring to the Rhinedaughters encapsulates the argument so far, in its implications concerning the themes of ownership and nature (who really owns the ring or whether ownership of a part of nature is acceptable), as well as concerning the issue of promises and contracts (Wotan expects Loge to keep his promise to him but does not feel an obligation to keep a promise to the Rhinedaughters, whom, like the giants, he sees as inferior). This kind of repetition by encapsulaton is a typical mode of development in the *Ring*.

Froh celebrates Freia's return with a brief arioso on the theme sung earlier by Fasolt as he mentions the golden apples; here it is accompanied by the strings conventional for such lyrical outbursts, though the color—limited to violas and cellos—is somewhat darker than required by convention. The point of this passage is the return of youthfulness to the gods, and it indicates Freia's importance as a goddess of youth. Her guardianship of the apples and her function as goddess of youth have to do with the Feuerbachian scheme of the twilight of the gods—since the gods exist only as reflections of the psychology of a people, they can remain young only as long as they are thought of as beautiful and gracious (a point made by Fasolt in scene 2 and by Alberich in scene 3 to Wotan, who does not seem to understand). As the cycle progresses and the richness of character of the people grows (in the persons of Siegmund, Siegfried, Sieglinde, and Brünnhilde), the need for gods of beauty and richness fades. Thus Froh and Freia (along with Donner) disappear from the cycle after this opera, their function over. They are simply superficial representations of man's need for love; beginning with *Die Walküre*, love finds a more profound and meaningful expression.

Erda's entrance momentarily distracts attention from the impasse the action has reached. She is usually interpreted as a nature god of a more fundamental sort than Donner or Froh. Certainly she is less superficial than they and represents in the overall cycle the earlier matriarichal culture that the anthropology of Wagner's day postulated as an outworn religion. She and her offspring, however, form an important strand in the development of higher states of consciousness, in the person of Brünnhilde. Yet she later becomes Wotan's slave (as Brünnhilde is at first); she is forced into a love relationship with him in order to bear him Brünnhilde (he claims he must try to force knowledge from her). Thus her situation parallels that of the unnamed woman whom Alberich rapes—

both create a child who is destined to take over the battle for the ring. However, Wotan, unlike Alberich, is not aware of this aspect; once again the assumption of the opera condemns domination motivated by greed or envy while sanctioning male domination in the name of knowledge and love. Erda represents woman as Other—she is as different as possible from Wotan yet shares his engagement with godhead and power. Her entrance is accompanied by a sudden and marked change of key, to C-sharp minor, and she is accompanied by lower brasses and bassoons. Thus she is provided with her own musical world, including her own motive which, while closely related to the Rhine music in the first scene, is quite different from the prevailing music of this scene. The musical devices of tempo, tonality, melody, and orchestration combine to emphasize her difference from the other gods. As she predicts the death of the gods, her theme, in a musical rendition of the spatial imagery of the *Ring,* is turned upside down, played in a descending rather than ascending scale. Her music dies out in the orchestra when she leaves the stage, and the prevailing tone returns (except when Wotan mentions her or the feelings of care and fear he now feels concerning the day's events).

Erda brings to Wotan the fear for his own existence that generates the suffering that finally enables him to come to understanding, and his character begins to change, even in the remainder of *Das Rheingold.* The relation of motives suggests the relationship between Erda and Wotan's change of character; the motive later associated with Wotan's wandering is a rhythmic diminution of the Erda motive. Erda brings doubt and fear to Wotan because she does not fit into his known world. Safe in his own commonsense rationality and reliance upon masculine dominance, ignoring the curse and Loge's and Fricka's criticism, he has not yet been shaken out of his complacency. In fact, at her entrance Erda is the only character in the *Ring* (with the possible exception of Loge) who does not occupy a position of slave with respect to Wotan. She appears to him spontaneously, not as someone who already belongs to his hierarchy of servants, and she withholds knowledge from him while making it clear that her knowledge is superior to his. As Woman or Other she represents a mysterious, natural force, and in conquering her (something Wagner deemphasizes by allowing it to happen offstage, between operas) Wotan reveals at once not only his need to dominate women but also to dominate nature. The matriarchal gods, Horkheimer and Adorno suggest, represent a regression of the self that the modern consciousness ultimately fears. At this point Wotan constitutes what they call "the self that is wholly comprehended by civilization" and that fears the loss of identity threatened by the older state of being in nature suggested by matriarchal nature gods such as Erda. These older forms, they think, were feared and denied by civilized man: "one after the other, mimetic, mythic and metaphysical modes of behavior were taken as superseded eras, any reversion to which was to be feared as implying a reversion of the self to that mere state of nature from which it had estranged itself with so huge an effort, and which therefore struck such terror into the self."[54] Not only Erda but also the Norns and to some extent Brünnhilde belong to the matriarchal origins that Wotan secretly fears, a fear that forces him to intensify his attempts to dominate them.

From Erda's disappearance until the end of the opera, the action merely works out the implications of what has already taken place, with the exception of Wotan's great idea. Donner's scene calling up the thunderstorm is an attempt to restore dignity, power, and ritual to the gods. But he can restore only imperfectly something that in reality was already gone when scene 2 opened: the search for origin, for authenticity has failed. All he can do is clear the mists and create a rainbow bridge, which helps point out, as Cooke says, that Valhalla is a place of illusion.[55] Donner's display of power is the empty power of the no longer viable nature gods. The music is as static as the action here; Dalhouse points out that the rainbow bridge theme is simply an extended G-flat major chord, but he feels that, unlike what he sees as the elemental simplicity of the E-flat at the beginning, here the single chord suggests reductivity and false simplicity.[56] However, Donner's music later forms the basis of the storm at the beginning of *Die Walküre*, and storms continue to be associated with the gods throughout the cycle. As the beginning of *Die Walküre*, the storm implies that Wotan is still controlling events, and the storm returns when he interferes in Siegmund's battle, when he seeks to punish Brünnhilde, and when he summons Erda.

After Donner's thunderstorm gives way to the rainbow, Wotan contemplates the castle. The stage directions say he looks as if struck by a great idea, and a motive later usually associated with the sword appears in the orchestra (example 3-12). Wotan then

Example 3.12

greets his castle, asserting that it is safe from fear and dread. The motive of example 3-12 is quite clearly intended to be associated, not with the stage property of the sword but with the entire scheme of redemption through heroic individuals that Wotan now conceptualizes but which is only revealed later. The appearance of this theme suggests the birth of the Hegelian notion of the hero, the world-historic figure who will effect the changes necessary for the world to move to a higher stage of consciousness. This theme, usually called the sword motive, is in fact meant to suggest the new consciousness that will develop in the world and later is a much more complex symbol than just a weapon; in the first act of *Die Walküre*, it is associated with Siegmund's love for Sieglinde; in *Siegfried*, it is reforged and recreated by Siegfried; and in *Götterdämmerung*, it is associated, along with the sword itself, with the problems Brünnhilde and Siegfried have maintaining their love in face of a corrupt society. At the end of *Das Rheingold*, however, Wotan's conception of the new consciousness is imperfect—his original notion of the army of heroes who will protect Valhalla is flawed and undergoes considerable change in the course of the cycle. With the apearance of this theme Wagner seems to be suggesting a Hegelian notion of history as a separate force that works its way in the world in spite of, though in a dialectic relation to, man's intentions.

But the opera does not end with Wotan's great idea (which implies the movement of the plot to the next stage of consciousness, presented in the first act of *Die Walküre*). Instead, it ends with two negative motions: Loge's aside in which he predicts that he will destroy the gods and the last cry of the Rhinedaughters. Loge's comments reflect his empty rationalizing that again, even though it is right, is right for the wrong reasons and therefore cannot lead to any positive development. According to Hegel, "The scepticism which ends with the abstraction 'nothing' or 'emptiness' can advance from this not a step farther, but must wait and see whether there is possibly anything new offered, and what that is—in order to cast it into the same abysmal void." He contrasts this with a true negation that does have content and creates the dialectical impetus to move to the next level (p. 137). The ending of *Das Rheingold* provides both types of negativity. The skeptic who ends with nothing is Loge, who only can threaten annihilation. The Rhinedaughters, however, lament a loss that has already set in motion events that will lead to a new stage of consciousness in which love is more important than power.

4

DIE WALKÜRE

In *Die Walküre* the theme of mutual recognition finds its clearest presentation. Siegmund and Sieglinde form the first and most passionately immediate of the various groups of lovers in the cycle, and they clearly present the image of the love that is only a potential in *Das Rheingold.* But the element of incest has disturbed many critics, who wonder why Wagner found it necessary to have made his lovers twins. Incest, according to Cooke's examination of Wagner's sources in the *Volsung* saga, is not an essential element.[1] However, as Rather points out, the symbolic significance of incest may have been suggested to Wagner by Greek tragedy: in *Antigone* the heroine is the child of an incestuous relation just as Siegfried is. Both Siegfried and Antigone are revolutionary figures because they violate the conventional, state morality even before they act.[2] Wagner explains this idea in *Oper und Drama,* where he argues that in *Oedipus* the natural ties between parents and children are a result of habit (*Wont*) rather than anything more essential and that to violate a habitual mode of thought is the real essence of incest. Incest, he argues, is only an accidental result of the real revolutionary essence of love:

> But the first attraction of sexual love is brought the stripling by an unwonted object, freshly fronting him from Life itself; this attraction is so overpowering, that it draws him from the wonted surroundings of the Family, in which this attraction had never presented itself, and drives him forth to journey with the un-wonted. Thus sexual love is the revolutionary, who breaks down the narrow confines of the Family, to widen itself into the broader reach of human Society. (PP. 181–82)

Siegmund and Sieglinde represent the revolution, but more importantly, they signal the movement of the drama into the wider realm of society. Wagner goes on to comment that Oedipus and Jocasta do not really commit a sin, since they did not know each other. Wagner holds that incest means nothing to nature, as sug-

Example 4.1

gested in the fact that Oedipus's children were perfectly normal. Incest was a problem for these characters when they became aware of it, and only then did their consciences cry out against it (p. 182).

Thus the motif of incest in *Die Walküre* represents a defiance of convention. However, not only do Siegmund and Sieglinde commit incest as brother and sister, but they are twins—they look alike. The importance of their looking alike is emphasized throughout the first act, from Hunding's noticing the similar look in their eyes to their final recognition of their memories of each other and their family relationship. Wagner is thereby stressing that they are true lovers, the first in the history of the world, because each finds in the other a recognition of the object as subject; each finds in the other another self with which he or she can identify. This identification, this recognition of the self in another, is the essential step in the Hegelian scheme of self-realization, and Wagner presents it metaphorically in the figures of his twins.

For Hegel, the most important step in the progression of self-consciousness is the subject's ability to find and recognize itself in another, a recognition that allows the individual consciousness to see itself as free and autonomous because the Other, which is identical to itself, is free and autonomous. For Wagner, Siegmund parallels Homer's epic hero, who in Hegel's description struggles against the limitations of his own society and blazes the trail into new consciousness. In *Lectures on the History of Philosophy* Hegel reiterates his idea that "freedom of self-consciousness emerges in Greece. In the West the spirit descends into itself. . . . In the brilliance of the East the individual vanishes; he is only like a sheen on the substance. In the West this light becomes the lightning-flash of . . . thought which strikes within itself, spreads from there, and so creates its world out of its own inner being."[3] The lightning flash of Siegmund's love creates the new world; lightning ushers him onto the stage of *Die Walküre* where his drama will begin. The lightning music of the prelude (example 4-1) grows out of the music associated with Freia in *Das Rheingold*, while the descending scales of the surrounding storm music suggest a relationship to the descending motive associated with contracts and Wotan's spear.

Siegmund, in spite of the advance in consciousness he represents, cannot succeed. Wagner finds the concept for Siegmund in Hegel, who suggests that the notion that man is free by essence (independent of birth, status, or religion) is a fairly recent one and a theoretical position that does not necessarily mean that the individual is free in practical terms.[4] Wagner attempts to suggest a historical progression that moves from Siegmund, who is free in essence but not in the development of the plot, to Siegfried, who though he also suffers in a world that is not ready for him, enjoys a good deal more freedom and love than Siegmund ever does. Fate, seen as the selfish decree of the gods (who are Feuerbachian metaphors for human desires), plays a much stronger role for Siegmund than for Siegfried. Siegmund remains the epic hero; Siegfried is the tragic hero of a later development of civilization.

The prelude to *Die Walküre* present metaphorically in the music the "lightning flash" that Siegmund will bring into the world and begins in D minor, with what Bailey calls an "expressive shift" up a halftone from the D-flat ending of *Das Rheingold*,[5] a shift that marks the intensification of plot as we move from the allegorical gods of *Das Rheingold* to real humans. The setting of the first scene is ambiguous because although it is enclosed (a room), it is penetrated by a huge tree that extends beyond the ceiling. Thus the enclosed space of the room also suggests in some ways an open space, where nature is wild and uncontrolled, something humans seek refuge from. This spot is where Hunding and his followers live, on the border of civilization. The ash tree growing in Hunding's home suggests an unspecified connection between this locale and the primeval place of Wotan's experience as later described by the Norns. Here, the ash tree, as in Wotan's story, signals a new stage of history about to begin; each tree is connected with a source of water, symbol of new life. In both cases, the symbol of the new stage of history is the weapon that will protect its owner, Wotan's spear signifying law—and its inadequacy—and Siegmund's sword suggesting the need for love. But Wotan's taking the spear begins the process that eventually kills his ash tree, while Siegmund's tree, befitting its role as symbol of the new, final stage, apparently lives on. Siegmund's withdrawing the sword in this act suggests that the rule by contracts has begun to fail and the rule by love is now in ascendancy.

Act 1

The first scene powerfully presents the attraction between Siegmund and Sieglinde, an attraction that represents the new force in
the world. Here Wagner works out for the first time his Feuerbachian materialism; gone are the bombastic rituals of *Das
Rheingold,* which are replaced with the simple and human physical
reality Wagner sees as the basis for love and self-consciousness.
The emphasis here, in contrast to *Das Rheingold,* is on the material
and sensual bases of life. Even the orchestral instruments prominent in the first scene suggest the human rather than the abstract.
In *Oper und Drama* Wagner discusses the human quality of some
instruments and its lack in others: the organ, for instance, suggests in its dead pipes not quite the living voice, and in an instrument like the "clavichord" one gets only the sound of hammering
(p. 123). In this scene the motives associated with Siegmund and
Sieglinde and their developing love are embodied in such instruments as cellos, English horn, and clarinets, which offer a contrast
to the inhuman hammering of such themes as the smith motive of
Das Rheingold.

An important prerequisite to the development of Siegmund
and Sieglinde's love is that she is miserable. Caught in the conventional morality of a precivilized culture, she has been captured
and forced to marry Hunding against her will. The point, a
realistic enactment of the allegorical capture of Freia in *Das
Rheingold,* is the subjugation of women. Sieglinde's captivity, like
that of Freia, has been implicitly approved by Wotan, as Sieglinde
inadvertently reveals later when she describes how he was present
at her marriage and although evidently sympathetic to her plight
and hinting at her eventual salvation, he did nothing to help her.
Rather, he allowed her to continue for a while in humiliation and
misery at Hunding's hands.

In presenting the misery of Sieglinde, caught in a traditional
marriage, Wagner is suggesting that women are forced into a role
like that of slave, at least in Hunding's culture. But this is not
without its advantages; for Hegel, it is the slave, not the lord, who
eventually wins self-consciousness. Sieglinde is ready for her great
adventure with Siegmund because in her humility she has come to
recognize herself in Hegelian fashion as an independent consciousness though she has not yet found an object worthy of her.
While she serves Hunding, she goes through the motions of love,
the self-sacrificing love that Wagner requires of women. She treats
Hunding well, waiting upon him, and knows the reality of phys-

ical things—food and shelter—that she deals with every day. Sieglinde is "at home" in the world in a way Hunding can never be.

Only Siegmund, who has suffered humiliation and defeat in the some of the same ways she has, can understand her. Siegmund and Sieglinde need each other in order to come to self-consciousness. And they do so in the quite personal style of the music that Wagner gives them in this scene, a style Porges characterizes as naive but strong, having the "power to convey sentimental emotions, in the deepest sense of the term, in a completely naive manner."[6]

Compassion, according to Cooke, forms the ideology of *Die Walküre* and is the root of the attraction between Siegmund and Sieglinde. Siegmund's opposition to laws has given him compassion for those who are its victims, and Sieglinde's situation as victim has given her compassion for the outlaw.[7] When she brings water, she refreshes Siegmund and makes him whole, combining the healing power Wagner implies is natural to women with the power of the water, the elemental force of the first opera. The combination of woman's love and water bring new life to Siegmund: this revival is emphasized in Siegmund's words after he drinks the water:

> Kühlende Labung
> gab mir der Quell,
> des Müden Last
> machte er leicht;
> erfrischt is der Mut,
> das Aug' erfreut
> des Sehens selige Lust.
>
> Cool and refreshing—
> now I am well;
> my load of care
> suddenly light;
> my spirits revive;
> my eyes enjoy
> a blessed, glorious sight.
>
> (P. 77)

Sieglinde brings life to Siegmund as she later does to Siegfried; woman, the creature of nature, is in Wagner's scheme the giver of life. She provides for Siegmund a revival of hope, as he does for her. Their names suggest not only that each is the counterpart of

Example 4.2

the other but also, ironically, what is important to them—their hope for victory over the unfair world that has so afflicted them.

Many of the motives associated with Siegmund and Sieglinde and their growing love have an organic or generalized relationship with one another, and the principal love theme (example 4-2) is derived from the second part of Friea's music in the first opera, usually known as a flight motive (example 4-3). It is played at length as Siegmund drinks the water Sieglinde has given him, and the stage directions specify that they look at each other. This music brings to mind the whole complex of ideas and emotions connected with Freia, but in a completely different mood. The result is a musical suggestion of dawning love in the characters.

Sieglinde's captivity is part of the ideological critique of property in the *Ring*. She tells Siegmund in response to his question:

> Dies Haus und dies Weib
> sind Hundings Eigen;
>
> This house and this woman
> belong to Hunding.

(P. 77)

The problem is that she literally belongs to Hunding, against her will, reiterating the theme of freedom from the story of Friea in *Das Rheingold*. Both women are treated as property (a variant of the motive associated with Wotan's spear and contracts accom-

Example 4.3

panies her words), and Wagner decries this attitude on the part of Wotan and Hunding and others as part of his general critique of property.

Siegmund is already immersed in the battle against treating women as things. His first narrative tells the story of a woman he was trying to save from a fate similar to Sieglinde's and establishes not only his compassion for the downtrodden but also explains the source of his quarrel with Hunding. His second narrative, which tells the story of his own origin, is more important because it extrapolates less obvious values from the events themselves. In this narration, Siegmund glorifies the individual and rejects the restrictive ethics of social life:

> Was Rechtes je ich riet,
> andern dünkte es arg,
> was schlimm immer mir schien,
> andere gaben ihm Gunst,
>
> For what I thought was right,
> others reckoned was wrong,
> and what seemed to me bad,
> others held to be good.
>
> (P. 83)

Siegmund's moral code is the rejection of the ideology of the society in which he finds himself. In rejecting it, he is evidently following Wotan's example, for he tells how he and his father roamed the forest living the life of outlaws. Later, of course, we learn that Wotan has in this way tried to teach Siegmund to be free and independent, but what Wotan learns of course is that freedom is not gained simply from refusing to follow laws. The laws themselves, as *Götterdämmerung* shows, must be destroyed. Wotan's notion of freedom, as exemplified in Siegmund, is inadequate, and Siegmund very rapidly moves beyond it.

Siegmund, however, clearly obeys, though he does not know it, the law of the need for love. In his narration, he details the fruitless search he has carried on for a companion, a person who can meet his needs. He foreshadows Siegfried in this emphasis on the social essence of human reality. Sieglinde unconsciously emphasizes this point, telling Hunding when he enters that need has drawn Siegmund to them: "Not führt' ihn ins Haus." Siegmund's need, of course, is the need for love and for mutual recognition, both of which she will shortly supply.

Hunding's entrance is marked with a motive (example 4-4) that

Example 4.4

is connected not only to many other themes in the *Ring* cycle but with a rhythmic topos that Frits Noske identifies as associated with death in a number of operas, including those of Verdi. In this case this topos of death, usually appearing in the *Ring* simply as a rhythmic pattern, constitutes the entirety of the Hunding motive. The musical allusion gives this character greater depth; the death topos connects him with much broader ideas, suggesting an epic dimension to his character.[8] The motive also suggests not only Hunding himself but the mood of fear or oppression he evokes in Sieglinde. This theme contrasts strongly with the other music of this act. It bears in its heaviness perhaps some resemblance to the music associated with the giants, who wanted to keep Freia in captivity in much the same way Hunding keeps Sieglinde. But the comparison of their two themes emphasizes that the giants are essentially innocent and nonthreatening, while Hunding is oppressive and dangerous.

In scene 3 the love that has been developing between Siegmund and Sieglinde becomes explicit, and Wagner presents his ideology of love in an unmistakable manner. The excesses of physical passion that Siegmund and Sieglinde allow themselves are, in spite of the fact that Wagner seems to approve of them, met with a swift death. Both of these characters are connected with nature and like much of nature are doomed to extinction in a modern world. Hegel emphasizes that the movement away from nature is a necessary one; mankind has to go through the stages of self-certainty in seeing nature as an object and undergo the master-slave relationship in which people are seen as objects by the master. Wagner sees the need for love, just as Hegel sees spirit, gradually becoming more important in these stages, and Siegmund and Sieglinde personify the first enactment of love in a hostile world.

As the third scene begins, the orchestra plays a combination of motives earlier associated with Wotan's great idea and with Hunding; the sword, which becomes associated with the great idea, will be prominent in this scene, but the Hunding theme serves the purely musical purpose of creating continuity with what preceded it. Siegmund's semiconscious awareness of the sword implanted in the ash tree, his confusing its light with Sieglinde's look, and the audience's awareness of the importance of the sword are all intermixed here. A hint of the contract motive appears in the orchestra when he remembers that his father promised him a sword. Although Wagner and Wotan perhaps do not quite think of this promise as a contract, and the text remains ambivalent, the music suggests it is.

The octaves Siegmund sings on *Wälse,* as he demands to know where his sword is, are related to the sword motive, which outlines an octave plus a third, and the *Nothung* theme on octaves that develops later, for octaves suggest a natural purity of musical expression. However, he changes his mood and thoughts when he sees the light from the fire reflected on the hilt of the sword, still not recognizing it as the sword. Instead, his thoughts turn to Sieglinde, though his vocal line almost outlines the sword theme again. He is thinking, influenced perhaps by the domestic scene and the light from the fire, of Sieglinde rather than battle, of love rather than killing. However, in the *Ring* the two are inextricably mixed. The sword, which appears in need, is named Nothung (Need) and is clearly related to the natural human need for love that according to Wagner is being articulated for the first time in the world, although Wotan conceived it and placed it in the tree in response to another need, his own need (as he sees it) to regain the ring. Thus in this remarkable scene in which Siegmund confuses the light from the sword with the light from Sieglinde's eyes, we move from Wotan's world of power and violence, where the sword suggests the necessity for heroic action and killing, to a more human world in which the sword instead represents the human drive toward love.

The contrast between darkness and light is prominent throughout this act. Siegmund arrives in the darkness of a storm, in early evening, and the first act progresses into the night. But at the height of the love scene between Siegmund and Sieglinde the door opens, and the stage is flooded with moonlight. Clearly, the set is on the side of young love. The firelight reflected by the sword in the ash tree reminds Siegmund of Sieglinde; the sword and Sieglinde literally light the darkness surrounding him, giving him hope for a way out:

Nächtiges Dunkel
deckte mein Aug';
ihres Blickes Strahl
streifte mich da:
Wärme gewann ich und Tag.

Shadows of darkness
covered my eyes;
but her radiant glance
fell on me then,
warming and lighting my heart.

(P. 87)

The looks exchanged between the twins in these early scenes indicate, along with the music, their mutual interest and understanding. Glances metaphorically suggest mutual recognition, and the importance of light here prefigues Siegfried and the awakening scene of Brünnhilde.

As Sieglinde tells Siegmund about the stranger who came to her wedding feast and left the sword, the orchestra plays the motive earlier associated with Valhalla. This music now becomes an evocation of the memory of Wotan, who Sieglinde implies brought them all a sense of magic. During Sieglinde's narration, the sword theme becomes intermixed with the Valhalla motive, demonstrating their similarity, in contrast to their presentation at the end of *Das Rheingold,* where the two motives seem quite different. The music hints that Wotan has in a way made a contract with Sieglinde, just as he has with Siegmund. However, Wagner does not emphasize this point in the text, nor does it appear in Wotan's argument with Fricka in the next act. The Valhalla motive develops as Sieglinde begins to think that she has seen Siegmund before, but the music is presented simply as a reminder of Wotan and their fatal connection with him. The love theme is also developed from the tentative theme in the orchestra at the beginning of this act to a full-blown and impassioned declaration of love between the pair. But earlier, in *Das Rheingold,* this theme is also associated with flight, fear, and captivity, all of which are important here as well and are presented in even more frightening and threatening terms than before.

Naming is also important in this scene and is obviously related to the Hegelian theme of self-recognition. Siegmund and Sieglinde do not finally recognize themselves in each other until the ecstatic moment of naming, which is the formal moment of their mutual recognition. Similarly, Siegmund's naming of the sword indicates his awareness and acceptance of his own need for another. Michael Ewans notes that the word *Not,* which Siegmund uses as he names the sword, indicates not only need but distress.[9] Siegmund's need for love that the sword and its name suggest also appears at the Hegelian moment of negativity, which will lead to the new stage. The descending scales in the orchestra as Siegmund claims both the sword and Sieglinde hint at the contract theme, emphasizing once again that the sword, after all, fulfills a contract. The sword for Wotan suggested the idea of the hero, but for Siegmund it is connected with the need for love and literally the need to save his life. Hegelian negativity, or need, has in this scene been moved from Wotan's world of law and power to the twins' world of emotion and human vulnerability. This moment is the final step in the process that began with the glances Siegmund and Sieglinde exchanged in scene 1 and continued in the narratives of scene 2, where Siegmund assumed a false name (Wehwalt) and discussed his identity only after gazing into Sieglinde's eyes. The process continues through the confusion between Sieglinde's eyes and the reflected light of the sword. Siegmund comes to full self-recognition in claiming the sword—and hence his identity as Wotan's hero—and in recognizing Sieglinde as his twin self. At this moment, he steps fully into two worlds, Wotan's and Sieglinde's. That the two identities he achieves are inherently contradictory is the source of his tragedy.

The mutual recognition the twins find in each other in this scene is clearly presented. Siegmund tells Sieglinde that she is just what he has long sought:

> Was je ich ersehnt,
>   ersah ich in dir;
>   in dir fand ich,
>   was je mir gefehlt!

> For all that I've sought
>   I see now in you;
>   in you, all things
>   I longed for are found.

(P. 89)

Throughout this scene the two reiterate that the hidden is now revealed and marvel in their physical resemblance, which gradually leads them to the final recognition of their identity. Physical resemblance is the emblem of the spiritual recognition of the Other as autonomous agent that in Hegel's scheme allows the individual to see himself or herself as free and independent also. Siegmund and Sieglinde, in their rejection of the conventional world of Hunding and Fricka, are the first man and the first woman. They are the beginnings of a new society, or the possibility of a new society, based on mutual recognition rather than exploitation.

Siegmund sings the need for love, or renunciation, theme (example 3-2) as he withdraws the sword from the tree:

>Heiligster Minne
>höchste Not
>sehnender Liebe
>sehrende Not
>brennt mir hell in der Brust,
>drängt zu Tat und Tod.

>Holiest love,
>highest need,
>yearning desire,
>longing need,
>burn bright in my breast,
>drive to deed and death.

(P. 94)

Clearly, this theme, like the sword, is connected with the need for love Wagner postulates, based on the model of Hegel's spirit, as the driving force in the universe. This theme appears frequently throughout the cycle. It is, as we have seen, first sung by the Rhinedaughters, who embody nature's lust for life—they speak of the need for love but understand it only in a most elemental way. Next, Alberich takes up the theme. Even though he forswears love in order to gain power, he still is subject to the universal need for love—thus the theme sounds in the orchestra at the very moment he rejects love. Loge next takes up this motive, cynically opining that people are too weak to give up love or pleasure for anything. He implies that men are selfish and value pleasure above everything. Loge understands the need for love only in a rationalistic way; he fails to grasp the passion with which humans experience it (and which enters the drama only with Siegmund and Sieglinde). At the end of act 1 of *Die Walküre*, however, the need for love ceases to be a negative force and becomes a positive one; even though the individuals who recognize in themselves and act upon the need for love do not survive, the overall movement of the *Ring* cycle suggests that the growth of love in the world is the growth of human potential. Brünnhilde, in her encounter with Siegmund, begins to understand the power of love, and she tells Wotan, who however does not understand. But Wotan himself begins to see his own real need for Brünnhilde at the end of this opera, though he refuses to go so far as to allow himself to forgive her. And of course Brünnhilde's final sacrifice is the ultimate proof for the need for love (the motive appears prominently during her last scene); she proves that the need for love is greater than the need for life, as Hegel argues that the need for rational fulfillment must be greater than the desire for life in order for humankind to progress.

Act 2

In act 2, we begin to see more clearly than we did in *Das Rheingold* what Wotan's problem is. His character has changed somewhat since *Das Rheingold*, but his new awareness is sufficient only to allow him, and us, to see the tangle in which he is caught, which is only more complicated than it was at the end of the first opera. During his discussions with Fricka and Brünnhilde at the beginning of the act, we see that Wotan is hopelessly involved as master in a master-slave relation with the other characters. As Hegel describes the problem, for the master, consciousness is mediated through that of another person; therefore the master gets recognition for his consciousness but fails to grow with it and becomes simply a consumer. This is because the master does not recognize the existence of the slave as an autonomous individual. Therefore he does not come to see that his own autonomy is the essential part of him. The master, because he views the slave as a thing and not a person, does not learn to value the other and hence himself as a total human consciousness. The slave, however, sees himself reflected as an autonomous Other, though he or she is hampered from acting freely and developing this knowledge. Wotan's relationship with Freia, the symbol of love, is that of master to slave; he merely consumes the apples and does not see love as a reciprocal relationship. Similarly, he views Brünnhilde as a slave, unable to understand her autonomous action later in this act, an action that he sees simply as rebellion and betrayal.

The prelude to this act, which consists of an alternation between the love and sword motives, finally changing to a rhythmic abstraction of the Valkyrie theme, lacks real musical structure, according to Peter Ackermann, because the isolation of the thematic

Example 4.5

materials in the leitmotif tends to break apart the musical form—a problem resulting from the opposition between the impulse toward symphonic organization and the impulse toward musical allegory that frequently appears in Wagner. That is, Ackermann argues that on the one hand Wagner attempts to create musical form based on the linguistic origin of the leitmotif, while on the other he cannot escape his tendency to stick to traditional forms.[10] If this is true, then Wagner perhaps unconsciously reflects in this prelude the ideological conflict he explores more directly in the first scene. This conflict, between new ideas and convention, is clear in the dialogue between Fricka and Wotan and is reflected in their music. Fricka's lines are accompanied by the Hunding theme, which as usual sounds repressive and threatening, while Wotan's words are accompanied by hints of the love music from act 1, suggesting that his consciousness has grown enough for him to begin to see the value of love. Fricka, however, has not changed and continues to abide by a conventional morality.

Wagner uses the textual associations of his motives to help advance the argument in this scene. The contract theme figures strongly as Wotan tells Fricka why he needs Siegmund. At this point, he fails to understand need as the need for love. Rather, he explains that the need of the gods is to have a hero. The contract motive also appears as Wotan protests that Siegmund won the sword for himself, the music suggesting that Siegmund was and is not, as Fricka knows, free. A variant of the spear motive appears for the first time as Wotan realizes that Fricka is right (example 4-5). Throughout the rest of the cycle this theme is associated with Wotan's dilemma; its placement here connects it with Wotan's first agonizing realization that he is caught by his own contracts.

Backed into a corner by Fricka's logic, Wotan rather lamely argues that Brünnhilde is free to do as she likes about Siegmund, but Fricka retorts that Brünnhilde is only an instrument of Wotan's will. As usual, Fricka is right in a narrow sense, but ultimately her limited understanding is inadequate, for Brünnhilde shortly proves herself to be indeed free. To view Brünnhilde, as Fricka does, as simply a function of Wotan is quite misleading, since it is from Brünnhilde that Wotan learns what it is to be truly free. Brünnhilde is not completely enslaved to Wotan—as a Hegelian slave, as a woman, her consciousness has already progressed beyond his.

Wotan is obviously beginning to see the inadequacy of his concept of law. In this scene, he contradicts his earlier stand on contracts, calling the marriage vows of Hunding and Sieglinde, which Fricka defends, unholy. Before, he was willing to use vows and contracts to his own advantage; now, he begins to see that they are too restrictive and he has fallen victim to the restrictive loyalties created by vows. Fricka accuses him of deceit in taking a new name; as Wälse, she says, he roams the world and betrays her. Like Siegmund at the beginning of act 1, Wotan attempts to escape his identity by changing his name, and like Siegmund he is unsure of his own identity because he lacks a love relationship, a relationship of mutual recognition. It is clear here and in *Das Rheingold* that the relationship between Fricak and Wotan is not based on love or mutual recognition of equals.

In the course of their argument, Fricka tells Wotan that in Siegmund she finds only Wotan, suggesting that Siegmund is not an autonomous agent. Read as allegory, this statement is a reversal of Feuerbach's views of the relationship between gods and people, but it reflects accurately the views of people who do not understand the place of religion. Such persons think, according to Feuerbach, that humans are made in the image of god, while Feuerbach holds that the reverse is true. Fricka reminds Wotan that people must act as slaves to the gods, and she claims Siegmund as her slave. But the Feuerbachian allegory of the *Ring* emphasizes the growing awareness of humans that the gods are simply false reflections of themselves.

The entrance of Brünnhilde in scene 2, after this dialogue, brings back a relaxed E-flat major for a brief respite in the tension. It quickly builds again, however, for this is the place of Wotan's great narrative in which he tells Brünnhilde the story of the ring. When Brünnhilde asks Wotan to tell his problems to her, the love music sounds in the orchestra, suggesting that this love theme refers not to sexual love but to the willingness to give oneself for another, a quality Brünnhilde has in abundance. The long-held E pedal point under both voice parts and the simple harmonies as Brünnhilde and Wotan speak just before his narrative begins suggest the unity of thought and mind between these two, just as changing harmonies and abrupt breaks earlier indicated the lack of unity between Fricka and Wotan.

Brünnhilde tells Wotan that in revealing his secrets to her he is simply telling them to himself, for she is his will. Wagner's emphasis on will and renunciation here is sometimes attributed to his reading of Schopenhauer but actually has its basis in Hegel. Indeed, this discussion of will cannot be influenced by Schopenhauer, since Wagner first read his work in 1854 but completed the text of the *Ring* in 1853.[11] In describing herself as an instrument of Wotan's will, Brünnhilde simply is expressing her own qualities of self-sacrificing love. Wotan, however, goes on to say that he longs simply to give up, suggesting a Schopenhauerian resignation. However, Wagner is probably relying on Hegel's description of the unhappy consciousness (Hegel's version of the self-deprecating Christian attitude toward selfhood). Describing this type of consciousness, Hegel says in the *Phenomenology* that it could ensure its own existence only in giving up the self: "For giving up one's own will is only in one aspect negative; in principle, or in itself, it is at the same time positive, positing and affirming the will as an *other*, and, specifically, affirming the will as *not* a particular, but universal" (p. 266). These terms anticipate Schopenhauer, though for Hegel this type of self-sacrifice is a false step in the progress of history, while for Schopenhauer (and later for Wagner) it is the essence of reality. In the *Ring*, Wotan's eventual self-sacrifice, foreshadowed here, is a necessary step toward love's making its way in the world, as belief in the gods must give way to belief in human potential. Wotan's concept here is also, as Hegel suggests, in some sense positive, for this is the first time Wotan has come to a sense of the universality of consciousness.

However, when Brünnhilde hints that she will disobey him, Wotan reverts unequivocally to his role as master. It seems that when he argued that Brünnhilde is his will, he meant she is his slave. Although he dislikes Fricka's attitude toward humans, he cannot see that as father or patriarch he too is playing out the part of the master. The contract motive appears in the orchestra when Wotan explodes at Brünnhilde; the moment has an ironic effect, for Wotan is so caught that he can no longer control even Brünnhilde. Again, the theme conveys the idea of his lack of freedom, though it also suggests his resorting to force or the threat of force, even with Brünnhilde. The motive associated with the need for love does *not* appear, however, when Wotan tells Brünnhilde of Alberich's forswearing love in order to master the ring, even though Wotan's narrative is otherwise filled with reminiscent motives from *Das Rheingold*. Perhaps the omission is meant to suggest that Wotan, as master, still is unaware of the need for love, even to the extent Alberich is.

Nevertheless, near the conclusion of Wotan's dialogue with Brünnhilde he laments that he can make only slaves: the other, the free agent he seeks, he cannot find. Wotan of course can never find the autonomous agent he seeks; only creatures who can find the other as equal can rise to self-consciousness. Wotan still seeks the other as an instrument of his own will, so freedom and love continue to elude him. Wotan's limitations do not allow him to recognize a true independent consciousness (Brünnhilde) when she is there. That recognition is left for Siegfried.

Brünnhilde's defiance of Wotan here is the crux of this act. In it she begins her reenactment of Antigone's drama, a reenactment completed in *Götterdämmerung*. Hegel discusses Antigone as one who obeys higher laws of social custom than Creon's tyrannical laws, a discussion Wagner echoes in *Oper und Drama*. Brünnhilde's defiance of Wotan's decrees parallels Antigone's defiance of Creon. Wotan's decision to destroy Siegmund is in accord with conventional morality as developed in the argument with Fricka but not in accord with the higher morality of the need for self-recognition that Siegmund has articulated. Brünnhilde acts from a nascent sense of the distinction between these types of morality. Furthermore, her rejection of Wotan's thinking here has other roots in Feuerbach's attempts to show that the relation between philosophy and theology is that between thought (reason) and fantasy, between healthy and unhealthy states of mind.[12] Brünnhilde's rejection of Wotan for Siegmund is a replacement of what Wagner implies is an unhealthy reason with a healthy one—god with human, fantasy with truth. Yet she is still subordinate; she does not win complete freedom from Wotan until the end of the cycle.

In scene 3, the two stories that have developed so far—Wotan's and Siegmund's—come closer together. At the beginning of the scene, the music associated with love reminds us of its original form, when it was associated with Friea's flight from the giants, as Siegmund and Sieglinde try to escape Hunding. The implication is that in a hostile world love must frequently seek refuge in flight. A little later, the threat of Hunding is clear in the orchestral use of the rhythm (Noske's death topos) though not the other details of Hunding's theme, as the two lovers talk. Eyes and seeing are again emphasized as Sieglinde, in her madness, loses sight of Siegmund

Example 4.6

and asks where he is, demanding that the light from his eyes again shine on her. She senses that their mutual love, symbolized by the exchange of glances, will fail.

In scene 4, the great question-and-answer passage between Brünnhilde and Siegmund furthers the progress of self-realization and love in the world. As Brünnhilde appears before Siegmund, the Valhalla theme sounds briefly in the orchestra, including the fatal cadence, suggesting the end of the gods is near. As Brünnhilde gives Siegmund, in answer to his questions, her most important piece of information, that he will be separated from Sieglinde in Valhalla, the voice part remains in E-flat minor while the orchestra is in D-sharp minor. This enharmonic writing suggests a kind of secret symbolism employed by Wagner in his use of keys here: Brünnhilde and Siegmund fail to recognize that they are alike, for although they approach the point of mutual recognition they do not quite achieve it. So their music is in an identical key that only seems to be separate.

As he voices his refusal to go to Valhalla, Siegmund sings a motive (example 4-6) prominent throughout this scene, which is frequently associated with the characters' sense of the inevitability of events and so usually called the fate motive. Wagner's concept is derived from Hegel's definition of fate as "uncomprehended necessity."[13] Siegmund's death is necessary because the negativity in his world must give rise to a new kind of world, to be sought by Siegfried, an individual who has been raised separately from Wotan's state. Mutual recognition and love, though lived out by Siegmund and Sieglinde, cannot survive in their still very conventional world, although their impassioned discovery of love is a necessary first step. They do not understand the larger historical forces that require their destruction. In *Oper und Drama* Wagner paraphrases Hegel's ideas on the Greek idea of fate, calling it "inner Nature-necessity" because, he says, the Greeks did not understand such necessity even when they pictured their tragic heroes as subject to it. Today, though, says Wagner, fate is "the arbitrary political State, which to us shews itself *as an outer necessity* for the maintenance of Society and from which we seek refuge in the Nature-necessity" (p. 179). Wagner pictures Siegmund as suffering from an inner Nature necessity—the need for love—that he does not quite understand. But he is the victim of another fate, the necessity for the message of love to be worked out in the social world. Siegmund suffers from this modern type of fate, the needs of the state morality to which, Fricka insists, he is subject, like every other character in the *Ring*. So the prominence of the fate motive in this passage suggests the movement of the plot toward love without the characters' knowledge, on the one hand, and the necessity for them to be sacrificed in a corrupt world, on the other.

Siegmund, however, seals his own destiny by rejecting immortality because it is cold and loveless, an action that leads Brünnhilde to reject it for the same reason.[14] These actions are again a Feuerbachian allegory of the rejection of religious ideas that are merely abstractions of human needs. Feuerbach suggests the psychological meaning of a belief in immortality as "an escape mechanism" that prevents humans from seeing clearly what they need to do to make society better. "Religion," he says in a phrase adapted by Marx, "is as bad as opium."[15] Siegmund is important in that he rejects the afterlife and so in effect destroys it; later, Siegfried is not even given the chance to choose an afterlife. Because of Siegmund's actions, belief in the afterlife has disappeared from the world.

Cooke rightly sees the moment of Siegmund's refusal to go to Valhalla as the "really the decisive one in the whole of *The Ring*," for this act motivates Brünnhilde's rebellion, which in turn leads to all the other events of the cycle.[16] The fear of death Siegmund rejects here is important in Hegel's work, and Wagner perhaps implies more of Hegel's notion than Feuerbach's (who sees fear of death as the reason people must invent religion). The fearful individual, according to Hegel, is self-absorbed; by contrast, the person who does not see his fulfillment in the particular but the universal does not fear death but is reconciled to it.[17] Siegmund has not perhaps reached the point of seeing fulfillment in the universal—that is left to Brünnhilde at the end of *Götterdämmerung*—but he does at least see beyond his own selfish interest.

den   hehr – sten Hel – den der Welt   hegst du, o

Weib, —   im   shir   – men-den Schoss!

Example 4.7

Act 3

The equation between need and love is continued when Brünn-hilde enters the gathering place of the Valkyries and begs her sisters for help "in höchester Not." They of course, refuse to help her, at least at first, because they are a part of the conventional world that Siegmund and Sieglinde—and now Brünnhilde—have defied. The eight Valkyries offer the standard of behavior against which Brünnhilde's behavior can be judged, according to Cooke, who sees them as "cold, hard, inhuman instruments of Wotan," who can only joke about human suffering.[18] They finally help Brünnhilde and Sieglinde in some small ways, since their loyalty to Brünnhilde is great, though not as great as their fear of defying Wotan. They agree to hide Sieglinde in the East because that is where Fafner lies protecting his gold, including the ring. It is consequently an area where Wotan never goes. Wagner perhaps meant to invoke Hegelian history here too; in the Eastern nations, according to Hegel, tyranny is the norm, and the progress of history stopped with the master-slave relationship. This loveless world is the climate in which Siegfried is to be raised by his mini-tyrant, Mime.

Sieglinde, of course, does not choose to try to save herself until she learns from Brünnhilde of the coming birth of Siegfried. As Brünnhilde tells Sieglinde that her son will be the world's greatest hero, a new motive (example 4-7) appears. This distinctive theme appears in this passage and throughout the act to herald the coming of the hero. According to Westernhagen, the germ of this motive, always associated with Siegfried and the establishing of his identity, appears in the composer's sketches at the point where Siegmund threatens to kill Sieglinde.[19] Brünnhilde also tells

Sieglinde what she is to call the new hero: naming is the mythical mode of calling something into being. In this way, Brünnhilde creates Siegfried.

The rhetorical and musical emphasis on the so-called redemption motive as Sieglinde sings of the great wonder of being a mother is a clear indication of Wagner's valorizing of woman in the role of mother (example 4-8). Sieglinde moves quite suddenly from suicidal depression to ecstatic affirmation. But Sieglinde greets Brünnhilde's news that she will bear the world's greatest hero with the words

> O herstes Wunder!
> Herrlichste Maid!
>
> O radiant Wonder!
> Glorious Maid.

(P. 137)

As the text indicates, Wagner saw this moment not only as an expression of Sieglinde's rapture over being a mother but as a hymn of praise to Brünnhilde. In it he pictures for Sieglinde, and for the audience, a moment similar to the moment of revelation he describes for himself in "A Communication to My Friends," when he discovered suddenly the essence of Elsa as loving, self-sacrificing woman. Sieglinde pays the same tribute to Brünnhilde when she realizes what Brünnhilde is risking to save the unborn Siegfried; Brünnhilde has decided to stay to face Wotan so that Sieglinde may flee. The motive with which Sieglinde sings words, "O herstes Wunder!" is then concerned not with redemption but with wonder. In *Oper und Drama*, Wagner devotes an entire section to wonder, which he defines as the poet's ability to condense motives and actions into one strongly-felt moment that says it all

Example 4.8

(pp. 218–21). For Wagner, Sieglinde's song of praise is such a moment: it is the central event of the cycle, the moment of self-sacrifice for love, and in it several threads come together—woman's sacrifice, motherhood, the new consciousness and the new hero, and the possibility of escape from the corrupt state. This motive, then, will reappear only one more time, at the end of *Götterdämmerung*, as a kind of summary of the main ideas of the *Ring*.

Brünnhilde's selflessness motivates her when she finally decides that Sieglinde should go on alone into the forest while she herself stays to absorb Wotan's wrath. She is again demonstrating her ability to give herself completely, this time to Sieglinde and the unborn Siegfried. At the same time, by staying and accepting Wotan's punishment, she is paradoxically defying his will. That is, by accepting his punishment freely, she asserts her own individuality and ability to choose. She further demonstrates her independence of Wotan by telling him what he does not know about the Völsungs: both how Siegmund acted when faced with death and about the anticipated birth of Siegfried. Here Brünnhilde and Wotan enact the essential elements of the Hegelian master-slave relationship—as Wotan's slave, Brünnhilde is closer to reality (in this case, the reality of human love) than he is, and the future development of a new consciousness arises out of her understanding and involvement with the fate of Siegmund and Sieglinde, while Wotan will never develop this type of understanding.

Wotan, demonstrating immediately after his entrance how far he is from Brünnhilde's self-sacrificing love, tells Brünnhilde that she has openly defied his will. He takes credit in a patriarchal manner for her very existence, saying that he created her. Earlier, in his monologue in act 2, he has told her that he received her as a gift from Erda (whom he enchained with love, he says). These attitudes toward the inception of human life can be contrasted with the rapture and wonder with which Sieglinde greets the news that she is pregnant—a woman's view of wonder and love at human life is much different from, and Wagner suggests superior to, the patriarchal ruler's assumption that a new life means simply a new subject, though of course Brünnhilde's devotion softens Wotan's attitudes a little later in this act.

However, now Wotan tells Brünnhilde that the bond that held them is broken, a fact he sees as tragic and a punishment to her. Wagner evidently intended Wotan's concept of love and the father-daughter relationship to be perceived as faulty. He is following Feuerbach, who argued that natural human relationships become allegorized into religion and in the process are transformed from ties based on love to relationships based on a fossilized ideology. In *Oper und Drama* Wagner echoes Feuerbach, arguing that family relationships turn into God and law—which are "chilling edicts of moral compacts" (p. 204). Not only is the father-daughter relationship broken, however; so is that of slavery. Wotan's refusal to allow Brünnhilde back into Valhalla is in fact what allows her to enter into a relationship with Siegfried and bring love into the consciousness of society. Wotan fails to understand; he tells the other Valkyries that Brünnhilde has broken the bonds of his love and betrayed him, not realizing that her move toward freedom is really an expression of her greater understanding of love.

Wotan's original scheme for punishing Brünnhilde is that she will become a wife—that she will become the slave of a man, as Sieglinde was before Siegmund arrived. Since Wotan cannot comprehend any other fate for her, as woman and his own subordinate, except some kind of master-slave relationship, he punishes her by ordering that her master be changed. (The effect is the same as if he had sold her in a market—something, however, reserved for Siegfried to do.) Brünnhilde's fear of Wotan is sincere and justified, a fact that is important in that it contrasts with Siegfried's lack of fear later. In the case of Brünnhilde, Wagner is following Hegelian thought more closely: for Hegel, only the total fear for one's life can give the slave a sense of self. Brünnhilde fears Wotan totally, yet she asserts her own sense of self when she faces him.

The other Valkyries, of course, are distraught when they hear that Brünnhilde is condemned to the fate of becoming a wife, subject to the will of a man rather than a god. However, Brünnhilde's subjugation to a man, though not quite in the form Wotan pictures it, becomes the catalyst for the rest of the action; she is the woman who is completely selfless, who turns out to be just the type of hero needed. Her sisters are too conventional to recognize the possibilities of this situation. Brünnhilde, on the other hand, has the imagination to see possibilities for saving herself. She begs Wotan to ensure that the man who finds and awakens her is no ordinary one but a man free of convention. The last words of the opera, in which Wotan proclaims that only a man brave enough to penetrate the circle of fire and challenge Wotan's spear can win Brünnhilde, reiterate that only one who is free of the fear of conventions and contracts is worthy of Brünnhilde. Brünnhilde asks, in essence, that Wotan promise her a person capable of mutual recognition with her, a person who will reflect the new consciousness instead of being the conventional husband Wotan at first describes to her. Wotan has not yet escaped his master-slave consciousness, for he insists on punishing Brünnhilde, but he relents to a degree that will at least allow the process of change in the world, already begun, to continue. Brünnhilde, even though put to sleep, will continue to act independently of Wotan's will, finally to the point of causing him to realize that his own self-destruction is inevitable. Ironically, Wotan calls in Loge to guard her—Loge, the image of the self-destructive tendencies of absolute or unloving freedom.

In the final moments of the opera, Wotan sings the motive earlier associated with the hero to come (example 4-7), echoed in the orchestra on trombones and other low brasses. Such trombone blasts are conventionally associated with gods and fate (as in *Idomeneo* and *Don Giovanni*) and suggest here that Wotan is no longer in control. A fate larger than he—love—has already taken hold in the world. This is, in fact, the last time we see Wotan as a god.

5

SIEGFRIED

The Hegelian themes of self-consciousness become even more important in this opera, in which Siegfried is not only introduced as a real character (he was only a possibility in the preceding opera) but is developed from a thoughtless, natural creature to full self-consciousness through his recognition of Brünnhilde as his counterpart. On the way, he goes through many of Hegel's stages of consciousness and rejects two father figures.

Wagner's demonstration of Hegel's point that the self is determined through the subject-object relationship is somewhat complicated in Siegfried, however. Preparing the text for the *Ring* cycle, Wagner found that in working backward from Siegfried's death to his origin he had to imagine a formative period for Siegfried. He tried to show in act 1 that Siegfried is created (following Hegel's *Phenomenology*) when he discovers nature as object, then language, and then the Other (at first in the shadowy figure of his mother and then in Brünnhilde). But Wagner has some trouble following the Hegelian steps of consciousness, which are of course simply an abstraction and difficult or impossible to dramatize. To some extent, Wagner also seems to be influenced by Rousseau and attempts to posit Siegfried in act 1 as a natural creature, independent of civilization. But in creating a childhood for his character, Wagner necessarily shows that Siegfried is a person determined by his civilization. In the formative period, Mime is his society, and Mime carries with him by implication, even though he has tried to escape to the woods, the whole corrupt society as it is set up in *Das Rheingold*. Siegfried fails in the end of the *Ring* because, although he constitutes himself in Brünnhilde, he does not remain faithful to that image; he is in spite of himself influenced by his childhood with Mime and his world.

The overall structure of *Siegfried* almost completely concentrates on the development of Siegfried's self-consciousness. In the course of this opera he will reach the highest stage of self-consciousness and freedom that the individual can reach, so that in the next opera he can bring that self-consciousness into society. Because at this stage his development requires no parallel changes in other characters (his counterpart Brünnhilde is already waiting for him), the plot affords greater unity than the other operas, which cannot concentrate so exclusively on a single character. Wagner himself saw *Siegfried* as a comic opera, first imagining it as the comic contrast to *Siegfrieds Tod*. The internal structure of the opera follows the three powers that Feuerbach outlined: "To a complete man belong the power of thought, the power of will, and the power of the heart."[1] Siegfried gains the power of thought when he learns to understand the real meaning of Mime's words, the power of will when he forges the sword, and the power of the heart when he gains Brünnhilde.

Act 1

In act 1, Siegfried works toward self-discovery by learning of his origins and his past and reenacting this past, making it his own, by reforging the sword. The prelude to this act is, according to Robert Bailey, probably the oldest music of the *Ring* cycle, going back to the earliest sketches in 1851.[2] Act 1 is set in a cave, a closed, dark space that contrasts with the relative openness of the forest from which Siegfried makes his entrance a little after the first scene begins; Mime's cave also contrasts with the more open scenes in *Die Walküre*. As the act opens, Siegfried is engaged in a master-slave relationship with Mime, though he quickly and easily overcomes the negative implications of this, reversing the slave relationship that Mime would like to force upon him.

The scene opens with Mime alone on stage. One of the frequently cited problems in producing this opera is how to prevent Mime from becoming a sympathetic character—he is obviously intended to be one of the most evil villains in the overall plot of the *Ring* cycle. If Siegfried is to be perceived sympathetically, the audience must see his killing of Mime as necessary and right, not the ungrateful murder of a benefactor. But the fact that Mime tends to be perceived sympathetically indicates a problem with Wagner's thought. That problem, for Adorno, is the composer's anti-Semitism; he cites the original description of Mime that Wagner left out of the final score and suggests that Wagner omitted it because in it he saw himself as Jew—the absurd physical characteristics Wagner assigns Mime ("small and bent. . . . His head is abnormally large, his face is dark ashen colour and wrinkled, his eyes small and piercing . . .") Adorno suggests, are remarkably similar to those of Wagner himself.[3] Adorno thinks that Wagner's own horror at seeing some of these qualities in himself was what prompted him to treat Mime so cruelly.

For whatever reason, Mime is frequently perceived more as a victim than a perpetrator of evil. Not only is he a victim of Alberich, he is presented as Siegfried's nurturer. Although from the first he has certain unpleasant characteristics, yet the fact remains that he has raised Siegfried and continues to take care of him. Thus in spite of Wagner's attempts to contrast him musically and dramatically with Siegfried's mother, we continue to see him in the role of mother. The contrast, of course, lies in the quality of love; Mime continually demands the loyalty that he believes Siegfried *owes* him as payment for his nurturing, while Sieglinde's sacrificing of herself demands no payment.

In addition, Mime is characterized by his music, which is conventional and repetitive, However, it is also pleasant and likable music, characteristically strophic and frequently melodic. The exaggerated A B A form of his first aria ("Zwangvolle Plage") reminds us of Wagner's criticism of formalism in older operas. Mime, he seems to suggest, is a character who belongs in Meyerbeer rather than in this historic development of the new consciousness. Mime's music perhaps indicates a negative value for his intellect, for although he has the outside trappings of cleverness he is really incapable of imagination. He lacks substance. Porges confirms this use of music to delineate the psychology of Mime's character: his part conveys "acutely conscious psychological processes of a very peculiar kind: the malignant dwarf, Mime, is in the grip of uncontrollable forces with which he cannot deal and so his mind is in a painful state of doubt and turmoil."[4] The repetitiveness of his music suggests obsession.

Mime begins with a characteristic speech, complaining about the wearisome and unending nature of his task, for Siegfried, if he is to slay Fafner as Mime hopes, needs a sword that will stand up to his strength. Mime's inability to forge a suitable sword, especially to repair the pieces of Nothung, is central to the ideology of the *Ring*—his unfruitful work is supposed to present him as a character in whom something is profoundly wrong (like Sieglinde's oppressors who could not draw the sword from the tree). The power of love already associated with the sword in act 1 of *Die Walküre* is unavailable to the selfish dwarf. Scale passages are unusually frequent in this act, though only some are seemingly significant because they are related to previous motives. McCreless points out that many of the melodic lines of *Siegfried* are constituted of *ascending* scale passages,[5] the most important and oldest of which is the dragon's melody. The scale passages form part of the general sound of this act, which is more tonal and more regular than anything in *Die Walküre*—indeed, one has to go back to the first scene of *Das Rheingold* to match it—and they are part of the folklike quality of this act. The scale passages perhaps provide an element of simplicity in the music or may illustrate Wagner's attempt, from the very beginning, to present a musical analogue to Siegfried's rising levels of consciousness. This act, much of which is concerned with Siegfried's rapid development through the first steps of self-consciousness, is often characterized as a *Liederspiel*. Wagner wanted the many songs here to suggest the natural quality of Siegfried's mind: he says in *Oper und Drama* that "only in solitude, where fractions of the Folk—far distant from the highways of associate life—found themselves alone with Nature and each other, was there preserved in its childlike simpleness and straitened indigence the *Folkslied*, so indivorcibly ingrown with Poetry" (p. 105).

The tonal structure of this act, according to McCreless, outlines the growth of Siegfried to maturity. Scene 1 is primarily in B-flat, associated with the Nibelungen and Nibelheim, for in a way Siegfried is rising out of Nibelheim; scene 2 is predominately in C, the key associated with the sword and Wotan, and scene 3 moves up to D, where the sword motive is presented prominently in D rather than its usual C. Act 1, then, as a whole exhibits a "progressive intensification by whole-steps."[6] The move from B-flat up to D demonstrates that Siegfried has risen not only above Mime's level but also above the level of Wotan; the transformation of the sword theme from C to D is the musical analogue for Siegfried's reforging of Wotan's weapon.

However, the musical and dramatic progress that Siegfried must go through makes it necessary for him to appear at first as a completely natural character, a feat Wagner was perhaps not quite able to pull off. Many audience members will agree with Adorno's description of Siegfried: "Siegfried, the man of the future, is a bully boy, incorrigible in his naivete, imperialistic in his bearing, equipped at best with the dubious merits of big-bourgeois self-confidence as contrasted with petty bourgeois pusillanimity."[7] However, Porges defends Siegfried, suggesting that the actor can prevent Siegfried from being perceived as a boor:

Siegfried should not create the impression of a character drawn with the conscious intention of violating the standards of civilized society; everything he says and does—even the rather crude aspects of his genuine boyishness—must be presented as the natural expression of an essentially heroic personality who has not yet found an object in life worthy of his superabundant strength.[8]

Thomas Mann sees Siegfried as a figure from a carnival, mixed as he is in the *Ring* with figures from philosophy and literature; noting that Wagner was delighted by carnival puppet shows, he refers to the "striking resemblance" between Siegfried and "the little fellow who wields the slapstick in the fairground booth." Yet, Mann continues, at the same time he is the "son of light, Nordic sun myth" and he is also the romantic new consciousness: "Harlequin, god of light, and anarchistic social revolutionary, all in the same person: what more could the theatre possibly ask for?"[9] Even Cooke, while he comments that Wagner intended Siegfried as a picture of the "man of the future," finds him "a very curious figure." Nevertheless he defends Siegfried as "Wagner's projection of a future regenerate type of man to supersede the corrupt Wotans, Alberichs, and Mimes of existing society."[10] Wagner himself perhaps realized that he had set out to do the impossible in portraying the early life of Siegfried. In *Oper und Drama* he writes, "The poet, then, who had to portray the battle of the Individuality against the State, could *portray* the State alone; but the free Individuality he could merely *suggest to Thought*" (p. 197). The reason he can only suggest rather than portray such a figure is that he does not yet exist. Wagner goes on to argue that such a figure could be drawn in the music drama, as opposed to the spoken drama, through the suggestive power of music. While Wagner felt that spoken drama can only present the individual as corrupted by society, the true individual is hidden away in a corner of the brain, as feeling, and so could possibly be denoted by the music in the music drama (pp. 197–98). Wagner here suggests his grasp of the Hegelian idea that consciousness is after all determined not by nature but society, though he reserved a romantic idea of a natural essence that *might* be accessible. What he attempted to present in Siegfried was a free individual formed as weakly as possible by the state, so that this influence is easily overthrown; but the idea that Siegfried is completely natural, driven by instinct alone, continues to surface throughout the next two operas in various ways.

Example 5.1

Thus to some extent Siegfried at the beginning of this opera is an avatar of the romantic natural man. But he has taken a shape informed by Wagner's understanding of the goals of Hegel and Feuerbach. Even Hegel suggests in the *Phenomenology* that there might be a state in which the subject is not limited by anything outside, a state in which men, seeing themselves as emanations of *Geist,* would no longer see the surrounding universe as a limit.[11] This unlimited individual is what Wagner attempts to depict in this first scene, though not, as Hegel suggests, in a utopian society, but in an attempted escape from society. Yet Siegfried is not a natural, wild creature. He is a creature whose consciousness is limited by Mime, whom Wagner then attempts to present as hardly a serious obstacle. More serious an obstacle is Siegfried's ignorance, but he is pictured in this scene at the very moment of conquering ignorance and regaining his own past. So on the one hand Siegfried is asocial, an unspoiled child of nature, yet on the other he submits necessarily, in simply living with Mime, to a social demand.[12]

When we first meet Siegfried, then, he is presented as an individual at the stage of Hegel's self-certainty; he is at home in the physical world without really being aware of himself and his position in it. Siegfried lives in the forest, but "the world" to which he escapes at the end of act 1, as well as his own consciousness, is at this point alien—this alienation is what he must overcome in the course of the action. Siegfried, on the verge of finding the natural world in which he lives no longer adequate to satisfy his dawning sense of himself, is ready to begin the next stage of consciousness and seek human ratification for his own consciousness.

Siegfried enters scene 1 to the accompaniment of a horn call (example 5-1), which is one of those motives that occur in the drama itself as instrumental music—that is, Siegfried is pictured as actually playing it on the horn he carries. At other times the orchestra plays this theme to remind us of Siegfried's presence or character. This motive shares some rhythm and shape with the hammering theme associated earlier with the Nibelungen and here with Mime (example 5-2). Rhythmically, both motives are in divisions of three (6/8 and 9/8), a resemblance that could be accidental, since both are derived from conventional musical presentations of real-world sounds (the hammer on the anvil and the hunting horn). However, their similarity is evident to the ear and adds to the profound ambivalence suggested in Siegfried's relation to Mime. Siegfried's rejection of Mime is the point of this act, yet the music suggests that Siegfried has so completely absorbed Mime's character and language (he is, after all, the only person the boy has ever known) that these pervade his own musical sound, even his own speech. The resemblance between the horn call and the hammering motive emerges in numerous ways in this act and undercuts Siegfried's overt rejection of Mime. In fact, however, as in *Götterdämmerung*, the music here suggests that after all, the idea of a person growing up independent of the dominant human culture is not possible.

However, Siegfried's horn call is not as static as the smith motive and suggests some contrast between the natural man and the drudge. The bear who accompanies him as he charges onstage has, he tells Mime, answered his horn call (as the dragon is to answer it later); he has called with his horn in an attempt to find a companion better than Mime. When we first meet him, then, he has already taken the first step on his road to self-consciousness in pursuing his desire to find companionship and love in an equal.

Siegfried's first words, an exuberant *Hoiho,* also bear out the contrast between him and Mime, for they are quite unlike the repetitious complaint to which Mime has just treated us. Siegfried's vocal lines tend, at least at the beginning, to outline triads and diatonic intervals, and he states the motive associated with his identity in the last act of *Die Walküre* (example 4-7), begun in the orchestra, when he tests and then breaks the sword Mime has made for him. The relationship implies how closely his own identity is connected with the right sword; the act of reforging the sword at the end of scene 3 is an act of self-realization.

Because Siegfried must establish his independence, his rejection of Mime is a constant theme. He says he dislikes even the sight of his foster father:

Example 5.2

Seh ich dir erst
mit den Augen zu
zu übel erkenn ich,
was alles du tust.

I am repelled
by the sight of you;
I see that you're evil
in all that you do.

(P. 161)

Once again sight stands as symbol of the subject-object relationship. The visual repulsiveness Siegfried finds in Mime suggests symbolically that Mime is an unworthy object in which
Siegfried might discover his own essence.

In answer to Siegfried's questioning, Mime asserts that Siegfried must love him. Mime tries to teach Siegfried the meaning of
love as well as the meaning of fear, though he fails in both; of
course Siegfried must wait for Brünnhilde in order to learn them.
Siegfried argues that Mime is lying when he says that he is father
and mother to Siegfried—young creatures look like their parents,
says the youth, and he has looked in a brook (repeating an image
from Die Walküre) and realizes that he does not look at all like
Mime. The self-recognition the subject needs in order to discover
his own self-consciousness is thus not available to Siegfried
through Mime—he must find someone who is like himself, just as
Siegmund and Sieglinde found each other.

That Siegfried has grown up in the hostile environment Mime
provides—an inversion of the hierarchical orderliness of the
realms of Das Rheingold—is important in the text here, for his
rejection of Mime is not only personal but cultural. Siegfried
rejects the conventional values that Mime embodies: power, intellect, control, and wealth. As smith, Mime exploits nature, although his song in Das Rheingold has already suggested that the
Nibelungen were originally happy and nonexploitative in their
employment of their craft. Now, however, as Mime's opening song
makes clear, his craft is only a means to the end of gaining power,
in the form of the ring. Siegfried, on the other hand, has a strong
and nonexploitative relationship with nature; in addition to his
friendship with the bear, he speaks of his respect for the family
life of foxes and birds. He also frequently communicates with
forest creatures, using his horn to call the bear and later the
woodbird, and he attempts to make a reed to imitate the bird.

Finally, of course, he learns to understand the very language of nature, under the tuition of the woodbird.

Mime has no such sympathy for nature. He attempts to dominate it by gaining control of the ring, just as he attempts to exploit Siegfried. Using physical force and mental cunning, Mime tries to establish dominance over Siegfried, or rather to maintain the dominance he once was able to hold when Siegfried was younger. Wagner seems willing to allow for a certain amount of superior cunning on Mime's part. The differences Wagner attempts to draw between the mental sets of these two characters lie not in their degree of intelligence but of morality: Siegfried is instinctively moral while Mime has been corrupted by the desire for the ring (that he had some claim to moral innocence at one time is suggested by his aria in *Das Rheingold*).

It is clear that Mime's connection with fear is supposed to characterize him as a despot. Near the end of *Die Walküre*, the Valkyries agreed that Sieglinde would be safest in the East, where Fafner's lair lay and hence an area Wotan avoids. The symbolism of the East is suggestive; in Hegel, the Eastern cultures are based on fear rather than on reason and create a state in which "there is only the status of lord and the status of servant. This is the sphere of despotism. When this is expressed in terms of feeling, it is *fear* which is the ruling category. . . . Thus fear and despotism are the dominants in the East. Either a man stands in fear, is afraid, or he rules by fear, and so is either servant or master. Both are on the same level. The difference between them is only the formal one of more or less force or energy of will."[13] Mime attempts to rule by fear, and Siegfried escapes him through superior force of will or energy.

The master-slave relationship that Mime is counting on goes awry, and Siegfried fails, in spite of Mime's best efforts, to learn fear. In Wagner's version of the history of consciousness, a relation of dependence must be based on love, and Wagner substitutes the relationship between mother and child for that between the master and the slave as a prerequisite for self-consciousness. Thus we see enacted on stage Siegfried's substitution of his new knowledge of his mother for the nurturing—the false nurturing—of Mime. In attempting to assume the role of mother, Mime is in fact only parodying it.

Throughout this scene, family and relationships with the past are stressed. Mime constitutes Siegfried's past, but it is a past that does not satisfy Siegfried, and he demands an alternative story of

Als   zul -len -des Kind   zog ich dich

auf,   warm-te mit Kleiden den klei – nen Wurm

Example 5.3

his life. Siegfried attempts to gain insight into his own being by
forcing Mime to tell him of his true origin in the story of his
parents and birth. Painfully, Siegfried forces from Mime the
name of his mother but accepts Mime's contention that he does
not know the name of his father. Mime finally complies at least in
part with Siegfried's demand for knowledge because he believes
he can use the knowledge he now imparts to Siegfried to control
his actions.[14]

Mime, trying to placate Siegfried, indulges in the appoggiaturas
that are characteristic of him here and in *Das Rheingold.* In his
song about how he has taken care of Siegfried (Siegfried calls it
the starling song), he tries to impress on Siegfried the debt the
young man owes him (example 5-3). Here and in his song at the
beginning of the act, he emphasizes his own labor. Mime tries to
sell himself as laborer, and like Alberich tries to barter for power.
However, Siegfried rejects the notion that Mime's labor on his
behalf needs to be repaid. Mime argues that Siegfried must love
his foster father because of what he owes him; while Siegfried
acknowledges the debt he rejects this definition of love as payment.

After Mime completes his song, Siegfried replies in music that
is simple and lyrical and contrasts with the cramped melodies of
the starling song that he has learned much from him. However, as
Siegfried enumerates the things he owes Mime, he adopts Mime's
melody, interspersing each of Mime's phrases with one of his own
in which he repeats how Mime's offices have repelled him. Siegfried internalizes Mime's music in order to reject it. He omits, of
course, in quoting Mime's melody, his grace notes; the effect is a
change from Mime's wailing tone of voice to a more lyrical one.
But the music shows how completely Siegfried has learned, even
if unconsciously, the lessons Mime has to teach. The music here
undercuts Wagner's apparent intention that Siegfried be pictured

as developing a consciousness independent of the influence of Mime and Mime's culture.

Siegfried asks Mime to explain why he always returns to Mime, even though he cannot stand him (the questions and answers here suggest that Siegfried still has a childish dependence on Mime, which he outgrows in the course of the act). Mime replies that it is love that brings Siegfried back—of course this is a false answer, but the orchestra begins a new theme derived from Erda's music in *Das Rheingold* that suggests how closely Siegfried (and even Mime) lives to nature (example 5-4). Musically, this variant of Erda's motive suggests that the dominant influence on Siegfried is nature, even though other evidence in the music argues for a strong influence from Mime also. This orchestral motive is that of the narrative voice: we are told that Siegfried is a child of nature, while his appropriation of Mime's music suggests otherwise in a perhaps more convincing form.

Siegfried sings part of the music earlier associated with his identity (example 4-7)—here, as is frequently the case, it is divided between voice and orchestra—as he says he saw himself in a brook. This image repeats the image of mirroring from *Die Walküre,* when Sieglinde compares Siegmund's face to her own image in a brook, and suggests again that self-definition is what Siegfried, like his parents before him, is seeking. His very next phrase, however, is a variant of a phrase from Mime's starling song. Again, the identity between foster father and son dramatically and musically is very strong, in spite of Siegfried's intentions.

Siegfried's ruminations after Mime tells him the story of his birth exhibit a typically patriarchal sentimentality toward the thought of his mother, expressed in the orchestra by the repeated use of themes associated with Sieglinde and her love for Siegmund in *Die Walküre,* usually with their characteristic orchestration intact. The mother figure is plainly supposed to be accepted by the audience as a figure for the self-sacrificing love that Wagner

Example 5.4

values in women, in spite of his insistence on equality, and Sieg-linde is presented in Siegfried's memory as the foundation of love and self-sacrifice. Thus we see on stage a mental process in which Siegfried replaces his false mother Mime with memories of his real mother.[15]

When Siegfried learns about his mother he seems to be strongly affected. In fact, in the Hegelian scheme of the *Ring*, he is recreating through these moments the earlier stages of consciousness: it is necessary for him to relive the important moments of *Die Walküre*, which of course Wagner can allow him to do through the leitmotif, explicitly designed to present just this type of meaning. Hegel suggests in the *Phenomenology* that the hero, the individual "whose substance is mind at the higher level," passes through all earlier stages, stages that mind in general has already gone through, not in actuality but "as shapes once assumed by mind and now laid aside, as stages of a road which has been worked over and levelled out" (p. 89). Siegfried, whose destiny is to learn the new consciousness through love, relives the past love of his parents in this scene through the reminiscent leitmotifs. Wagner is also drawing on Feuerbach, to whom memory was very important. In *Thoughts on Death and Immortality*, Feuerbach explained the Hegelian concept of self-consciousness through mutual recognition as a process of memory:

> A person becomes personal only with the determinate comprehension and grasp of himself. A person has the measure of his being and duration only with and in this personhood. You know, not from yourself, but only from others, that you were once a child and that you are the same being that you were as a child. Others are entwined and woven into your own life, into the unity of the consciousness of your own particular personhood, to such an extent that your knowledge of yourself is mediated by others' knowledge of you.[16]

Siegfried's consciousness of himself, however, cannot be mediated by that of his parents, who are dead. In spite of himself, his consciousness is mediated to some extent by Mime's; more fully, however, his consciousness is later mediated by Brünnhilde, who serves in some way as both parent and lover.

The confusion between lover and mother applies not only to Brünnhilde, however, but also to Sieglinde. The musical reminiscences of Sieglinde that the orchestra presents in this scene suggest Siegfried's first object of desire is not Brünnhilde but his mother. Hegel argues that in order to be conscious of one's own existence one must experience desire for the things of the outer

world.[17] Desire is the essential element for Hegel, the element
that leads from a stage of unawareness of the self to the next level,
self-consciousness. Desire is the connection with the other. Siegfried's experience of desire here, first for his mother and the love
she could have offered him, is what allows him to begin to experience himself as different and is what motivates him to begin to
seek the next level of consciousness. In a moment foreshadowing
modern psychology, he connects desire with the mother first,
before the lover. Thomas Mann has suggested that in this passage
we witness the beginnings of Siegfried's love life. "What we have
here," he says, "rising up from the dark depths of the unconscious, is a presentient complex of mother fixation, sexual desire
and *Angst* (by which I mean that fairy-tale fear that Siegfried seeks
to know)." Mann also suggests that this passage and later ones
connecting desire, mother, and fear indicate an intuitive affinity
between Wagner and Freud: "The way that Siegfried's thoughts of
his mother slide into eroticism in his reverie beneath the linden
tree, or the way in which, in the scene where Mime tries to instruct
his ward in the meaning of fear, the motif of Brünnhilde slumber-
ing in the fire moves through the orchestra like a dark, distorted
presence—this is pure Freud, pure psychoanalysis."[18]

The emphasis on naming that was so important in *Die Walküre*
continues in the next scene, for when the Wanderer enters, Mime
demands his name. Mime's failure to recognize Wotan indicates
his inability to see the Other in any form. However, instead of
giving his true name, Wotan, like Siegmund, gives a descriptive
pseudonym that, he says, the world knows him by: "'Wanderer'
heißt mich die Welt." As Wanderer, Wotan can observe the events
of history but not take part in them. Yet he retains enough of his
identity as god here to attempt to manipulate events: in an excess
of generosity he hints that he can tell Mime how to forge the
sword he needs, but Mime (whose false self-confidence is a parody
of true self-consciousness) does not accept. Later, in the series of
questions he asks Wotan, Mime again has the opportunity to find
out what he needs to know, but he fails to ask the right questions.
The Wanderer tells Mime that he rules the world with absolute
power, through the agency of the spear and the contracts written
on it. We know, of course, that Wotan no longer completely believes in the power of contracts and violence, as he has told his
most private thoughts on the subject to Brünnhilde. But here he is
simply trying to impress Mime and sticks with the old fiction of
absolute power. Law and contracts return as a theme when the
Wanderer tells Mime that, since he answered three questions,

Mime too is obliged. This is another example of the kind of false contract—law reduced to bargaining—that has gotten Wotan into trouble before, though he is arrogantly sure of his ability to deal with Mime.[19]

The Wanderer sings part of the theme associated with Siegfried's identity (example 4-7) as he asks the third and fatal question, Who can forge the sword? In this way he gives the answer in the music, but Mime of course does not hear it. Throughout this dialogue, the orchestral motives suggest the things the participants are thinking about, usually their shared knowledge of events, but here the crucial knowledge is of course not shared. The music becomes very agitated as Mime realizes that this is the very question he cannot answer. The orchestra plays (and Mime sings part of) a version of the need for love motive as Mime admits he does not know how to forge Nothung. Now, however, the feeling/thought objectified in the orchestra is not the need for love but the great need Mime had for the one piece of information he did not ask for.

The magic fire music appears as Mime imagines he sees all sorts of things in the forest, out of his fear of losing his head. Mime experiences the fear he must try to teach Siegfried if he is to save his own life (whereas earlier he only needed to teach Siegfried fear in order to gain the ring). The issue of fear is turned on its head now—fear is not only what Mime must teach Siegfried, but what he himself experiences.

Wagner turns Hegel on his head in dealing with the issue of fear. For Hegel, the master-slave relationship is based on fear, and fear is necessary to self-consciousness. That is, the individual (in this case the slave) must know and conquer fear; he must feel what it is to have his life in danger and must reach a stage of believing that some things are more important than simply preserving existence before he can rise to the next, higher state. Wagner rejects fear for Siegfried, however, who becomes self-aware only through love, first through the example of love among the forest animals and in his mother, then in actual experience.

Attempting to explain the somewhat confusing place fear plays in the plot of this act, Ernest Newman details the differences between *Der junge Siegfried* and the finished text on this point. The theme of fear is more fully explained, he says, in the earlier version of the text. There, Mime tells Siegfried that the wise man is always on the lookout for things that threaten his life; "fear it is that teaches us craft: this is fear's fruit." This echoes Hegel, who argues that fear for one's life teaches reason by allowing the individual to realize that there is something beyond the here and now. According to Newman, it is clear in the earlier poem that Mime attempts to conquer the ring and the world not through Siegfried's courage but through Siegfried's fear. But much of this argument is left out of the final version. In the final version the Wanderer says "He who to fear / was ne'er a slave / forges Nothung anew." Wagner, in his attempt to create the romantic superhero in Siegfried, will not allow him to go through the experience of fearing for his life.[20] Instead, Wagner apparently dropped the Hegelian argument so that Siegfried could realize his own finiteness in the love relationship rather than through fear of death.

Mime's fear at the beginning of scene 3 finds a specific object: he fears a glow that he imagines he sees in the forest and associates with Fafner. Fear is specifically related to the fear of fire here, not only in the text but also in the orchestra, which plays a variant of the music associated with Loge in *Das Rheingold* and with the fire that surrounds Brünnhilde at the end of *Die Walküre*. The fire Mime fears, then, is exactly the fire that Siegfried must not fear in order to win his way to Brünnhilde. The magic fire music serves as the basis of the scene in which Siegfried forges the sword, and the hero's intimate relation with fire is made clear. Mime comments, watching him, that he forges the sword with great power and without tiring, recognizing that an element of natural power is at work, an element to which Mime himself has never had access. Siegfried rejects Mime's skill as a smith, going in fact against all traditional knowledge of forging in order to recreate the sword in a new way. Siegfried's rejection of the conventional ways to mold the sword advocated by Mime parallels Siegmund's earlier rejection of conventional society. Siegfried must completely destroy the sword, reducing it to splinters, an action that forecasts the complete destruction of society itself at the end of *Götterdämmerung*.

The forging scene has intimate connections with Hegelian dialectic, especially in its connections to Marxism. This is in no way to suggest that Wagner was a closet Marxist, but it seems clear that some of the issues in Hegel that Marx seized upon were also impressive to Wagner. In Hegel, labor has a central importance in the development of the new consciousness, though of course not nearly the position it has in Marxist theory. Similarly, for Wagner, labor, the physical transformation of objects, plays an important though not central part in Siegfried's development. Siegfried's relation to the sword, which is the emblem of Wotan's ideal of the

hero, leads to its transformation as an object and the transformation of Wotan's plan for power and dominance into Siegfried's as
yet unformed objective of freedom and equality. Siegmund's
equating of the sword with Sieglinde's look began the process of
transforming it from a symbol of power to a symbol of love, a
process Siegfried has taken a step further.

Reforging the sword is the symbolic gesture that suggests that
Siegfried has, after rejecting Mime, recast his own identity in the
image of the mother and father he has finally learned about.
Earlier the sword was contaminated by Wotan's touch, but the fire
at the end of this act purges it of convention and the failed
contract with Siegmund. It is now ready to help Siegfried in his
quest for love.

Act 2

Just as act 1 was built on a series of songs, act 2 is constructed of
a series of dialogues that deal with the issues of language and
understanding. The first dialogue, between Wotan and Alberich,
is one of discovery for Alberich and thus serves to foward the
plot; Wotan, on the other hand, participates in it, as he did in his
dialogue with Mime in act 1, from an ironic distance. These two
characters represent contrasting types of understanding, both of
which Siegfried must go beyond. The dialogue between Mime
and Alberich at the beginning of scene 3 similarly demonstrates a
mode of being that contrasts with Siegfried's: the lack of love
between two creatures of the same kind is the issue here. But the
relationship between the two dwarfs is the opposite of the love
relationship Siegfried seeks; similarly, as Fafner dies he recalls the
lack of love between himself and Fasolt. Wagner assumes that the
love that must exist between two creatures of the same kind is
most likely to be sexual love; brotherly love in the *Ring* cycle is a
failure (which is later repeated between the half-brothers Hagen
and Gunther).

But the dialogues in which Siegfried himself is involved in act 2
are particularly interesting; in one he attempts to learn the language of the bird, and in the other, with Mime, he finally comes to
understand what Mime means. In both cases he discovers meanings previously hidden; these examples objectify the rapid growth
of his consciousness. He learns to read the signs of nature and
begins to see nature as a manifestation of the force of love that
impels him on to Brünnhilde. But he also learns to see that

human language is often duplicitous; Mime does not mean what he says. However, neither type of learning is powerful enough to resist Hagen's potion; in *Götterdämmerung* Siegfried can no longer understand the birds or comprehend Hagen's treacherous language.

The second act in general is somewhat more chromatic and harmonically complex than the first because it less often attempts to create a folklike atmosphere. As the curtain goes up, the scene is dark, with a cavern at the back. The place, of course, is Neidhöle. Alberich wanders about in the dark asking when the gloom will lift; the day enters with Siegfried, of course, but first a false light appears as Wotan enters.

Alberich, like Mime in act 1, tells the Wanderer to go away. It is characteristic of both dwarfs that they do not feel the need for companionship felt by the other persons in the drama. The Wanderer replies that he only watches but does not participate. This assertion is somewhat questionable, and Adorno points out that the purity of Wotan's motives here demands a closer look: not only does he pretend neutrality but he also appears on the one hand to defend rebellion and on the other to continue to defend his own imperialistic concept of law.[21] Alberich understands Wotan's motives, reminding him that he dare not break his treaty by attempting to get the ring from Fafner, for the spear would break. The Wanderer replies that no treaties bind Alberich to obey him; rather, he says, it is force:

> dich beugt' er mir durch seine Kraft;
> zum Krieg drum wahr ich ihn wohl.

> By force I bent your will to mine;
> my spear brings victory in war.

> (P. 194)

Wotan still is unable to see that the force that eventually will break the spear is Siegfried himself; the world is not progressing in the direction of laws and contracts—Wotan's direction—but toward freedom and love.

In spite of his protestations of neutrality to Alberich, Wotan still seems eager to have his hand in the plot. The music is suggestive; the Valhalla motive, associated with Wotan's power and pretensions of grandeur, marks the Wanderer's first phrases. However, the harmonic progression associated with Wotan's guise of neutrality (example 5-5) sounds as he tells Alberich he will not participate. These chords serve here, as they do in act 1 and later in the

Example 5.5

scene between Erda and Wotan in act 3, to make a dramatic
change of pace with the person to whom the Wanderer is talking,
always helping to suggest an aura of detachment for Wotan. Here,
Wotan's presence, imaged as distant and calm by the slow-moving
chords, is opposed to Alberich's eager interest. In this case, however, the distinction between the pace and tone of the two voices
lessens as the conversation develops, as if Wotan, in spite of how
much he wishes to remain aloof, is not able to do so.

Freedom is constantly presented as the issue in this scene;
Wotan makes a point of telling Alberich that he is free. But this
type of freedom is empty and meaningless; here as in *Das
Rheingold,* Alberich refuses to act free. His bondage is greed.
Wotan also tells Alberich that Siegfried is free—he is the hero the
gods need. Here Wotan insists on the freedom of everyone to act
as they wish, yet he knows that freedom is difficult to win and
difficult to keep. Whether or not Siegfried is really free is the
question behind all others, a question answered negatively by
Brünnhilde at the end.

As the conversation continues, the Wanderer tells Alberich that
all things follow their own course. He seems to be quoting Erda,
and indeed, music earlier associated with her not only sounds in
the orchestra but appears in Wotan's part. However, the Wanderer does not give her credit but lets Alberich believe that it is his
own philosophy he is citing. Wotan does not acknowledge superior wisdom from a woman, even though he willingly uses it. His
use of her music, which is also associated with nature and the
Rhine (as it is derived from the prelude to *Das Rheingold*), suggests
that he too conceives of her as a nature goddess. This traditional
aligning of women with nature, to which Wotan subscribes, is a
tool of domination, for to assign Erda to an outgrown mode of
consciousness is to dismiss her, as he shortly does in actuality.

Alberich responds to the new information the Wanderer gives

him in somewhat the same way Wotan responded to Erda in *Das Rheingold;* after the Wanderer leaves, Alberich notes that he leaves him in care and sorrow ("Sorg' und Spott"). Here as in several instances in the cycle the stages of consciousness are repeated from character to character, suggesting their universality. However, although Alberich now repeats some of the insights Wotan gained earlier, his consciousness never progresses any further, and he remains at the stage at which Wotan is left at the end of *Das Rheingold.*

The entrance of Mime and Siegfried, bickering, returns the tone to the comic for the moment. Mime, after one more fruitless attempt to teach Siegfried fear, retires to a nearby spring in order to wait for the end of Siegfried's battle with the dragon. This spring reminds us of the water that provided new life for Siegmund in *Die Walküre.* However, this water is an inversion of that one; it does not signal the beginning of a new stage of consciousness for Mime. Similarly, the "refreshing drink" Mime has prepared for Siegfried not only repeats the potion that Sieglinde gave Hunding, it repeats the idea of sleep, for Mime makes a feeble and aborted attempt to put Siegfried to sleep as Wotan put Brünnhilde to sleep (it also anticipates the potion that is successfully given Siegfried in *Götterdämmerung*). As with almost everything Mime touches, however, the spring and drink are not symbols of life but death. Mime goes down to the spring to await his own death, though he thinks it is to await that of Siegfried.

As Siegfried is left alone on the stage, he is still thinking of the question of his own identity. He expresses satisfaction that Mime is not his father, and in wondering what his father would have looked like, he realizes that he would look like himself, as Mime's son would look like Mime. Siegfried's thoughts return to his mother, and the Sieglinde music again sounds in the orchestra, the music again indicating the character's thoughts. The transition in his mind to a new subject is imaged in the music; he notices that the bird is talking and singing with creatures of its own kind, and Siegfried decides to try to learn its language. The music sung by the bird is derived from the Rhinedaughters' song of *Das Rheingold,* indicating an elemental connection with nature in both cases. Indeed, this scene emphasizes Siegfried's own connection with nature and continues the process of separation from Mime.

The horn with which Siegfried attempts to communicate with the bird awakens the dragon (just as later Siegfried awakens Brünnhilde; in each case he rises to a new level of consciousness). The slaying of the dragon is derived not only from Hegel's pages

on the master-slave relationship but from Greek epic. In the
Phenomenology, master-slave relationships are established after a
battle, and Hegel describes the battles of Greek epic as engage-
ments in which two heroes acknowledge one another briefly as the
Other; but at their stage of civilization, one of the two must be
either enslaved or killed.[22] Siegfried echoes this pattern; in bat-
tling Fafner, he implicitly acknowledges him as a worthy oppo-
nent and hence, however briefly, as an independent consciousness. In killing him Siegfried ensures that he must find still
another relationship in order to find recognition.

After fatally wounding the dragon, Siegfried returns with
characteristic stubbornness to the problem of his own identity.
Seeking self-knowledge, he tells the stricken Fafner that he does
not know who he is. Siegfried naively seeks recognition from the
dragon, but Fafner is not prepared to give him this sense of self.
Fafner however does attempt to help him, first by warning him
with the story of two brothers who tried to destroy each other
(their battle parodied by Alberich's and Mime's heated argument
later), and next by warning that he who urged Siegfried to kill him
will also kill for the ring. Siegfried's encounter with the Other
fails, for Siegfried does not fear the dragon, as Mime had hoped,
so he does not come to see himself as mortal and therefore see his
essence as being more than simply life—this awareness must await
the mutual recognition of a love relationship.

The dragon represents a stage of consciousness that Siegfried
will not have to suffer; Fafner, as he indicates at his death, has
been wrong to destroy his brother and guard the treasure rather
than simply go on living. Fafner presents the image of a life lived
in fear, in this case fear aroused by ownership of property. In *Oper
und Drama* Wagner cites an episode from *Antigone* in which the
dragon's attitude toward property is paralleled, arguing that the
dispute between Antigone's brothers was essentially based on the
unthinking acceptance of property as a right: "Each citizen who
recognized in Property the guarantee of wonted quiet, was ipso
facto an accomplice of the unbrotherly deed of Eteocles" (p. 185).
Fafner too is guilty of participating in the crime of Alberich
because he wants to enjoy the gold quietly, without facing the fact
that it represents an injustice. His returning it to the earth, in his
cave, is not a substitute for returning it to the river.

Siegfried's new interest in the bird after Fafner's death indicates
a new stage in his growth; in spite of his failure to learn his
identity from the dragon, he has gained a new interest in others as

independent consciousnesses rather than as things. This is what enables him to understand the bird; the other characters cannot understand the bird's language because they still see him as an object. At this level of consciousness, it is given to Siegfried to understand that other creatures may exist as a consciousness distinct from his own even though he has not yet found the independent consciousness that will mirror his (this attitude toward animals parallels Brünnhilde's respectful understanding of Grane).

The bird predicts the unhappy fate Brünnhilde and Siegfried will experience; his song includes love and grief in the same phrase:

> Lustig im Leid
> sing ich von Liebe;
> wonning aus Weh
> web ich mein Lied:
> nur Sehnende kennen den Sinn!

> Gaily in grief
> I sing of love;
> joyful in woe,
> I weave my song;
> only lovers can tell what it means.

(P. 218)

This song repeats what Siegfried has already said about the bird—that he and his fellow creatures sing in laughter and love. But the bird's song also hints that for the humans of the drama, a simple happy existence is not possible, for the world they must enter is already corrupt. Love must be met by suffering, for only through suffering may the higher stages of self-consciousness be reached.

As Siegfried, on the birds' advice, enters the cave to examine the hoard he has won by killing the dragon, Mime and Alberich appear. Characteristically, Mime uses a fragment of his starling song from the first act as he asks Alberich to treat him like a brother and share the booty. The music earlier associated with Siegfried's impatience with him plays under this rapid argument between the brothers, suggesting that not only Siegfried but everyone appears to be impatient with Mime. The dialogue between the two dwarfs as to who will get the ring, who made the tarnhelm, and who deserves what is a parody of the interests of property and is contrasted with Siegfried's innocent attitude toward wealth.

When Siegfried leaves the cave with the ring and helm, the key changes to C major, and the original version of the greeting to the Rhinegold theme plays, providing a contrast to the chromatically altered version now associated with Alberich. As Siegfried contemplates the gold, a good deal of the Rhinedaughters' song is heard, hinting that Siegfried has the same nonpolitical attitude toward property that they did. This passage connects Siegfried to the Rhinedaughters, although they will be opposed in the next opera, where the crucial issue of fear again arises.

The use of language in this act is very interesting. First, Siegfried reveals that a dwarf once told him that he could learn to understand the words of the birds, and he attempts to do so with pipe and horn. Later, the dragon's blood gives him power not only to understand the bird's speech but also the hidden meaning behind Mime's words. Siegfried learns from Fafner not fear but language; that is, he learns how language really works. In the remarkable passage in which Siegfried finally understands Mime's character, the audience must guess what Mime is actually saying, for what we hear is what Siegfried hears—the words the actor sings reflect the intent behind Mime's words. This passage is a parody of dialogue and in some ways duplicates the function of the leitmotifs, which also often tell us the intent behind the text. Wagner is perhaps employing a Hegelian idea of language here. Hegel suggests that only language allows the individual to move from being trapped in the present and the immediate: language moves us instantly from the specific, from hereness and nowness, to the general. Words make the world into things or symbols. The bird has taught Siegfried to use words as symbols and in doing so reveals a world that is not the world of here and now but a more general and social world—a world of ideology—which Siegfried is about to enter.

As Siegfried deals with the dead bodies on stage, the motive earlier associated with Mime and the Nibelungen sounds on a repeated F-sharp, forming a pedal point that alternates with Siegfried's horn call, which occurs on various pitches (example 5-6). The rhythmic similarity between the two motives is emphasized in a musical restatement of the relation between these two characters—Mime always on the same sinister theme, with Siegfried always reacting to it, trying to escape but not quite able to do so. Even Mime's death does not completely free the hero, for Mime's

Example 5.6

consciousness continues to influence his own, and Mime's world remains ready to destroy him.

Act 3

This act, of course, marks the point at which Wagner resumed composition of the *Ring* after a long hiatus during which he completed both *Tristan* and *Die Meistersinger.* McCreless notes that the new, post-*Tristan* compositional techniques displayed in this act are largely tonal. In Wagner's new compositional technique, an act no longer consists of a series of closed tonal units (scenes or periods). Rather, each act is structured between the polarities of two tonalities, the problem being how to get from one tonality to the other in the course of the act. One way Wagner does this is to undercut the importance of cadences within the act and to weight the final cadence more strongly in order to make it function structurally as a cadence for the whole act.[23] Wagner's growing dependence on pairs of tonal centers to structure acts develops from purely musical considerations in *Tristan,* which is influenced more by the metaphysics of Schopenhauer than of Hegel. However, Wagner did not hesitate, when he returned to the more Hegelian ideas of *Siegfried,* to employ the new musical structures when they seemed to fit the meanings of the text. Even though to a large degree the tonal structure of this act is independent of the text, the tonal structure moves, as McCreless shows, in complex ways to the final scene where the C associated with Wotan's great idea, and hence with Siegfried himself, is paired with the E-flat associated in various ways with Brünnhilde. The act as a whole moves Siegfried from the youthful callowness he exhibited in previous acts toward his discovery of the autonomous subject as lover in Brünnhilde.

The act opens in a wild place in a thunderstorm, near Erda's home. She is sleeping, her state suggesting that she is an outgrown goddess whose time is past. Like Brünnhilde's, however, her sleep is not permanent; she sleeps only to be awakened to consciousness by a man. Wotan embodies the male god, the patriarchal culture that has taken over and destroyed the older matriarchal power. That he is greatly more powerful than she (even though his power too is already on the decline) is reflected in the fact that he can call her at will. After cruelly awakening her, Wotan switches to music usually associated with Erda herself as he describes her. She enters, however, accompanied by chords associated with Brünnhilde's sleep at the end of *Die Walküre*. The tension between Erda and Wotan, according to William Kinderman, is expressed in the tension between her tonality (E-flat, with which she has been associated since *Das Rheingold*) and his (G);[24] the contrasting tonalities are expressive of a tension that cannot be resolved in a conventional way.

Musically and in the text the discussion with Erda suggests a double image of domination: the supersession of Wotan's male gods over the female gods of Erda and her family, and the domination of Erda herself by Wotan. The music changes to the rising passage associated with the Rhine and with nature in general in the prelude to *Das Rheingold* as Erda tells him to go find the Norns, emphasizing an affinity between them and the Rhinedaughters, based in part on their mutual helplessness and the ease with which Wotan ignores them. Wotan in reply says that the Norns are in the power of the world, rather than the other way around, and thus they are useless as guides. He admits that these gods have been replaced by human nonreligious values (the need for love theme sounds as he says their knowledge can do nothing), but he has not quite accepted his own replacement. His peremptory treatment of Erda and his scorn for the Norns suggest that he still believes in the trappings of his own power. Erda apparently complies with his assessment of her own position, saying that men's deeds have clouded her mind. She admits that she was once conquered by love, a statement that, just to make everything clear, is accompanied by the Valhalla theme. We cannot escape the implication that she came to love unwillingly.

The mood of the conversation changes somewhat as Wotan begins to attack Erda angrily. Wotan wants still more out of her and accuses her of bringing fear and shame into his own life with her prediction of his downfall. Now, however, he does not want her help but wants to gloat, hinting that he knows what she does not, that she will perish with him. He implies she has lost all her former value and strength; he calls her the unwise one (*Dir Unweisen*). Still, he also calls her mother, but tells her, as mother of dread (*Urmütterfurcht*), to return to sleep. His rejection of the mother, of matriarchy, here parallels Siegfried's upcoming rejection of him as father-figure. Wotan seems to feel that he must force Erda into retirement (in spite of the fact that she was roused unwillingly from her sleep), in contrast to his own, wiser resignation; he tells her that what he once in anguish saw was inevitable he now freely wills to pass. Wotan's characterization of Erda as a negative force seems to be in retaliation for his inability completely to dominate her. In *Das Rheingold*, Erda evoked woman as Other, who was not self-sacrificing or a slave to Wotan and represented an older but still viable power. Wotan's gratuitous cruelty here suggests how strongly Wagner rejects the possibility of matriarchal power.

In scene 2, Siegfried, having bullied a diminutive and unworthy father-figure, must now prove himself against a stronger one, his grandfather Wotan.[25] Here another question-and-answer series occurs, this time between Siegfried and the Wanderer. The effect is comic, but the final result is the breaking of Wotan's spear, the last step in his loss of power. In his discussion with Erda Wotan has claimed to be ready for this step, but in fact he finds it difficult. He begins to feel angry toward Siegfried and warns him of the anger, saying it could undo both of them. Wotan seems unable to control his anger, a quality he perhaps owes to the likeness Wagner intended between him and Oedipus. Indeed, this scene at the crossroads, so to speak, where the son destroys the father who would stand in his way, owes much to *Oedipus*, though as the father Wotan is parallel to Laius rather than to Oedipus. In *Oper und Drama*, Wagner had commented that Laius's sin against Oedipus goes unpunished because the Greek society pictured in the play valued the relationship to the father more than it valued the life of the son. In this scene Wagner seems determined to reverse these values; the spirit he glorifies in the *Ring* would value love between man and woman above all other relationships and the son above the father. This contrast suggests Wagner's idea that the new society of the *Ring* is superior to that of the Greeks, a point he borrows from Hegel, who believes that modern society has progressed beyond the best of its predecessors, the Greeks.

Siegfried's rejection of Wotan also indicates, as Wotan's rejection of Erda did in the previous scene, a step in the Feuerbachian allegory of the *Ring*. The action in these two scenes metaphorically suggests humanity's total rejection of religion, which Feuerbach argued was necessary; he argued that gods are simply an abstraction of human characteristics and are inimical to the full development of human consciousness. Part of his argument is based on the idea that only humans create gods; animals have none.[26] Siegfried has been raised with a simple, animal-like consciousness, ignorant of the religious ideas imposed on most people by society. This simplicity in his background, part of the natural, nonsocial world Wagner attempted to create for him, enables him to laugh at Wotan's pretensions.

The imagery of seeing appears in this scene, though it does not as before chronicle a meeting of equals. Siegfried and Wotan exchange glances. Siegfried, however, does not understand what is happening, and when he makes fun of the Wanderer's single eye, Wotan replies:

> Mit dem Auge,
>   das als andres mir fehlt,
> erblickst du selber das eine,
> das mir zum Sehen verblieb.

> Yet be careful,
>   for with eyes quite as blind
> as that I've lost, you are gazing
> on the eye that is left me for sight.

(P. 228)

Wotan's voice part here, as he finishes this rather cryptic statement, duplicates or almost duplicates the closing part of his greeting to Valhalla from *Das Rheingold* and hints at his own awareness of the coming end. The text suggests that both Wotan and Siegfried are defective in seeing, Siegfried temporarily and Wotan permanently. Wotan's patch is the emblem of what he lacks, the ability to see the Other as equal (as he has just proved in the exchange with Erda). Siegfried has two eyes still, but his behavior here is enough to prove that he too is blind, a symbolic blindness that the last scene, with its heavy emphasis on the sun, eyes, and awakening, will clear up.

Scene 3 contains the second and most important appearance in the *Ring* of a love relationship as mutual recognition. Siegfried finds the Other, the equal subject whom he must come to regard as both like himself and separate from himself, in this scene.

Feuerbach's description of the basic Hegelian notion seems to be the model Wagner had in mind:

Man is nothing without some "objective." The great models of human-ity, such men as reveal to us the essence of man, have attested the truth of this proposition by their lives. They had only one dominant pas-sion—the realization of the aim which was the essential object of their activity. But the object—at least the object to which a subject stands in a necessary and essential relation—is always the subject's own nature "objectified." We know man by his object; and in it his nature and his true objective self.[27]

Brünnhilde is Siegfried's true self, as this scene makes apparent. However, while Feuerbach's version of Hegel is quite clear, it implies that the object is most important for what it reveals about the subject rather than for its own independent existence, sug-gesting that Wagner perhaps created Brünnhilde from the first as a reflection of Siegfried's character. The "glorious maid," seen in this light, is nothing more than the image of the kind of woman who could inspire Siegfried's love. Siegmund could only love his own self reflected back to him, and Siegfried is not much better, loving a woman who has already displayed heroic qualities, who indeed has been a goddess and given up her godhood only for him.

This scene, in which Siegfried gains his own true identity through coming to know Brünnhilde, reflects a stage of growth of consciousness described by Feuerbach:

Your consciousness of yourself was originally outside of you; others were your consciousness, were the knowledge of you; your being was taken up into the knowledge of others. Only later, when you objec-tified yourself bodily and externally, did you also become inwardly independent. At that point the knowledge that others had of you became your own knowledge, the external consciousness of you be-came your inner consciousness. . . . You received from the hands of others, as it were, a consciousness that had already been prepared for you.[28]

This is the real significance of the wisdom that Brünnhilde im-parts to Siegfried. Siegfried, receiving the consciousness prepared for him by Brünnhilde's understanding of Siegmund and by her prescience, is transformed from the innocent bumbling boy of acts 1 and 2 to the mature hero who will live out the tragic fate of the new consciousness in a corrupt world.

Scene 3 opens with a statement of the motive associated with Siegmund's death (example 4-6), indicating a sense of foreboding even though everything on stage seems good so far. A long solo violin passage as Siegfried approaches the sleeping Brünnhilde is based on the love music first hear in association with Freia in *Das Rheingold,* strongly reminding us of the earlier connections made between love and freedom. An important point of scene 3 is that Brünnhilde finally, freely accepts Siegfried and in this way presents a contrast with the coercion Erda experienced earlier from Wotan. Another parallel between these two scenes is the sleep out of which both Brünnhilde and Erda are aroused. Sleep is connected with the elemental natures of Brünnhilde and Erda, suggesting they both dwell in a state of unconsciousness out of which they must be awakened by a man. Wagner believed that woman exists in a state of perfect instinct, that she embodies pure feeling and passivity as opposed to man's activity. This instinctiveness he objectifies as sleep.

Sleep, however, is not exclusively associated with females. Siegfried, discovering Brünnhilde sleeping on the rock, also realizes that he himself has existed in an unconscious or less conscious state. Recognizing that Brünnhilde represents the possibility for a new type of consciousness, Siegfried says that if he is to awaken himself, he must first wake her. He realizes that his own understanding of self, his own rising to self-consciousness, depends on her. However, when he tries to awaken her Wotan-fashion, by crying, "Erwache, erwache, Heiliges Weib" (p. 234), he is of course unsuccessful. He must abandon Wotan's heroic posturings; only a kiss will awaken the sleeping woman.

As she awakens, Brünnhilde greets the day and the sun. Then she calls on Siegfried as the bringer of light ("Du Wecker des Lebens, / siegendes Licht!" [p. 236]). The light imagery is of course conventional, but Wagner is preceded by others who used light imagery to suggest the new consciousness. Hegel describes the self-conscious individual in terms similar to Brünnhilde's: "The element in which individuality manifests and displays its form and shape, is simply the day, in whose light consciousness wants to display itself" (p. 415).[29]

The moment of awakening is emphasized not only in the text but in the music. The pairs of tonalities that Wagner frequently used for dramatic effect in his compositions after *Tristan* now control the musical structure. The music for Siegfried's awakening of Brünnhilde is based on the paired tonalities of E and C. The first of these, E, is the key in which Brünnhilde is put to sleep at the end of *Die Walküre* and was associated with her there, while C, the key of the sword motive and of Wotan's great idea, is frequently associated with Siegfried. The two keys alternate during the first part of the scene, until the moment of maximum musical tension is reached, at the moment of Brünnhilde's awakening, when C major is affirmed, having grown out of a tonal context of E, with the effect, in William Kinderman's words, of "the falling away of one perspective, and the simultaneous opening out of a new one."[30] The key that dominates, finally, is C, Siegfried's key (the key in which the act ends), and the perspective that has fallen away is Brünnhilde's. Musically, this startling and effective use of tonality serves to support the ideology of domination. The music suggests that after mutual recognition is acted out, in the mutual importance of C and E in the first part of the scene, it is replaced by the hegemony of Siegfried's consciousness and key and the effacement of Brünnhilde's.

Brünnhilde at first easily agrees to the love that she is destined to hold, telling Siegfried that she will be one with him: "Du selbst bin ich." She immediately accepts the oneness of the situation; Siegfried is a step behind her as he replies that he does not understand her. Having lost her status as god, Brünnhilde is passing rapidly through phases of humanness here. She already knows fear; she cries out (like Mime) against the darkness and her loss of wisdom. Brünnhilde has a vision of death and destruction in this scene; like Sieglinde before her, she worries about seeing, and what she sees is destruction. But Siegfried uncovers her eyes ceremonially, and the emphasis on eyes continues as she asks him if he has seen himself in a stream, suggesting the self-reflection she knows he has sought. As in *Die Walküre,* seeing is the emblem of mutual recognition.

The fear that Hegel postulates as a necessary step in self-realization shows up in a number of ways in this duet. Not only does Siegfried admit to finally feeling fear as he hesitates before the sleeping woman (though his fear passes quickly), but both he and Brünnhilde stress how unprotected they are. Wagner, like Hegel, sees fear as an important step in gaining self-consciousness, for fear represents the loss of egoism. But Wagner feels that the fear of losing the self lies in commitment to love, not in fear of death. Both Brünnhilde and Siegfried hesitate before taking the final leap into the loss of self demanded by love. Brünnhilde momentarily rejects love entirely, begging Siegfried not to disturb her own equanimity, before finally giving in to his passion.[31] The symbolism of the clothing develops this idea: with her armor, Brünnhilde is a goddess, without it, a vulnerable woman. Her vulnerability is emphasized in a number of ways. One of Siegfried's first acts is to remove her helmet, and he uses the sword to remove her breastplate (later, the sword stands between them when he returns as Gunther). Siegfried says he has brought her to life by removing her helmet, suggesting that this is part of her awakening to her new role as woman. She too sees him as vulnerable, comparing herself to Siegfried's shield as she explains to him how she protected him before he was born.

Siegfried embodies both the happiness of giving up the self, which Wagner always sees as the true character of love, and the contrary tendency to maintain the self through power and domination. Brünnhilde embodies a more complete understanding of giving up the self, perhaps—or at least she will by the end of *Götterdämmerung*. Siegfried has persuaded her to accept a relationship of love and passion, when she wanted to settle for mutual respect. Nevertheless, she accepts his domination over her, as Wagner expects his best women to, joyfully.

The act ends, however, as a number of people have pointed out, on the word *death*—the last words ("leuchtende Liebe, / lachender Tod") seem to suggest a sinister mood encroaching on this celebration of mutual recognition in love. However, death may be taken metaphorically here—both Siegfried and Brünnhilde have gone through a very brief stage of fear for their own lives; they have gone to the next Hegelian step of realizing that the individual life is not worth much and now have given up the self into love. At the end, death is mentioned because it has to do with loss. What they have lost is egoism, extreme self-interest and the belief in protecting the individual life no matter what. Love and death are equated in Wagner because both lead to this conclusion. However, Wagner may have been drawing more directly from Feuerbach than Hegel in this scene. Feuerbach argued in *Thoughts on Death and Immortality* that

> your life, as a continuing process of recollection and spiritualization, is the uninterrupted process of canceling the boundary between you and others and therefore of canceling your personal being and with it your personhood. In death, the result of this process, those boundaries for the cancellation of which you have worked in and by Spirit throughout your entire life completely disappear. The last word you speak is death, in which you totally express yourself and impart yourself to others. Death is the ultimate act of communication.[32]

Death will indeed be the last moment of communication between Siegfried and Brünnhilde, and death is the last word of

Siegfried. However, in the Hegelian scheme, it is necessary that one should be aware of oneself as one among others—and self-certainty does not achieve this; it is purely self-centered. The pleasure that Siegfried and Brünnhilde have given themselves over to is forbidden in our culture, like the song of the sirens that represents the absolutely forbidden pleasure for Odysseus as described in *The Dialectic of Enlightenment:* it is the call of man to complete submersion in nature, and the sirens "threaten the patriarchal order which renders to each man his life only in return for his full measure of time" (that is, only by giving oneself fully to the dominant culture can life be maintained).[33] Pleasure is a stolen moment and self-sufficiency, even for two lovers, is forbidden. So Siegfried and Brünnhilde move on to *Götterdämmerung*.

6
GÖTTERDÄMMERUNG

In *Götterdämmerung* the Hegelian scheme of the world-historical figure embodied in Siegfried begins to break down, while the Feuerbachian model of memory and death as the culmination of love as mutual recognition is emphasized. As Siegfried enters society, he loses the sense of self he has gained from Brünnhilde, and mutual recognition turns out to be temporary. Wagner uses the trick of Hagen's potion to trigger this regression and loss of self. The potion seems intended as primarily positive, as the first step of Siegfried's loss of individuality and his immersion into community. But the potion is also negative; it turns Siegfried into a conventional person as he appears to Brünnhilde in the form of Gunther and causes him temporarily to lose the new consciousness he has attained. Siegfried and Brünnhilde on one level are victimized by the corrupt society into which they are thrust, a society influenced by the false love of power and honor—Wagner's "state."

But this Hegelian allegory of mutual recognition in a social setting is superimposed upon a more mystic formulation Wagner derived from Feuerbach. To some extent, the difficulty in *Götterdämmerung* lies in the fact that Wagner attempted to combine in it a Hegelian notion of the place of the individual in history with a Feuerbachian notion of memory and spirit. Wagner may have had in mind throughout *Götterdämmerung* the emphasis on love as abandonment of self that he found in Feuerbach (an idea that was no doubt the genesis of *Siegfrieds Tod* and therefore the entire *Ring*). Feuerbach argued in *Thoughts on Death and Immortality* (which is heavily influenced by Hegel's *Phenomenology*) that spirit works through the willingness of each individual to give him or herself up completely to the other. Love, he said, is the ultimate human experience, and its strength and value are judged by its unselfishness:

> the more you sacrifice yourself, the greater and more genuine is your love. For one cannot love without self-sacrifice. In loving, I love myself

162

in another, I locate myself, my essence, not in myself, but in the object that I love. I bind my being to the being of another; I exist only in, with, and for another. If I am not in love, I exist only for myself. But when I am in love, I posit myself for another; I no longer possess my own being, my being-for-self; the being of the other is my being.[1]

That is, the individual gives way to a spiritualization that is others' consciousness of him. This process overtakes Siegfried during this last opera; his individuality gives way first in Hagen's potion, which causes him to lose his own memory and sense of self. Later, when memory is restored to him, he gains a new sense of the universality of love in his own recollections of Brünnhilde. But the process is still not complete. At the end of act 3, Siegfried is posited as a spiritualized being by Brünnhilde's love and self-sacrifice. Siegfried has throughout his lifetime worked toward developing himself as spirit (self-consciousness or love); he is the essence of Brünnhilde's love working itself out in human form. When he dies at the end, and the significance of his life becomes clear, the melody earlier associated with Brünnhilde's sacrifice for Sieglinde and for love at the beginning of act 3 of *Die Walküre* returns as the emblem of what his existence means as spirit. In *Götterdämmerung*, both Siegfried and Brünnhilde are constituted as spirit, their lives complete, so that the onlookers—both the Gibichungs and the audience—can experience love as an abstract, complete essence rather than the individual experience it has been up to now.

Prelude

Götterdämmerung begins its prelude on Brünnhilde's rock, where the Norns, described as wearing dark drapery, are keeping their vigil. They are obviously related to the three witches of *Macbeth*, and the ensuing drama, with its murders and ruthless battle over power, bears some resemblance to this play also. Like Erda, the Norns represent a natural world, but one radically transformed by human consciousness; they are, in addition, part of the universe of gods that will perish forever at the end. In the Feuerbachian allegory of the *Ring* the Norns represent not the powerless and slightly silly nature gods that Froh and Donner suggest but the still-viable ancient belief in matriarchal gods. They are important to Wagner's allegory because they suggest the power of love and self-sacrifice just as Brünnhilde does (and this is reflected in their family relationship with Brünnhilde). But their essential powerlessness is also important; as gods, they cannot act to further the new human consciousness. The Norns can only, as Wotan has already told Erda, reflect events—they cannot influence them.

The prelude begins on an E-flat-minor chord, a chord that relates it, with the negative implications of a shift to the minor, with the beginning of *Das Rheingold*. The elemental water music from the first scene of *Das Rheingold* (repeated in Erda's scene with Wotan in act 3 of *Siegfried*) forms the musical ground for the Norns, making the connection between the Norns and the Rhine-daughters clear (this opera will begin with the Norns and with their destruction and end with the triumph, of sorts, of the Rhine-daughters). But the elemental music here is disturbed by the music previously associated with Brünnhilde's annunciation of death to Siegmund. The melody Brünnhilde used then, the "song of death," recurs throughout this scene, hinting at an alignment of the Norns with the role Brünnhilde played before her dawn of self-consciousness as unthinking messenger of fate in the abstract world of the gods rather than actor in the human drama. To some extent, the Norns' music helps provide a mythic depth to the events of *Götterdämmerung*, the most unmythical of the four operas. The stories they tell in this prelude are history become myth, and the function of the music is to connect, as Dalhouse puts it, the events of the present with "their primeval premises and origins."[2]

The Norns, in fact, give not one but three interrelated narratives here, reflecting the structure of the cycle into three operas (excluding *Das Rheingold* as a prelude) and the division of the world into three levels—gods, humans, and underworld. The first story the Norns tell is that of Wotan and his loss of an eye. As a number of commentators have pointed out, their version of this story contradicts the account Wotan himself gives in *Das Rheingold*. Wotan lost his eye, they say, when he took a branch of the World Ash tree to make his spear, the spear by which he rules the world. The loss of an eye was the price he had to pay for drinking at the spring guarded by the Norns. However, this story supplements rather than contradicts Wotan's version. The eye Wotan loses corresponds to the eyes with which Siegmund and Sieglinde regard each other in *Die Walküre:* Wotan's loss of an eye symbolizes his inability to regard another as equal. In other words, the loss of his eye that the Norns here narrate is the loss of his ability to love, and his suggesting to Fricka that he lost it for her is not a contradiction at all but simply his way of saying that he gained her through force, not love. For in return for the eye, he gained power, the antithesis of love because it is based on subjugation rather than equality.

Furthermore, the spring at which Wotan drinks in the Norns' story suggests the source from which Sieglinde provides the water that reawakens Siegmund to life; in the beginning of *Die Walküre* Siegmund and Sieglinde relive Wotan's history as it is told here—with spring, ash tree, and weapon—but with a vastly different outcome. Wotan, as god, begins a cycle of history based on power, while Siegmund and Sieglinde begin the cycle, recounted in the *Ring*, of history based on human love.

The ash tree in both scenes symbolizes the life force itself. Sieglinde lives beneath the ash tree in Hunding's house, suggesting her connection with the natural source of life itself, and the sword Siegmund draws from it becomes a symbol of love whose removal does not seem to hurt the tree. However, Wotan in his quest for power robs the ash tree of a branch in order to make the spear, and this theft, which parallels Alberich's theft of the Rhinedaughters' gold, eventually results, according to the Norns, in the loss of life for the tree itself, the dead branches of which now provide the material for the fire of the final conflagration.

Another familiar set of images in the Norns' narrative are those of fire and light. The second story they tell is of Loge and his imprisonment by Wotan. Just as Wotan's theft of the ash branch results in eventual loss, his refusal to abide by the dictates of reason, suggested by Loge and the fire, has the same result. As instrumental reason, Loge represents freedom based on logic and practicality rather than love, a type of freedom Wotan endorsed until he met Alberich. Now Wotan, the Norns tell us, in his efforts to retain power has enslaved Loge, forcing him to guard Brünnhilde's rock. The Norns' concern with fire and day here repeats an image from act 2 of *Siegfried*, where Alberich expressed his fear of the day (as a symbol of reason or consciousness) when watching by Fafner's lair. That image in turn repeated the scene from act 1 of *Siegfried*, where Mime feared the coming of the light in the forest, for it was through light (in the person of Siegfried) and fire (Loge's fire, the fire of freedom and reason that allowed Siegfried to reforge the sword) that he met his destruction. This portion of the Norns' story then reiterates an idea important throughout the *Ring*, that reason is often helpful but inferior to love as a force in human history.

The third story told by the Norns is of their rope itself and of Alberich, for his curse is what causes the rope, which represents

Example 6.1

the soon-to-be outmoded sense of fate as something controlled by the gods, to frazzle and break. The rope of fate they control for the moment is related to the mythic knowledge the Norns represent. However, like Erda earlier, they suggest the uselessness of such mythic knowledge. In the *Ring*, knowledge is only available as it is lived out, in the doing; therefore Brünnhilde has to give up her own knowledge to Siegfried, since as woman (rather than goddess) she is no longer active in the world. The Norns and Erda represent some aspect of knowledge that does not develop but is destroyed rather than changes. The story they tell about the rope seems to be in the present rather than the mythic or historical past of the other two, and placed last, it is in a privileged position. When the rope breaks, the Norns see it as an end to their wisdom and say that the world will no longer hear from them; they return "Zur Mutter," presumably sinking back into the elements from which they arose. Their disappearance is the second step in the death of the gods (as Erda's sleep imposed by Wotan was the first).

The Norns' appearance here is the negative side of the positive action that follows, Brünnhilde's and Siegfried's love scene. In some ways the Norns offer a parallel to the Nibelheim scene in *Das Rheingold,* though their tales show how far we have come since then. Now world history is concerned with more human things— political power or convention versus love, rather than, as in *Das Rheingold,* sensuality and greed as the negative of Wotan's cold practicality and dependence on reason. The Norns prepare the way for the social world of the Gibichungs.

In the interlude leading to the second part of the prologue, a new theme appears, associated with Siegfried in his new guise of maturity (example 6-1). It is a variant of Siegfried's horn call, but the presentation is all pomp and bluster, as befitting Siegfried's new status. This theme perhaps foretells trouble, for it is infected with the spirit of the Valhalla music and suggests Wagner's inability to escape a patriarchal prejudice in favor of power, in spite of his story line. The second scene of the prelude opens with the break of a new day, an indication of still another moment in the progress of the new consciousness. Brünnhilde tells Siegfried that her love for him requires that he be allowed to leave; Brünnhilde gives him his freedom, out of love, whereas the women captured earlier for "love" had no freedom—Brünnhilde's attitude here contrasts with that of Wotan in the first opera or Hunding later. It also, of course, is opposed to (and assumed to be much preferable to) Fricka's desire in *Das Rheingold* to keep Wotan at home. Brünnhilde the exceptional woman is contrasted with the less desirable and more conventional Fricka, who ridicules Wotan's desire to wander the world and act the hero.

Brünnhilde emphasizes her own loss of individualism in the love relationship in this scene. In spite of the fact that the music glorifies love and disguises the reality of the situation, Brünnhilde has entered into the life of wifehood that the Valkyries found so distasteful when Wotan threatened it in *Die Walküre*. Although the music here presents a positive and emotionally charged inner experience for both Siegfried and Brünnhilde, the text suggests something altogether different. Brünnhilde remains passively on the rock while Siegfried goes out into the world, armed with her knowledge and equipped with her horse. Furthermore, not only has Brünnhilde given Siegfried her knowledge but the act of giving it has left her without wisdom:

> Des Wissens bar,
> doch des Wunsches voll;
> an Liebe reich,
> doch ledig der Kraft.

> I'm wise no more,
> though my heart is full:
> in love I'm rich,
> though emptied of power.

> (P. 253)

Wagner's ideology of love includes exalting emotion and sensuality and ignoring the concomitant subjugation of the woman. This pattern is common in Western culture as Horkheimer and Adorno summarize it when they call love "the human emotion proper" and note that it always involves the deification of the man. The boundless admiration that the male lover is expected to receive from the woman is, according to them, a means of glorifying slavery for woman and reconciling her to forgetting the better times that existed in matriarchy. They suggest that the battle of the sexes was settled in the thralldom of the female partner and read marriage as a type of property arrangement.[3] Wagner too, in spite of the overt ideology of the *Ring*, which abjures property, sees the relationship between Brünnhilde and Siegfried as having its basis in property; he finds it necessary that Brünnhilde give up her wisdom as payment to Siegfried for bringing her love.

The wisdom Brünnhilde imparts to Siegfried is of two kinds: her previous consciousness of him, which goes back to her involvement with Siegmund, and her present reflection of his consciousness in her own. Feuerbach argues in *Thoughts on Death and Immortality* that the individual is actually created in the consciousness of a loved one; in such a relationship "you received from others, as it were, a consciousness that had already been prepared for you."[4] This is the meaning of the wisdom Brünnhilde imparts to Siegfried—what she gives him is simply consciousness itself, his consciousness of his own essence, which is a consciousness he can get only from others. Brünnhilde emblemizes the gift of wisdom when she gives Siegfried her horse; as a living creature, Grane represents the love and faithfulness that ironically Siegfried will betray.

Brünnhilde, however, gladly accepts her new status as a powerless individual required not only to stay at home while the hero Siegfried goes into the world for great deeds but to give him a cheerful and loving farewell. That she may, however, have some intuition about what is to come is reflected in the emphasis she places on memory as she recounts the love they have for each other. She voices Feuerbachian theory when she suggests to Siegfried that their love is a part of history; it has passed from the immediacy of sense experience into the fullness of self-consciousness. She emphasizes the relationship of equality, of self-recognition, which exists between the two lovers as she tells Siegfried, "You are Brünnhilde." Siegfried replies in kind, saying that he will remain with her in spirit even as he leaves her in search of adventure. These are intended, however, as more than simply conventional lovers' pledges. Rather, they suggest a reiteration of the theme of self-consciousness, in spite of the emptiness of Brünnhilde's new life and the richness of Siegfried's that the words imply.

The music often works toward the glorification of the hero in this scene. Brünnhilde sings the theme associated since the last act of *Die Walküre* with Siegfried when she remembers Siegfried's taking off her helmet, and he repeats this melody a little later when he talks about the deeds he performed. His identity as hero is at stake here and is stressed, as if Wagner has some idea of the problematic nature of the relationship he has allowed between Siegfried and Brünnhilde. Siegfried also sings part of his song about going out into the world from the first act of *Siegfried* as he says he is no longer Siegfried, suggesting the transformation of the sword in that act is now fulfilled as the transformation of Siegfried himself from child to hero.

The mutual recognition, then, that works between Siegfried and Brünnhilde is theoretically a relationship of equality but actually is not. However, Wagner seems satisfied with the stage his new consciousness has reached, and following Hegel, who said that mutual recognition must finally exist among all people, he sends Siegfried out into the world (a moment that has been delayed since the first act of *Siegfried*). For Hegel, equality is a social, not an individual, relationship: "And this implies that others are equal to me too, because they are just as universal as I am. I am free only inasmuch as I allow the freedom of others and am recognized as free by them. Real freedom presupposes the freedom of many; only among several people is freedom actual and existent."[5] Siegfried must leave Brünnhilde's rock and go into the world as harbinger of freedom, though he leaves an unfree Brünnhilde behind.

The freedom that Siegfried represents is not, however, absolute. Both he and Brünnhilde are bound by promises; Siegfried specifically pledges in this scene not to forget Brünnhilde, even if he forgets everything else. Brünnhilde emphasizes that they have made promises to each other—but these of course are promises freely given, unlike Wotan's contracts. Although promises have been presented earlier as having a negative value, in the *Ring* cycle nothing remains the same—promises can be, of course, the basis for an equal love relationship. In spite of Brünnhilde's faith, however, the promises, oaths, and contracts remain a problem; Siegfried's identity as hero, (like Brünnhilde's as goddess) is about to be taken from him in a contract. The two are caught, in spite of everything, in the inescapable fact that social life is based on contracts that must be freely upheld by all concerned.

Yet the question remains as to why Siegfried must leave the rock, why the lovers' happiness and their mutual self-recognition must be betrayed. Hegel attempts to rationalize the suffering and destruction common in history by arguing that such things are necessary to the development of his world spirit; Horkheimer and Adorno find it in the nature of the myth of the Enlightenment, where, they say, ". . . the title of hero is only gained at the price of the abasement and mortification of the instinct for complete, universal, and undivided happiness." That is, the instinct for domination they find at the base of Enlightenment thought is antithetical to happiness. Western thought finds excuses, they argue, for destroying happiness.[6] Hegel justifies suffering in the name of the development of reason, while Wagner attempts to justify it in the name of love, which is often a disguise for aggrandizement of the male ego at the expense of the female. Thus Brünnhilde lets Siegfried leave her in the prelude to *Götterdämmerung*, and he seeks to act out his role as hero at the sacrifice of their happiness.

Act 1

In the first act, Siegfried moves into society to test his new self-consciousness. For Hegel, this movement into society is necessary: the individual at first exists in social naïveté, unaware that the self is universal, that what the individual is for himself is what all others are as well. But when for some reason such a naive individuality becomes aware that his own self is in some ways different from others, that he exists alone (as must inevitably happen in the course of historical progress), he loses confidence, a confidence he can only regain in a relationship of mutual recognition.[7] But for Hegel this mutual recognition must be from all persons to all persons; he imagines a utopian state of society not yet reached. Contesting Kant's idea that morality is independent of social existence, Hegel believed that man's moral nature is developed only in society and that such a moral nature must be inadequate in a flawed society. Wagner apparently attempted to show this kind of moral development in *Götterdämmerung*, suggesting that Siegfried's character is still incomplete when he depends only upon a relationship with Brünnhilde. He needs to develop his native good feeling and the self-consciousness he has found with Brünnhilde into an ethical, socially-based mode of conduct.

Hegal and Wagner pictured in an ideal society some kind of universal relationship of mutual support and recognition. However, the social bonds described in the master-slave relationship, which isolate individuals and set them against one another, are still, in Hegel's and Wagner's world, the most common types of human intercourse. Hegel argues in the *Phenomenology* that the realm of universal recognition must develop in the world of ethics, which he calls *Sittlichkeit*, derived from *Sitte*, or custom. Therefore, for Hegel, the customs of a people are what constitute each person's individuality, what makes him or her ethical—the ways of a people that have been absorbed by the individual and constitute a part of his or her consciousness (p. 72). This natural ethics, Hegel argues, appears in the most spiritually advanced societies, and Wagner contrasts it with what he calls the state, symbolized in the *Ring* by Wotan and Alberich. In "A Communication to My Friends," Wagner expressed a very Hegelian notion of the role of the individual in society, arguing that society itself constitutes a force: "By no means, that associate, communistic force is only brought into play through the medium of the individual force; for it is, in truth, naught other than the force of sheer human Individuality in general." This generalized "sheer human individuality" and "individual force" are parallel to Hegel's spirit. Wagner goes on to argue that the form in which individual force—what he elsewhere calls the life-bent—manifests itself is not the actions of the individual but the group as a whole.[8] That is, the individual has no real power apart from society, yet the power of society is simply the power of the individual taken in aggregate. Therefore, Wagner felt that individual self-expression, even at the intense level he pictures it between Siegfried and Brünnhilde, is still incomplete, and individuality can only find its true expression within society. In *Oper und Drama* he argues that an unformed individuality, the physical life force, is after all not enough, that "A *conscious* individuality,—i.e. an individuality which determines us in this one particular case, to act *so* and not otherwise" is something we can gain only in society, because it "brings us first the case in which we have to form decisions" (p. 195). Wagner goes on to suggest that this unformed individual is inevitably put into conflict with society: the individual force is "open to arbitrary interpretings" in a society formed as part of a corrupt state. The life-force of the unformed individual and the habit and convention *(Wont)* of the state then come into conflict: "Wherefore the 'view' of Society, so long as it does not fully comprehend the essence of the Individual and its own genesis therefrom, is a hindering and a shackling one; and it becomes ever more tyrannical, in exact degree as the quickening and innovating essence of the Individual brings its instinctive thrust to battle against habit" (p. 170).

Hegal, however, dismisses the kind of instinctive goodness that Wagner here seems to suggest for his unformed individual, Siegfried. Hegel calls the ethical view of individuals like Siegfried "the law of the heart" and suggests that it is doomed to fail because it is not a universal social law. The two realms, individual feeling and social reality, have at this stage not yet come together. By working according to the dictates of the law of the heart, or sentimental goodness, the individual brings about, according to Hegel, "not *his* law, but—since the realization is inherently and implicitly his own, but explicitly alien and external—merely this: he gets involved and entangled in the actual ordinance, and, indeed, entangled in it, not merely as something alien to himself but as a hostile, overpowering dominion" (p. 393). This then is the problem of this last opera of the cycle; Wagner retains for Siegfried a sentimental law of the heart instead of a philosophically rigorous ethic based on mutual recognition. In pledging friendship to Gunther Siegfried gets hopelessly entangled in a society he experiences as hostile and overwhelming. Mere good will is not enough to save him; even the wisdom he has gained from Brünnhilde is not enough to allow him to resist it. Siegfried, who has reached the highest possible measure of self-realization through his relationship with Brünnhilde and who expresses physical life force, must seek an even higher self-realization ("a *conscious* individuality") by seeking a similar relationship with all people. He is compelled by the need for love to find his way into society. But the society he finds is ruled by convention or habit *(Wont)*, and fails to understand the new consciousness Siegfried and Brünnhilde bring to it; Hagen's society attempts to impose the tyranny of power and property on Siegfried.

The opening dialogue of act 1 of *Götterdämmerung* shows the conventionality of the social world Siegfried will enter. Wagner apparently attempted to reproduce in the exchange between Gunther and Hagen, in brief outline, the whole image of a society hopelessly embroiled in convention. Gunther's concern for his reputation is empty and meaningless, and Hagen cynically manipulates for his own ends his half-brother's ambition. That the problem will once again be with contracts is clear from the music; Hagen's words are accompanied by the characteristic dotted rhythms and scale passages of the spear motive. Like Wotan in *Das Rheingold*, Gunther here is told of something he cannot have: Hagen's story about Siegfried and the ring creates envy, just as Loge's did earlier, though with the difference that Loge always remains an observer or narrator whereas Hagen is very much a participant in the action. The chords associated with the tarnhelm appear as Hagen begins to work on Gunther, creating a spell in which to hold him. The essence of the tarnhelm, of course, is to make other people see what they did not see before or see what is not there. Hagen brings in another memory from *Das Rheingold* when he sings the need for love melody as he says that he has a potion that will bind Siegfried to Gutrune, suggesting that in his

corrupt world this need has been transformed from mutual recognition to physical attraction. Gutrune, like Gunther, represents
the conventional; she seems to be Wagner's portrait of official
womanhood. She is sensual yet stupid, manipulative yet easily
manipulated by Hagen and Gunther, and the music associated
with her is particularly lyrical, perhaps to suggest a natural beauty
for her that will help explain Siegfried's infatuation.

The set of act 1 (the palace of the Gibichungs) is open toward
the back, but the openness is deceptive and helps to confuse
Siegfried, who innocently believes that appearances reveal truths.
When he arrives in his quest for adventure, Siegfried says he has
no property to exchange with Gunther as a pledge of friendship;
he has only his body:

> Nicht Land noch Leute biete ich,
> noch Vaters Haus und Hof:
>   einzig erbt' ich
>   den eignen Leib;
> lebend zehr ich den auf.

> No land nor men have I to give,
> no father's house or hall:
>   all my birthright
>   my sturdy limbs,
> useless things when I'm dead.

(P. 264)

However, a snatch of the forging music from act 1 of *Siegfried*
appears when Siegfried mentions that he does have one small
piece of property, a sword he forged himself. This music recalls
the entire scene in which he recreated the sword, detailing the
importance of his own forging of the self through physical labor.
In this way the essential connection between property and contracts is reiterated, and Siegfried paradoxically shows himself not
indifferent to either property (in the sword) or contracts after all.
Indeed, Siegfried willingly enters into contracts when he swears
casually on his sword to be Gunther's friend, and later when he
takes an oath of truthfulness on Hagen's spear; the imagery of
sword and spear here recall *Das Rheingold*. Cooke feels that Siegfried's problem is that he loves people too indiscriminately; his
first action, after leaving Brünnhilde and meeting Gunther, is to
give friendship and service.[9] Yet what Wagner shows is his strong
instinctive natural man claiming not to be influenced by social
customs of property and contracts and yet accepting both un-

critically. This is Siegfried's dilemma: he is the individual whose natural bent is to avoid these things, yet society presents them to him in a deceptively innocent light. Siegfried's problem is his innocence; in presenting him as a natural man raised apart from society, Wagner has prepared him to forget the lessons learned form the woodbird, from Mime's treachery, and from Brünnhilde herself. Siegfried is tested in the self-recognition of society. The problem is that he does not find reflected there his own goodness or innocence.

The instrument whereby Siegfried is destroyed is Hagen's potion; Gutrune's offer of a drink to Siegfried repeats the image of Sieglinde's offering water to Siegmund. But the differences are great. In the earlier opera the love relation was established naturally, by an intuitive recognition of the self in the other. In this opera, the relationship between Gutrune and Siegfried is established by trickery and deception. It is only when Siegfried loses his self-identity through losing his memory that he becomes involved with Gutrune. The already familiar imagery of eyes and looks is introduced here yet again: immediately after taking the potion, he notices Gutrune's eyes and says her look sets him afire; she lowers her gaze, however, unable to meet him in a relation of equality.

The potion in this scene is the negativity of the spiritualization and abstraction of the individual through memory so important to Wagner through his study of Feuerbach. The potion represents the first step in Siegfried's loss of individuality, a loss that culminates in his own and Brünnhilde's death. Feuerbach emphasizes the importance of this loss of individuality:

> The boundary between you and others is your personal existence, which is proper to you and immediately identical with you as a particular person. But if recollection is grasped as universal activity of Spirit (as it is in essence and truth), there is no boundary between the recollection in you and the recollection of the other. Rather, as your personal being (to which you can attribute, for example, actions, experiences, suffering, as those realities alone in which your personal being has existence and activity) passes away and is transformed, is taken up into Spirit, and as that which is person becomes impartible and universalized, as the boundary between you and others is canceled. As much as you are, so to speak, recollection, to that extent you are not person, are not excluding, unimpartible being-for-self. As much and as far as your being is recollection, it is spiritual, represented, impartible, detachable from you, and no longer personal being that is identical with you.[10]

With the potion, the personal boundaries which are Siegfried the individual begin to give way, and he begins the process of becoming Siegfried the abstraction of love. As an abstraction (or spiritualization) of love, he forms love relationships with everyone around him, especially Gutrune and Gunther. But because the potion comes from Hagen and is permeated with conventional values of property and greed, the loss of selfhood created by the potion proves false, and the true abstraction of individualism into love comes only with Siegfried's death.

Hagen's potion, as Adorno puts it, absolves Siegfried from civic responsibilities.[11] The potion causes Siegfried to lose himself; in losing his memory, especially his memory of Brünnhilde, he loses the self-realization he has gained. The new consciousness is a fragile thing, it seems, subject to the wiles of a tyrant like Hagen. The potion, then, rather than culminating the process of spiritualization, becomes the emblem of conventional social values (Wagner's *Wont*), which literally invade the body of the hero, making a mockery of his claim that his body is his only property. While the potion implies the transformation of the individual into spirit on the one hand, on the other it begins the transformation of the natural hero into the social man, a transformation that will be completed in Siegfried's change into Gunther by the agent of the tarnhelm. Contaminated by the potion, Siegfried leaves his innocence and learns to value property as much as anyone. He desires Gutrune and all her wealth.

Under the influence of the potion, even love fails, and women are treated more overtly as property than in *Das Rheingold*. The bartering of women is quite brutal in this scene:

Gunther. Gutrune gönn ich dir genre.
Siegfried. Brünnhilde bring ich dir.

Gutrune I'll give to you gladly.
Brünnhilde then is yours.

(P. 267).

Siegfried attempts to buy social standing and happiness with Brünnhilde's person, assuming that she is property, something he claims to have eschewed. That Wagner intended this to be an example of treating people as things is suggested by the fact that Alberich's curse theme sounds just before Siegfried asks Gunther if he has a wife. The curse, of course, is the curse of property, and here it infects human relationships more fully than ever before.

In this scene, Siegfried sacrifices Brünnhilde before she offers
herself, in a secular parody of the sacred significance of her final
self-sacrifice. Ironically, however, Siegfried offers to sacrifice not
to the gods but offers a god herself; he, as human hero, has in
Wagner's mythology the power to reverse religion and myth.
However, as usual in Wagner, it is the woman who suffers. In
effect, Siegfried is offering Brünnhilde as sacrifice in the power of
her own wisdom and strength (which she has given to him).
Wisdom, transferred from god to man, from woman to man, has
lost its original meaning and become the sign of treachery and
deceit. Consequently, Siegfried offers his own power to Gunther
as if it really were his own, forgetting where it came from. The
vow of blood brotherhood that the two men take parodies the
promises exchanged between Brünnhilde and Siegfried in the
prelude, promises based on love. Here the promise is based on
property for the purpose of the exchange of women and the
defense of property in a feudal system.

At the beginning of scene 3, music associated with Hagen's
potion (a variant of the tarnhelm theme) sounds as the curtain
rises on Brünnhilde, reminding us ironically how she earlier emphasized the importance of memory to Siegfried and how quickly
he has forgotten. When Waltraute enters with her story of Wotan's
despair, Brünnhilde listens eagerly. Waltraute's narrative is filled
with reminiscent melodies from earlier operas, indicating perhaps
not only her conventionality but also a world of memory and myth
that acts on her even though she does not understand it. Here as
in the other great narratives of the cycle, the point is the education
of the person listening. The *Ring* is full of narratives like this one:
Loge's narrative about love and the ring, Siegmund's stories of his
own history, and Wotan's exposition of his dilemma to Brünnhilde
in *Die Walküre*. These narratives outline the social world against
which the characters are to act. The narratives suggest the cyclical
nature of history; Hegel argues in the *Phenomenology* that events
and thoughts that cost individuals great effort in the past become,
as culture progresses, mere educational exercises for children. In
these forms, he says, we can see the history of the world's culture
delineated in faint outline: "This bygone mode of existence has
already become an acquired possession of the general mind,
which constitutes the substance of the individual, and by thus
appearing externally to him, furnishes his inorganic nature" (p.
90). This suggests a theory of myth similar to Bakhtin's theory of
language: Waltraute's narrative with its reminiscent melodies
forms an objectification of history as it appears in Brünnhilde's

consciousness. From Waltraute Brünnhilde learns what has happened to Wotan, but the outline is faint to her, for she has other cares and other purposes more important to her now. Wagner does not suggest that Brünnhilde is simply selfish but that her thoughts and feelings, concentrating on human love, represent the direction in which the culture is developing. So the story of Wotan and the gods, with its accompanying reminiscent music, seems somewhat distant and cold in Waltraute's narrative; these are already outgrown modes of thought.

In this narrative as before, seeing continues to be a symbol of the self-recognition of individuals in the other. Waltraute says that Wotan is now blind (completing the process begun with the loss of one of his eyes as a symbol of his inability to love). He does not see the Valkyries who gather around him and attempt to help him. Repeating Erda's advice to Wotan earlier, Waltraute advises Brünnhilde to give up the ring. But Brünnhilde refuses to give up what has now become for her an emblem not of power but of love.

Brünnhilde puts love before everything; human emotion has finally conquered religion. However, Brünnhilde's simple message seems to be that love will make everything all right, an idea that proves inadequate. While for her the ring has changed from a symbol of power to a symbol of love, it has also taken on the quality of a rune; it is as Siegfried's *Liebesfand* that Brünnhilde refuses to give it up, suggesting again that even love must depend on contracts. She sings almost the entire two-phrase need for love theme in its original key—reaffirming the ideology of the cycle— as she firmly says she will not give up love. In this way she rejects Waltraute and Wotan, repeating Siegmund's action when he rejected Valhalla, and, like him, she makes her own death a certainty.

As Brünnhilde hears what she thinks is Siegfried returning to her rock, we hear snatches of his characteristic horn call and other music previously associated with him; the music indicates that she is right. But as the disguised Siegfried speaks to her, the complexity of the situation is indicated in the orchestra by a tangle of motives associated with the tarnhelm, forgetfulness, and the Gibichungs. Siegfried has been transformed from heroic into human form, and as human he resembles Gunther. The tarnhelm that changes Siegfried into Gunther is simply a further stage of the process begun by Hagen's potion. The tarnhelm, formed as it is of the original gold, is suggestive of the transformations the greed for property causes. In a world ruled by property values, Siegfried the hero becomes Gunther the feudal lord. Brünnhilde, of course, must come to the difficult realization that Siegfried the individual is already lost to her, spiritualized into a Feuerbachian abstraction of love that is now let loose upon the corrupt social world. But at the moment she is a long way from recognizing or accepting this point.

The false Gunther takes the ring away from Brünnhilde just as Wotan takes it away from Alberich in *Das Rheingold*. The ring is now reified as a symbol of love, as a commodity rather than the real thing, but whether as a symbol of love or power, it inspires theft.

Act 2

Until act 2 of *Götterdämmerung*, it is easy enough to misread the *Ring* cycle as advocating emotion in place of reason, individuality in place of society. In fact, the cycle as a whole is usually read as a romantic defense of love. However, in this act love proves inadequate in a corrupt world. Wagner, following his models Hegel and Feuerbach, understood the necessity for placing his lovers into a social context. He did not, however, place them in a modern society, for the society Brünnhilde and Siegfried destroy is that of feudal Germany. Nevertheless, we cannot help reading some modern constructions in this ancient society, as the composer no doubt intended. In this society as in Wagner's own, Brünnhilde's position is ambivalent: in spite of Wagner's insistence on equality and freedom, she has in fact assumed a position of traditional dependence and subordination. Wagner assumes that ancient society was based on the subjugation of women; the ideal society that, he implies at the end of act 3, grows out of it is built on woman's willing self-sacrifice in the name of a glorifying but finally destructive love.

Hagen's sleep in the first scene parallels that of Brünnhilde and Erda, sleep being throughout the *Ring* an important symbol of the absence of the new consciousness. Hagen's dream suggests the mystical power of the unconscious, yet the emphasis in the dream conversation between Alberich and Hagen is instead on contracts and the social situation. Hagen, in spite of Alberich's repeated demand for his oath of loyalty, refuses to swear to his father; he says instead that he swears only to himself—he promises himself to gain the ring. Hagen's denial of his father here duplicates that of Siegfried earlier; Alberich is overthrown, in the dream sequence, just as Wotan is when Siegfried breaks his spear, and in both cases the new generation expresses contempt for the old.

Hagen, in refusing to make a promise to his father, insists on acting individually, thereby dooming himself to failure. The ring has previously been associated with individuality; the greed it inspires does not allow for cooperation. Similarly, Siegfried acts as an individual when he forgets about Brünnhilde. In both cases the individual has been conditioned by the state (in Siegfried's case through the medium of the potion) to act as he does. Individuality is therefore opposed to love on the one hand and to society on the other: Hagen betrays society by acting as an individual, while Siegfried, the great heroic individual, betrays love.

With the entrance of the chorus in scene 3, society officially enters the *Ring*. The people whom Hagen calls with his horn duplicate the people whom Hunding commands and the society Siegmund has tried to escape. To some extent, they represent conventional morality, and their unquestioning acceptance of Hagen's leadership is a measure of their moral emptiness. Yet Wagner gives them stirring and delightful music, causing them to make a claim to the affections of the audience. Once again, Wagner's essential ambivalence toward the role of society in the working out of the hero and of love surfaces; Hagen's serfs represent the *Volk* and as such are naturally good. But they are also necessarily corrupted by the state under which they live. Wagner attempts to represent in their music that spirit of the people that Hegel found important and to which Wagner dedicated the *Ring*, as Porges suggests: "It is as though the poet had conjured up from their graves the ancient Germans of Tacitus. The words and the music, charged as they are with defiant self-assertiveness, fearlessness and a strange, almost frightening humour, express the unique character of the German race."[12] If it is true that Porges paraphrases Wagner himself, it can be noted that the spirit of these people duplicates what Wagner has postulated as the "natural" heroic qualities of Siegfried: self-assertiveness and fearlessness. Thus the music suggests for these people a genuine spirit, which Wagner felt was perhaps naturally good but corrupted by Hagen.

When she enters with Gunther, Brünnhilde at first does not see Siegfried—she keeps her eyes down until his name is mentioned. The symbolism of looks suggests her inability to recognize Siegfried as he appears under the influence of the potion. When she sees the ring on Siegfried's finger, she exclaims that she has been betrayed, as Alberich did when Wotan stole the ring, and the Rhinedaughters did when Alberich stole the gold. Of course, it is not ownership of the ring that concerns her, but what the ring represents, Siegfried's faithfulness. Yet previously a symbol of power, the ring has now become a symbol of the power of love, and Brünnhilde's concern over it for a while becomes as possessive as Alberich's desire for the gold. Indeed, Brünnhilde is so caught in conventional morality that she accuses Siegfried of being a thief. Theft, of course, as Wagner made clear in *Das Rheingold,* is the essence of property, and Brünnhilde, like Siegfried, has become a victim of conventional morality when she comes to see the ring as property.

Accusing Siegfried, Brünnhilde says that he forced love from her ("Er zwang mir Lust / und Liebe ab"). She is willing now to characterize the love relationship as one based on force, though she sings the need for love melody as she does so. A slippage between the need for love and domination has occurred. Siegfried has no recourse to Brünnhilde's accusations but to swear an oath, and with it his regression to the corrupt morality of *Das Rheingold* is complete. Brünnhilde swears an oath in reply, repeating the notes of Siegfried's oath almost exactly. Her notes are echoed by the trumpet in a parody of the flute-soprano duets of conventional operatic mad scenes; the trumpet has been associated throughout the *Ring* with a kind of heroic purity, and here it implies the purity of Brünnhilde's motives even though the situation is confusing.

The trumpet suggests an ideology of honor for Brünnhilde that goes beyond the conventional concept of honor that Gunther and now Siegfried hold. Their honor is shown to be an empty value when Gunther worries that Siegfried has betrayed it. It is this conventional role of honor that Hagen is banking on. Wagner draws on Feuerbach, who argues that men may love anything—power, honor, or money—but that only love for another human is creative.[13] Gunther is presented as a well-meaning but misguided person who loves honor more than he loves individual persons. This kind of love fails in the end as surely as the more pernicious love of power and money exhibited by those who love the ring.

Brünnhilde's reaction to Siegfried's betrayal is perhaps psychologically believable, yet she has been presented throughout the *Ring* cycle as the goddess, the "glorious maid," the one person who is worthy of Siegfried because she understands more even than Wotan. Her anger at her betrayal reflects Hegel's "law of the heart," which he sees as a common cause of dissension in history—

when the person of a good heart and virtuous habits comes to realize that these things are not enough, when the individual realizes that the law of the heart must be overthrown, he or she rages and puts the blame on others. Her excuse is moral outrage and passion; in Wagner's view, women, being exclusively instinctual, are always motivated by feeling. Brünnhilde, his example of a great woman, is one who feels everything greatly, first in love and now in betrayal.

The self-realization and confidence brought about by the mutual recognition of love fails, then, in this bigger world, and Brünnhilde like Siegfried at the beginning of act 1 reverts to a lesser stage of consciousness. She replays Wotan as the force seeking revenge for betrayal. Through the action of the potion, she has lost Siegfried as subject, or equal; what is left is only Siegfried as alien, and she attempts to destroy him as Wotan was determined to destroy her when she disobeyed him. Her faith in love and in Siegfried undergoes a severe test, which she in some ways fails; yet the result is her final understanding, which could not have happened without the betrayal. For, as Hegel believes, individuality is to be canceled and superseded in the development of true virtue: "True cultivation and discipline consists solely in the surrender of the entire personality, as a way of making sure that in point of fact individual peculiarities are no longer asserted and insisted on. In this individual surrender, individuality, as it is found in the world's process, is at the same time annihilated" (*Phenomenology*, p. 402). Thus Brünnhilde is called upon to sacrifice her own individuality to the good of the group, though she does not see this yet. Siegfried and Brünnhilde are acting out a drama that is bigger than either of them can realize: according to Hegel, the purpose of individual self-realization is to "transmute again the perverted world's process" in order to bring true virtue into the world. Although the virtuous individual is bound to fail, love itself will win out. Brünnhilde's rage is an assertion of individuality that is understandable but wrong; she finds the right path a little later when she gives up her own individuality, her life, for the good of the world.

In scene 5, the connection between the actions of the drama and the larger forces at work becomes clear in the music. Brünnhilde's first words are sung to a new melody that continues to be associated with her betrayal, but the orchestra has only the descending notes of the need for love theme, which turns into the last phrase of the melody in which she originally announced Siegfried's fate to him. The need for love is now, finally, seen as

inevitable and identical to fate. Only by suffering can she come to
understand her own need for love and come to understand that
this need is universal, more than a need for the immediate pleasure she and Siegfried have already celebrated. The fate of humankind is this need for love, and the motive associated with fate
in the orchestra indicates that here, as when it first appeared in *Die
Walküre*, a force is at work larger than simply the intentions and
desires of the participants.

However, in her moment of rage Brünnhilde in effect wills
Siegfried's death, joining with Hagen and Gunther in their plan to
take revenge. The scene is a conventional operatic trio, with the
three characters singing together of their differing reasons for
seeking revenge. (Hagen's music uses diminished fifths consistently, against the perfect intervals of the other two parts). The
very conventionality of the scene suggests its meaning: Brünnhilde has become an ordinary—and very angry—woman. Without
the Hegelian framework, it is difficult to explain her actions in this
scene. Porges argues that they stem simply from her passionate
nature; reflecting Wagner's ideas about the nature of women, he
sees her as essentially emotional. He feels that Brünnhilde's revenge is a "rebellion springing from the core of her personality
against the rapturous love which had once impelled her to give
herself to Siegfried."[14] Although Brünnhilde's will asserts itself,
she later recovers her sense of the larger meanings of her actions.
In a letter to Mathilde Wesendock about this scene, Wagner later
interpreted "will" in a non-Hegelian fashion: "I want to demonstrate that there is a saving way that leads to the complete pacifica-
tion of the will through love, which no philosopher, especially not
Schopenhauer, has ever recognized; it's not an abstract love of
mankind, but real love, the love that blossoms from sexual love,
that is, from the attraction between man and woman."[15] Self-
sacrifice as the essence of love and the hope of humankind is the
theme that remained constant throughout Wagner's interest in
Hegel, Feuerbach, and Schopenhauer.

Act 3

If Brünnhilde is to overcome individuality and progress beyond
the assertion of her own will to reach this kind of expression of
real love at the end of act 3, Siegfried comes to it a little earlier. At
the beginning of this act, as he encounters the Rhinedaughters, he
is at first willing to give them the ring because to him it means

nothing. Their desire for the ring suggests that, after all, they consider it property, and it is as property that he refuses to give it to them, especially when they threaten him. But he picks up a clod of dirt and flings it away, saying he would gladly give up life and limb. He is still unafraid; he knows that individual life is not worth anything. This is the essential point that he has reached; he does not value his own individual existence and so is unable to fear for it. Wagner made this Hegelian notion clear in a letter to Röckel in 1854, where he discussed the new consciousness that Siegfried has attained by the time he reaches this scene: "Here we see that infinite wisdom has come to Siegfried, for he has grasped the highest truth and knows that death is better than a life of fear: knowledge of the ring, too, has come to him, but he does not heed its power, for he has something better to do; he keeps it only as a proof that at least he has never learned what fear means."[16] The issue of fear is somewhat confusing once again; Wagner seems to contradict Siegfried's idea that he indeed learned fear in observing the sleeping Brünnhilde. Wagner continues to insist, in spite of Hegel, that progressing beyond fear is not necessary, that the individual is not really heroic because of development but because of his innate quality of fearlessness.

However, in spite of the insight Wagner has Siegfried exhibit here, the hero notes as the Rhinedaughters leave that he would like to have one of them if he were not married—a very conventional sentiment and unworthy of Siegfried. Siegfried, not having learned fear, has also not really learned love, at least not yet; he has not learned that love is universal, the reflection of human rather than his own individual need. This lesson is reserved for Brünnhilde at the end. Siegfried continues to be the object of love and suffering but not the subject; here he fails to convince us that he exhibits the new consciousness Wagner claims for him.

However, in scene 2, Siegfried regains his memory of himself and finally of Brünnhilde. A good many reminiscent melodies from the whole cycle are repeated as Siegfried tells of his childhood. A snatch of Mime's music appears even before Siegfried begins, while he prepares his story, and he quotes a good many tunes from the first act of *Siegfried* during this conversation, including Mime's starling song. The Sieglinde motive is also important in this scene, sounding first under the words as Siegfried tells about tasting the dragon's blood. Siegfried is recapitulating the steps in his own rise to consciousness, in preparation for death. He receives Hagen's new potion restoring his memory of

Brünnhilde as simply another step in helping to return his past to him.

The long section of Siegfried's memories about Brünnhilde just before he dies recapitulates music from the last scene of *Siegfried*. The hero Siegfried has not gone through the reversion to elemental selfishness that we have seen in Brünnhilde; he does not rage at her or at his murderers. Wagner as usual protects Siegfried from suffering; at the moment of death he is lost in a beatific vision of love and beauty. In this vision of Brünnhilde, Siegfried emphasizes eyes and seeing and asks who has put her to sleep again. He means, of course, why she has reverted to selfish individuality and conventional morality. In dying, he says that he frees her again, breaking her fetters. The imagery of his words reminds us of the armor from which Siegfried freed Brünnhilde in the love scene; by dying he is making it possible for her to return to a selfless devotion and, on a larger scale, to a realization that individual life does not matter. His death will awaken her to new consciousness.

Siegfried's remembering of Brünnhilde's awakening in *Siegfried* is a dramatization of Feuerbach's theory of memory. In *Thoughts on Death and Immortality*, Feuerbach asserted that

> Recollection, as living, effective, universal activity of Spirit, in which Spirit negates single or sensibly independent existence, recollection, in this negation of independence and sensible shape, assimilates and collects itself into its self-consciousness. Thus, recollection, as something identical with time itself, is also the ground of your death; in recollection, your being is glorified and transformed into ideal being, in the being of representation.[17]

In this scene, Siegfried's memory of Brünnhilde makes her complete, at least to him, and brings her to the spiritualization we will see later. Musically, this scene suggests the importance of the reminiscent motives Wagner has employed throughout the *Ring*. However, rather than recalling specific melodies here, in this most important moment of recollection, the orchestra recalls large sections of the music from the awakening scene in *Siegfried*. The music of this scene indicates that the hero reaches a new understanding of his relationship with Brünnhilde, just as she reaches a new understanding of him in her immolation scene.

The funeral music continues the spirit of memory and recapitulation; Thomas Mann calls it "an overwhelming celebration of thought and remembrance" that presents the outline of Siegfried's life in the orchestra.[18] The death rites that take so long at the end of *Götterdämmerung* are necessary to the realization of the meaning of death; the emphasis on the funeral here and in the next scene is also related to Wagner's use of Greek tragedy as a model for the *Ring*. Funeral rites, according to Hegel, were very important to the Greeks and indicated their high level of consciousness; the rites surrounding death rescue it for self-consciousness.[19] The funeral rites for Siegfried dramatize his transformation—for Brünnhilde, for the Gibichungs, and for the audience—from Siegfried as individual to Siegfried as memory, as the spiritualized abstraction of the possibility of love.

The ending of the *Ring* cycle has continually been a puzzle for many people. The rising self-consciousness of the hero and the triumph of love seem to be rescinded in the last scenes. Peter Conrad, for example, feels that the final holocaust is "puzzlingly gratuitous," for the ring has been returned, and while the orchestra "asserts the redemptive power of love, . . . there is no one left for it to redeem."[20] This interpretation is partially based on the assumption that the motive the orchestra brings back from *Die Walküre* at the end is the "redemption" motive, though in *Die Walküre* it is more a summary, a moment of wonder at Brünnhilde's sacrifice and love. Other critics argue that Wagner was suggesting, in the many parallels between *Götterdämmerung* and *Das Rheingold*, the cyclical nature of history, that we never learn anything and are doomed to repeat the past.[21] But this leaves out the importance of the Hegelian concept of history that influenced Wagner so fully; Hegel in no sense thought that we do not learn from history. He argued that history is not something that happens to people, to individuals who are essentially unchanged by events. Rather, for Hegel history creates individuals, though not completely or deterministically. History is an interaction between inevitable processes (spirit) and individuals who are both dependent upon and yet independent of that process. Wagner adopts a similar attitude: in the *Ring* history is the series of events that happen to individuals in the inevitable progress of love in the world, and individuals both cause and are transformed by these events. The ending of *Götterdämmerung* suggests not redemption so much as the end of one stage of the progress of love and the beginning of the next, one that is transformed by the events chronicled in the four operas.

It is clear that Wagner had in mind the model of *Antigone* for the ending of *Götterdämmerung*. In *Oper und Drama* he explains that when Antigone revolted against the corrupt self-serving society ruled by Creon, she was acting (in burying her brother) out of love and a deeper sense of human right. Her love, he argues, was rational and fully conscious; she acted not out of the emotion of the moment but out of a higher morality nevertheless rooted in personal love. Antigone knew, he says, that "she had no choice but to act according to love's Necessity." But for Wagner there is an immediate slippage from love or morality into self-sacrifice. Antigone knew "that she had to listen to this unconscious, strenuous necessity of *self-annihilation in the cause of sympathy.*" He then asserts that in listening and acting according to the dictates of self-annihilation in the name of love she was "the perfect Human Being, the embodiment of Love in its highest fill and potence" (p. 189). Thus Brünnhilde's self-sacrifice is presented as the highest moment of human action.

The words and music sung by Brünnhilde in the final scene attempt to draw to a close several of the ideas developed throughout the cycle. The death of the gods is very much in mind; Brünnhilde expresses allegorically the anger of humans when they realize that the gods they have created and trusted have betrayed them. The musical phrase associated with fate reaches its most important statement when she sings "alles, alles" ("All things now I know") on notes that outline the fate chords playing in the orchestra; fate is no longer unconscious need but has become need raised to consciousness. The Valhalla music is prominent as she mentions the death of the gods; allegorically, she reminds us of the death of the hope of immortality in Siegmund's refusal of Valhalla, the turning point of the entire cycle, for this was the point at which humans found a higher hope and need, in love of one another, than what they had depended on before. Brünnhilde is simply living out the consequences of that moment, as the last god herself, seeing to the death of all the gods. She is finding her way to a new higher state of consciousness, a state Wagner attempts to present here.

That Wagner changed his mind about the ending is well known. Apparently he originally intended to present Brünnhilde as going on to a new stage of consciousness in a dramatic and literal way. In a letter to Röckel he said that he once attempted to show this intention: "to wit, in the tendentious closing phrases addressed by Brünnhilde to those around her, in which she points away from the evils of possession to all-redeeming love, without (unfortunately!) making absolutely clear the nature of that love, which we have seen, in the course of the myth, to have appeared fundamentally destructive." But the destruction is the destruction only of selfish individuality and leads to a new stage of consciousness for society. Wagner continues in this letter by saying that he originally intended an optimistic ending emphasizing love over greed. Then he wrote a new passage that would explain the new, more philosophical idea, but finally left even that out.[22]

The idea that Wagner decided to omit this ending after reading Schopenhauer was first suggested by Nietzsche in *The Case of Wagner*.[23] Dalhouse agrees, arguing for the influence of Schopenhauer in the ending, because Schopenhauer condemned "optimism as 'wicked.'" The original ending had Brünnhilde repeating these lines:

> Nicht Gut, nicht Gold,
> noch göttlich Pracht;
> nicht Haus, nicht Hof,
> noch herrischer Prunk;
> nicht trüber Verträge
> trügender Bund,
> nicht heuchelnder Sitte
> hartes Gesetz:
> selig in Lust and Leid
> läßt—die Liebe nur sein.

("Not goods, not gold, nor godly splendour; not house, not land, nor lordly pomp; not the cheating covenant of cheerless contracts, not the harsh laws of lying custom: rapture in pleasure and pain comes—from love alone.") In 1856, Wagner replaced these lines, which summarize the opposition between property and love prominent throughout the cycle, with the following ending he described to Röckel, which is obviously based on a Schopenhauerian concept of the loss of individualism rather than on a Feuerbachian idea:

> Aus Wunschheim zieh ich fort,
> Wahnheim flieh' ich auf immer;
> des ew'gen Werdens
> offne Tore
> schliess ich hinter mir zu:
> nach dem wunsch- und wahnlos
> heiligsten Wahlland,
> der Weltwanderung Ziel,
> von Wiedergeburt erlöst,
> zieht nun die Wissende hin.
> Alles Ew'gen
> sel'ges Ende,
> wißt ihr, wie ich's gewann?
> Trauernder Liebe

tiefstes Leiden
schloß die Augen mir auf:
enden sah ich die Welt.

("I depart from Wish-home, I flee Delusion-home for ever; I close behind me the open doors of eternal becoming: where there is no wishing or delusion, to the holiest chosen land, the goal of world-wandering, released from [the cycle of] rebirth, made wise I now go. Know you how I accomplished the blessed end of all eternal things? Sorrowing love's deepest suffering opened my eyes: I saw the world end.")[24]

But these lines were finally rejected also, and Wagner settled on the final version, in which Brünnhilde simply jumps on her horse and enters the fire. The *Ring* at the end is completely ambiguous: even Wagner could not determine what it meant. But the problem is caused not by Wagner's turning to Schopenhauer but by the fact that he could not resolve the problem of love versus power in his own mind. He could not accept Brünnhilde as the heroine of his story but kept trying to make her fit his own notions of self-sacrificing woman. Horkheimer and Adorno criticize the whole tradition of sacrifice from which Wagner is working, suggesting that self-sacrifice is an "impressed pattern according to which the subjected repeat upon themselves the injustice that was done them, enacting it again in order to endure it."[25] Brünnhilde, in destroying herself, is working out her fate by accepting it. She has been changed from Wotan's unconscious slave to Siegfried's conscious one, asked to give up consciousness itself in the name of a new consciousness, and finally asked to give up self-affirming love in the name of self-destroying domination.

CONCLUSION

Brünnhilde and Siegfried seem simply to fail at the end of *Götter-dämmerung;* the new consciousness they are supposed to represent is unconvincing after all. Although Wagner apparently wanted to emphasize the deaths of Brünnhilde and Siegfried as a means to a new life for society, their deaths have a sense of utter finality about them. Neither the philosophy of spiritualization through memory borrowed from Feuerbach nor the idea of a new consciousness for society through mutual recognition borrowed from Hegel seems fully persuasive in the end. Nor is the orchestral postlude, with its linguistically-loaded motives associated with love and self-sacrifice, enough to lead us unfailingly into a positive interpretation of the ending of the *Ring.*

Wagner's ideology of the annihilation of the self for the good of all remains unconvincing partly because it is so one-sided. Brünn-hilde seems to suffer because her consciousness is so much greater than that of the other characters: Siegfried is saved from con-sciousness of how wrong things have gone at the end by the potion, and even after he is stabbed he seems unaware of the present while he lives for a few moments gloriously in the past. Never in the entire *Ring* does he have a moment of pain—he not only feels no fear (except for his fleeting moment of confusion when he first encounters the sleeping Brünnhilde) but experi-ences none of the anger of Brünnhilde or Alberich, no moments of the panic Gunther or Hagen felt, no sense of tragic loss that Wotan suffers. Therefore, audiences sometimes find it difficult to take Siegfried seriously or believe in the depth of his passionate love.

The annihilation of self, then, is only for women. The male characters reach their inevitable deaths, true, but the modes of death generally seem mild compared to immolation, except of course for Wotan, who however has been so far removed from being a real character at the end that he is only a dream, a figment of Waltraute's imagination. Siegmund gives up immortality for Sieglinde, but the fact that the Valhalla he repudiates is a cold and unpleasant place is part of the Feuerbachian point. His death, like

Siegfried's, is short and swift, while Sieglinde is punished by experiencing great pain and a lingering death. Wagner exalts the pain and suffering of Brünnhilde and Sieglinde by arguing that such suffering will redeem society, ignoring the fact that the corrupt society they must destroy was in fact created and controlled by Wotan and other men who have driven out Erda and matriarchy.

Wagner's music glorifies not only women and their suffering but also, of course, love. In the emotional importance he assigns love, Wagner wanted to celebrate freedom and equality, abstract ideas that imply an escape from domination and humiliation—the very things Freia needs release from at the beginning of the cycle. But Wagner cannot escape patterns of sexist domination. He seems sometimes to identify with Siegfried and is unable to give up his image of the hero. Wagner's claims for Siegfried's self-consciousness just are not convincing; in denying Siegfried fear Wagner denies him any real humanity. The hero, paragon of the new consciousness, remains a wooden god, representing the deification of the male in our culture, and it is impossible to forget that Brünnhilde, the symbol of self-sacrificing love, is the product of rape. Even though Wagner understood to some extent that values are socially defined, that historical individuals are created by their culture (ideas he learned from Hegel), he is unable to escape his own culturally derived ideas; any concept of real equality escapes him because he insists on seeing women as naturally passive and self-sacrificing and men as naturally strong and active.

Wagner uses language in music to make music work to support this ideology. Music is an important and influential material sign in the West that reflects cultural values and, because of its peculiar psychological effects, seems to invade the listener's mind. Wagner's music uses all the considerable resources of Western musical tradition plus the innovations and variations he himself introduced to make us feel, to encourage us to define feeling as pleasure and pleasure as love, and to help us forget that this love is after all a product of domination. Wagner sanctions emotion at the expense of reason but uses emotion as the emblem for power. The musical idiom of the *Ring* has come into our vocabulary of musical thinking. The passion Wagner images in music is a fiction, a somewhat pernicious one that continues to serve the purpose of disguising and glorifying domination. The audience is likely to leave the theater humming the "redemption" motive without considering who is being redeemed and at what cost.

A new consciousness based, as Wagner seems to suggest

through the end of *Die Walküre* that it will be, on mutual recognition, freedom, and equality and on the idea that human love rather than human reason is the driving force creating history is an intriguing utopian image, presented in a complexly devised drama and compelling musical idiom. But from the moment Wagner attempts to create a hero who would embody these concepts, he falls into patriarchal stereotypes of male self-aggrandizement. So the last part of the *Ring* cycle remains a confusing work, playing to the emotional response with which we as listeners and viewers protect and hide some of our most sacred and personal values. Love, freedom, and equality are emotionally loaded by Wagner's music and structured into an artistic form that reflects back to us some of Western culture's best and worst ideas and values.

NOTES

Introduction

1. Thomas Mann, *Pro and Contra Wagner,* trans. Allen Blunden (Chicago: University of Chicago Press, 1985), p. 107.
2. Ibid., pp. 107–8.
3. Andrew Feenberg, *Lukács, Marx, and the Sources of Critical Theory* (New York: Oxford University Press), p. 5.
4. Ibid., p. 11.

Chapter 1. Wagner, Hegel, and Feuerbach

1. John Edward Toews, *Hegelianism: The Path Toward Dialectical Humanism, 1805–1841* (Cambridge: Cambridge University Press, 1980). Toews gives a detailed history of the deep influence of Hegel in Germany during the period when Wagner's ideas were being formed.
2. Martin Gregor-Dellin, *Richard Wagner,* trans. J. Maxwell Brownjohn (San Diego: Harcourt Brace Jovanovich, 1980), p. 164.
3. Friedrich Engels, *Ludwig Feuerbach and the Outcome of Classical German Philosophy* (New York: International Publishers, 1941), p. 15.
4. Ibid., p. 19.
5. Friedrich Nietzsche, *The Case of Wagner,* trans. Anthony M. Ludovici, vol. 8 of *The Complete Works,* ed. Oscar Levy (New York: Russell and Russell, 1964), p. 31.
6. Friedrich Nietzsche, *The Gay Science,* trans. Walter Kaufmann (New York: Random House, 1974), p. 153.
7. George Windell, "Hegel, Feuerbach, and Wagner's Ring," *Central European History* 9 (1976): 40.
8. Ibid., p. 38.
9. Ibid., pp. 38–39.
10. Richard Wagner, *My Life,* trans. Andrew Gray (Cambridge: Cambridge University Press, 1983), pp. 429–30.
11. Ronald Taylor notes that Wagner also sketched a drama on the life of Jesus that was based on David Strauss's book on Jesus as well as on Feuerbach; both of these sources looked to Hegel, whom Taylor reports Wagner was reading at the time (*Richard Wagner* [London: Panther, 1979] p. 151).
12. Wagner, *My Life,* p. 130. One of Feuerbach's major ideas is an expansion of this Hegelian idea of the historical desacralizing of the world. That is, Hegel felt that religion embodied a historical moment in the movement from myth to dialectical humanism. Feuerbach, developing the implications of Hegel's position, argued that humans create gods in their own image and that religion is simply the reflection of human aspirations and values transferred to the gods:

"Hence the historical progress of religion consists in this: that which during an earlier stage of religion was regarded as something objective is now recognized as something subjective, so that that which was formerly viewed and worshipped as God is now recognized as something human" (Ludwig Feuerbach, *The Essence of Christianity,* ed. E. Graham Waring and F. W. Strothmann [New York: Ungar, 1957] p. 11.) Thus Brünnhilde goes from goddess to woman, Wotan from god to Wanderer. The *Ring* is Feuerbachian in that it records a movement from ancient mythology to modern self-awareness in love (it skips Christianity, a topic Wagner took up in other operas) in the spirit of the German people. The *Ring* follows Feuerbach only in general: in it Wagner implies that the spirit of the German people has always been to reject religion for heroism, metaphysics for love.

13. Wagner, *My Life,* p. 431.

14. Ibid., p. 509.

15. Engels, *Ludwig Feuerbach,* p. 18.

16. Charles Taylor, *Hegel* (Cambridge: Cambridge University Press, 1975), p. 97.

17. Richard Wagner, "The Art-Work of the Future," in *Richard Wagner's Prose Works,* trans. William Ashton Ellis, vol. 1, 2d ed. (London, 1895), p. 69. All other references to this essay will be from this translation.

18. Amerongen may be close to the truth when he suggests of Wagner, "In his guise as philosopher, he was a typical exponent of the nineteenth-century desire for a complete, self-contained view of the world, in which everything had its proper place and function. His writings form a half-baked mishmash of one particular brand of socialism and conservatism, Hellenism and Teutonism, anti-Semitism and vegetarianism, Proudhon, Hegel, Feuerbach, Gobineau and Schopenhauer" (Martin van Amerongen, *Wagner: A Case Study,* trans. Stewart Spencer and Dominic Cakebread [New York: George Braziller, 1984], pp. 24–25). However, I would argue that Hegelianism is the most important of these influences.

19. Charles Taylor, *Hegel,* p. 103.

20. Judith N. Shklar, *Freedom and Independence: A Study of the Political Ideas of Hegel's "Phenomenology of Mind"* (Cambridge: Cambridge University Press, 1976), p. 1.

21. Hans-Georg Gadamer, *Hegel's Dialectic,* trans. P. Christopher Smith (New Haven, Conn.: Yale University Press, 1976), p. 40.

22. Engels, *Ludwig Feuerbach,* p. 12.

23. Richard Rorty, *Consequences of Pragmatism* (Minneapolis: University of Minnesota Press, 1982), p. 148.

24. Ronald Gray puts it nicely (without acknowledging the specific debt Wagner owed to Hegel): "If we go with Hegel, we believe that certain great individuals are capable of knowing the essential spirit of the world, and that these great individuals gain a following precisely because lesser individuals recognize in them the spirit which they are unable to realize effectively in themselves" ("The German Intellectual Background," in *The Wagner Companion,* ed. Peter Burbidge and Richard Sutton [New York: Cambridge University Press, 1979], p. 41).

25. Richard Wagner, "A Communication to My Friends," in *Richard Wagner's Prose Works,* vol. 1, p. 366. All further references to this essay will be from this translation.

26. Thomas Mann finds this emphasis on receptiveness one of Wagner's most interesting ideas (*Pro and Contra Wagner,* trans. Allen Blunden [Chicago: Univer-

sity of Chicago Press, 1985], p. 286). It anticipates ideas Wagner later found in Schopenhauer.

27. Richard Wagner, *Oper und Drama*, in *Richard Wagner's Prose Works*, vol. 2, p. 194. All further references to this work will be from this edition.

28. Ronald Taylor, *Richard Wagner*, p. 189.

29. Charles Taylor, *Hegel*, p. 79.

30. Skhlar, *Freedom and Independence*, p. ix.

31. Ibid., p. 65.

32. However, not all interpretations of the *Ring* cycle see love as a positive force. Michael Tanner points out that love makes Siegfried more naive and stupid, not less, because he figures out Mime but not Hagen ("The Total Work of Art," in *The Wagner Companion*, p. 175). He goes on to suggest that "the motif of the educated Siegfried, which is a transformed version of his horn motif in Siegfried, shows a sturdiness and pride, but hardly an advance in consciousness. What happened is that the force of love has turned out to be much weaker than anyone expected, including Wagner."

33. Shklar, *Freedom and Independence*, pp. 11–12.

34. G. W. F. Hegel, *The Phenomenology of Mind*, trans. J. B. Baillie, 2d ed. (London: George Allen and Unwin, 1931), p. 225. All further references to this work will be from this translation.

35. Cited in L. J. Rather, *The Dream of Self-Destruction* (Baton Rouge: Louisiana State University Press, 1979), p. 66.

36. Shklar, *Freedom and Independence*, p. 61.

37. George Bernard Shaw, *The Perfect Wagnerite* (New York: Brentano's, 1909).

38. Charles Taylor, *Hegel*, p. 158.

39. Rather, *Dream of Self-Destruction*, p. 52.

40. Adorno, however, believes that, the new self-consciousness not withstanding, most relationships in the *Ring* are based on domination derived from a belief in "natural kinds"—dwarfs and giants, for example: "the dialectic of instinct and domination is reduced to a difference of 'nature' rather than one socially caused. The absolute distinction drawn in the *Ring* between the different natural kinds becomes the basis of the life and death struggle, its apparent historical structure notwithstanding. If in the social process of life 'ossified relationships' form a second nature, then it is this second nature at which Wagner gazes transfixed, mistaking it for the first" (Theodor Adorno, *In Search of Wagner*, trans. Rodney Livingston [Manchester: NLB, 1981], p. 26).

41. Ludwig Feuerbach, *Principles of the Philosophy of the Future*, trans. Manfred H. Vogel (Indianapolis, Ind.: Hackett Publishing Co., 1986), pp. 52–53.

42. Feuerbach, *The Essence of Christianity*, p. 39.

43. Horkheimer and Adorno read the self-sacrifice common to the ideology of love in our culture as the instrument whereby people are punished for their own pleasure: "In the world of commercial exchange, he who gives over the measure is in the wrong; whereas the lover is always he who loves beyond measure. Whereas the sacrifice that he brings is glorified, jealous care is taken to ensure that the lover is not spared a sacrifice. Love itself is the very place where the lover is made to do wrong and punished for his wrongdoing. The incapacity for domination over himself and others to which his love bears witness is reason enough to deny him fulfillment" (Max Horkheimer and Theodor W. Adorno, *Dialectic of Enlightenment*, trans. John Cumming [New York: Herder and Herder, 1972], p. 73). Siegmund and Sieglinde both give too much, as do Siegfried and Brünnhilde, and each is punished for his or her failures at self-control. Love, in spite of how much Wagner felt it to be the essential need of human society, is

punished in the *Ring* cycle. Wagner follows Hegel on this point; Hegel argues that suffering is necessary before the self can reach complete realization. Horkheimer and Adorno, however, would simply see this idea as rationalization of the status quo, a society built on domination and suffering.

Chapter 2. Language and Music in the *Ring*

1. Porges, *Wagner Rehearsing the "Ring."* p. 2.

2. Mann, *Pro and Contra Wagner*, p. 45.

3. Phillippe Lacoue-Labarthe and Jean-Luc Nancy, *The Literary Absolute*, trans. Philip Barnard and Cheryl Lester (Albany: State University of New York Press, 1988), pp. 29–35.

4. Curt von Westernhagen, *The Forging of the "Ring*," trans. Arnold and Mary Whittal (Cambridge: Cambridge University Press, 1976), p. 386.

5. Raymond Furness, *Wagner and Literature* (New York: St. Martin's Press, 1982), p. 7.

6. Deryck Cooke, *I Saw the World End: A Study of Wagner's "Ring"* (London: Oxford University Press, 1979), p. 4.

7. Deryck Cooke, "Wagner's Musical Language" in *The Wagner Companion*, p. 227.

8. Julia Kristeva, *Revolution in Poetic Language*, trans. Margaret Waller (New York: Columbia University Press, 1984), p. 62.

9. Furness, *Wagner and Literature*, p. 5.

10. James A. Massey, Introduction to *Thoughts on Death and Immortality* by Ludwig Feuerbach (Berkeley and Los Angeles: University of California Press, 1980), xxx.

11. Cited in Westernhagen, *The Forging of the "Ring*," p. 4.

12. Cooke, *I Saw the World End*, pp. 44–45.

13. Mann, *Pro and Contra Wagner*, p. 46.

14. Carl Dalhouse, *Richard Wagner's Music Dramas*, trans. Mary Whittall (Cambridge: Cambridge University Press, 1979), p. 115.

15. Adorno, *In Search of Wagner*, p. 46.

16. Cooke, *I Saw the World End*, p. 39.

17. Helene M. Kastinger Riley, "Some German Theories on the Origin of Language from Herder to Wagner," *Modern Language Review* 74 (1981): 629.

18. Charles Taylor, *Hegel*, pp. 19–20.

19. S. K. Land, "The Rise of Intellect in Wagner's Ring," *Comparative Drama* 5 (Spring 1971): 21–43.

20. Rather, *Dream of Self-Destruction*, pp. 86–87.

21. Charles Taylor, *Hegel*, p. 141.

22. Shklar, *Freedom and Independence*, p. 15.

23. L. S. Vygotsky, *Thought and Language*, trans. Eugenia Hanfmann and Gertrude Vakar (Cambridge, Massachusetts: MIT Press, 1962), p. 5.

24. M. M. Bakhtin, *Marxism and the Theory of Language*, trans. Ladislav Matejka and I. R. Titunik (Cambridge: Harvard University Press, 1986). This book was published under the name of V. N. Volosinov. However, a number of authorities attribute it to Bakhtin, and I have chosen to follow this common practice. All further references to this work are from this edition.

25. Vygotsky, *Thought and Language*, p. 74.

26. Ibid., pp. 6–7.

27. Cooke, *I Saw the World End,* pp. 4–12.
28. Adorno, *In Search of Wagner,* pp. 38–45, 31.
29. Ibid., pp. 67–68.
30. Robert Bailey, "The Structure of the *Ring* and its Evolution," *Nineteenth-Century Music* 1 (July 1977): 54.
31. Adorno, *In Search of Wagner,* pp. 119, 66.
32. Patrick McCreless, *Wagner's Siegfried* (Ann Arbor: UMI Research Press, 1982), p. 95.
33. Bailey, "The Structure of the *Ring*," p. 51.
34. Ibid., pp. 51–53.
35. William Kinderman, "Dramatic Recapitulation in Wagner's Götterdämmerung," *Nineteenth-Century Music* 4 (Fall 1980): 103–4.
36. Adorno, *In Search of Wagner,* pp. 71, 77–79.
37. Ibid., pp. 117–19.
38. Bryan Magee, "Schopenhauer and Wagner," *The Opera Quarterly* 1 (Autumn 1983): 156.

Chapter 3. *Das Rheingold*

1. Peter Ackermann, *Richard Wagners "Ring des Nibelungen" und die Dialektik der Aufklärung* (Tutzing: Hans Schneider, 1981).
2. Max Horkheimer and Theodor W. Adorno, *The Dialectic of Enlightenment,* trans. John Cumming (New York: Herder and Herder, 1972), p. 27.
3. Mann, *Pro and Contra Wagner,* p. 189.
4. L. J. Rather argues, however, that the opening of *Das Rheingold* is a realization of Schopenhauer's theory of music as he expressed it in the following passage from *The World as Will and Representation:* "In the lowest harmonic tones I recognize the lowest stages of the objectification of the will: the mass of the planet, inorganic nature. As is well known, all the higher tones, moving easily and dying away more rapidly, are considered to arise from secondary vibrations of the fundamental bass tone; when it sounds they always sound gently along with it. A law of harmony requires that a bass note be accompanied only by the higher tones that are already of themselves sounding with it, due to secondary vibrations. These are its *sons harmoniques* or overtones. Now this is analogous to the necessary origin, by stepwise development, of the totality of bodies and organizations in nature from the mass of the planet, which is their support and source. The higher tones have a similar relation to their ground bass" (*The Dream of Self-Destruction,* pp. 134–35).
5. Richard Wagner, *My Life,* p. 499.
6. Porges, *Wagner Rehearsing the "Ring,"* p. 7.
7. Robert Bailey, "The Structure of the *Ring* and its Evolution," p. 50.
8. Ackermann, *Richard Wagners "Ring,"* pp. 12, 23.
9. Westernhagen, *The Forging of the "Ring,"* pp. 21, 17.
10. John Deathridge, "Wagner's Sketches for the '*Ring*': Some Recent Studies," *Musical Times* 118 (May 1977): 387.
11. Ackermann, *Richard Wagners "Ring,"* p. 25.
12. G. W. F. Hegel, *Introduction to the Lectures on the History of Philosophy,* trans. T. M. Knox and A. V. Miller (Oxford: Clarendon Press, 1985), pp. 166–67.
13. Porges, *Wagner Rehearsing the "Ring,"* p. 9.
14. Horkheimer and Adorno, *Dialectic of Enlightenment,* p. 111.

15. But most critics still insist on seeing the Rhinedaughters as innocent, natural creatures. Richard David argues that "the Rhinemaidens are animal, mischievous, but not evil" ("Wagner the Dramatist," in *The Wagner Companion*, p. 130). And Michael Tanner agrees, saying that the song of the Rhinedaughters is "the song of innocent, pre-moral Nature," contrasting with Valhalla in the next scene, which is "the symbol of human creativity and the urge for immortality, both for oneself and for the products of one's labours" ("The Total Work of Art," in *The Wagner Companion*, p. 172).

16. Richard Wagner, *The Ring of the Nibelung,* trans. Andrew Porter (New York: Norton, 1977), p. 5. The quotations from the text throughout are from this book. I have followed Porter's translations for the most part, modifying them for greater adherence to the original only where necessary.

17. Fredric Jameson, *The Political Unconscious* (Ithaca, N.Y.: Cornell University Press, 1981), p. 171.

18. Cooke, *I Saw the World End,* p. 214.

19. Horkheimer and Adorno discuss the song of the sirens in *The Odyssey,* saying the giving over of the self to pleasure has always been forbidden in our culture. Because Fricka likens the Rhinedaughters to the sirens in the next scene (by suggestion), Horkheimer and Adorno's point seems to apply to them (p. 59). They are representative of physical pleasure as evil, Wagner's claims to the contrary.

20. Dalhouse, *Richard Wagner's Music Dramas,* p. 117.

21. Richard David, noting the many times the renunciation theme is used, also feels that it is misnamed. He argues, however, that it occurs at "nodal moments" in the drama which have to do with difficult or important choices the characters make, so he calls it the theme of "serious or heroic choice" ("Wagner the Dramatist," in *The Wagner Companion*, p. 127).

22. The connection of this need for love is related to Siegmund in another way. Frits Noske points out that when Woglinde sings the words to the need (renunciation) motive, another motivelike entity, which he calls a topos, appears in the orchestra as a characteristic rhythm. This is what he calls the death topos, which Wagner has borrowed from other operas and used here as prophecy under Woglinde's words; it is also prominent when Siegmund withdraws the sword and, Noske thinks, foretells his death there ("Das exogene Todesmotiv in den Musikdramen Richard Wagners," *Musikforschung* 31 [1978]: 295).

23. Westernhagen, *The Forging of the "Ring,"* p. 29.

24. Ibid., p. 31.

25. I am indebted to Robert Bailey for this observation.

26. S. K. Land, "The Rise of Intellect in Wagner's *Ring,*" *Comparative Drama* 5 (Winter 1983): 26.

27. Horkheimer and Adorno, *Dialectic of Enlightenment,* p. 21.

28. Pierre-Joseph Proudhon, "Readings from *What is Property,*" in *Social Reformers,* ed. Donald O. Wagner (New York: Macmillan, 1949), p. 316.

29. Adorno, *In Search of Wagner,* pp. 117–18.

30. Ibid., p. 119.

31. Shklar, *Freedom and Independence,* p. 6.

32. Adorno and Horkheimer, *Dialectic of Enlightenment,* p. 57.

33. Shklar, *Freedom and Independence,* p. 58.

34. Feuerbach, *The Essence of Christianity,* p. 33.

35. Adorno, *In Search of Wagner,* p. 117.

36. Cooke, *I Saw the World End,* p. 148.

37. Ibid.

38. Charles Taylor, *Hegel*, p. 137.
39. Westernhagen, *The Forging of the "Ring*," p. 37.
40. Cooke, *I Saw the World End*, pp. 49, 53.
41. *Ibid.*, p. 28.
42. *Ibid.*, p. 156.
43. Hegel, *Lectures*, p. 83.
44. Richard Norman, *Hegel's Phenomenology* (New York: St. Martin's Press, 1976), p. 52.
45. Cooke, *I Saw the World End*, p. 169.
46. Hegel, *Phenomenology*, pp. 245–46.
47. Cooke, *I Saw the World End*, p. 187.
48. Westernhagen, *The Forging of the "Ring*," p. 43.
49. Cooke, *I Saw the World End*, p. 218.
50. Horkheimer and Adorno, *Dialectic of Enlightenment*, pp. 105–6.
51. Cooke, *I Saw the World End*, pp. 218–24.
52. Bailey, "The Structure of the *Ring*," p. 60.
53. Cooke, *I Saw the World End*, p. 225.
54. Horkheimer and Adorno, *Dialectic of Enlightenment*, pp. 30–31.
55. Cooke, *I Saw the World End*, p. 162.
56. Dalhouse, *Richard Wagner's Music Dramas*, p. 111.

Chapter 4. *Die Walküre*

1. Cooke, *I Saw the World End*, pp. 282–96.
2. Rather, *The Dream of Self-Destruction*, p. 55.
3. Hegel, pp. 171–72.
4. *Ibid.*, p. 75.
5. Bailey, "The Structure of the *Ring*," p. 54.
6. Porges, *Wagner Rehearsing the "Ring*," p. 44.
7. Cooke, *I Saw the World End*, p. 305.
8. Noske, "Das exogene Todesmotiv," pp. 298–89.
9. Michael Ewans, *Wagner and Aeschylus* (Cambridge: Cambridge University Press, 1982), p. 125.
10. Ackermann, *Richard Wagners "Ring*," pp. 31–37.
11. Land, "The Rise of Intellect in Wagner's *Ring*," p. 22.
12. Eugene Kamenka, *The Philosophy of Ludwig Feuerbach* (New York: Praeger, 1970), p. 37.
13. Charles Taylor, *Hegel*, p. 175.
14. Tanner suggests that Valhalla, "which is clearly Wagner's image of any desirable life after death," is given a serious blow by Siegmund (Michael Tanner, "The Total Work of Art," in *The Wagner Companion*, p. 166). However, Valhalla is most emphatically not Wagner's idea of a perfect life, for it has no women (except as servants), therefore no mutality and no love.
15. Feuerbach, *The Essence of Christianity*, p. 47.
16. Cooke, *I Saw the World End*, pp. 336–37.
17. Charles Taylor, *Hegel*, p. 164.
18. Cooke, *I Saw the World End*, pp. 343–44.
19. Westernhagen, *The Forging of the "Ring*," p. 98.

Chapter 5. *Siegfried*

1. Feuerbach, *The Essence of Christianity*, p. 7.
2. Robert Bailey, "The Method of Composition" in *The Wagner Companion*, p. 326.
3. Adorno, *In Search of Wagner*, p. 24.
4. Porges, *Wagner Rehearsing the "Ring,"* p. 79.
5. McCreless, *Wagner's "Siegfried,"* p. 121.
6. Ibid., p. 100.
7. Adorno, *In Search of Wagner*, p. 140.
8. Porges, *Wagner Rehearsing the "Ring,"* p. 81.
9. Mann, *Pro and Contra Wagner*, p. 31.
10. Cooke, *I Saw the World End*, p. 26.
11. Charles Taylor, *Hegel*, p. 148.
12. Adorno, *In Search of Wagner*, p. 131.
13. Hegel, *Lectures*, p. 169.
14. As Siegfried tries to get Mime to tell him about his past, a new motive, sometimes called Siegfried's impatience, appears in the orchestra; it is very regular in rhythm and indeed suggests hurry or impatience. This figure is sometimes alternated with or accompanied by scale passages, and Siegfried's voice rises on a scale as he expresses his impatience with Mime, culminating on a high G. Wagner in *Mein Leben* tells a story about the conception of this theme; he was, he says, composing *Siegfried* in a house where the neighbor, a tinker, was constantly hammering—so in a fit of anger at the irritating disturbance caused by his neighbor he composed the melody for Siegfried's outrage at Mime's bungling. In this anecdote, Wagner clearly identifies with Siegfried, in spite of his claims elsewhere to identify with Wotan (Wagner, *My Life*, p. 537).
15. The confounding of Jewish and female stereotypes here foreshadows the connection Horkheimer and Adorno find between the problem of the subjugation of women with the problem of anti-Semitism. They argue that the justification for the hatred for woman, which is based on the idea that she is intellectually and physically inferior, is equivalent to the motivation behind the hatred for Jews: "Women and Jews can be seen not to have ruled for thousands of years. They live, although they could be exterminated; and their fear and weakness, the greater affinity to nature which perennial oppression produces in them, is the very element which gives them life. This enrages the strong, who must pay for their strength with an intense alienation from nature, and must always suppress their fear" (Horkheimer and Adorno, *Dialectic of Enlightenment*, p. 112). In this light, the figure of Siegfried, who exaggerates the cultural need to suppress fear, openly exhibits his hatred for Mime and disguises his hatred of women in sentimentality.
16. Feuerbach, *Thoughts*, p. 115.
17. Hegel, *Phenomenology*, p. 46.
18. Mann, *Pro and Contra Wagner*, pp. 97–98.
19. Adorno points out that the racism of which Wagner has often been accused appears in this scene, in the complete security in which Wotan describes the world as being divided into completely separate types of beings, each with its own incontrovertible nature (*In Search of Wagner*, p. 25).
20. Ernest Newman, *The Life of Richard Wagner*, vol. 2 (Cambridge: Cambridge University Press, 1933), pp. 331–33.

21. Adorno, *In Search of Wagner,* p. 15.

22. Shklar, *Freedom and Independence,* p. 60.

23. McCreless, *Wagner's "Siegfried,"* p. 188.

24. Kinderman, "Dramatic Recapitulation," p. 106.

25. Robert L. Jacobs, "A Freudian View of the *Ring,"* in *Penetrating Wagner's "Ring,"* ed. John Louis DiGaetani (Rutherford, N.J.: Fairleigh Dickinson University Press, 1978), p. 119.

26. Feuerbach, *The Philosophy of the Future,* p. 9.

27. Feuerbach, *Essence of Christianity,* p. 8.

28. Feuerbach, *Thoughts,* p. 115.

29. In addition, L. J. Rather notes that Wagner himself suggests that Siegfried is a sun god (*The Dream of Self-Destruction,* p. 42). Further, S. K. Land reminds us that in the Wibelungen myth Siegfried is a sun god, though in the Oedipus-like myth Land argues Wagner is also using, he is the revolutionary ("The Rise of Intellect in Wagner's *Ring,"* pp. 30–31).

30. Kinderman, "Dramatic Recapitulation," pp. 102–3.

31. Peter Conrad finds her reaction to Siegfried's demands for love somewhat sinister: "Brünnhilde's reaction when Siegfried awakens her on the rock expresses the coincidental terror of Wagnerian time and the claustrophobia of Wagnerian space: she is, despite her elation, appalled by the neatness and inevitability of the design which has sent Siegfried unknowingly to release her from a punishment which she incurred to save his life. Wagnerian providence leaves his characters with the afflicted sense of being immured in a forbiddingly unified work of art" (*Romantic Opera and Literary Form* [Berkeley and Los Angeles: University of California Press,1977], p. 23.

32. Feuerbach, *Thoughts,* p. 121.

33. Horkheimer and Adorno, *Dialectic of Enlightenment,* p. 33.

Chapter 6. *Götterdämmerung*

1. Feuerbach, *Thoughts,* p. 122.

2. Dalhouse, *Richard Wagner's Music Dramas,* p. 135.

3. Horkheimer and Adorno, *Dialectic of Enlightenment,* pp. 106–7.

4. Feuerbach, *Thoughts,* p. 115.

5. Hegel, *Lectures,* p. 173.

6. Horkheimer and Adorno, *Dialectic of Enlightenment,* p. 57.

7. Hegel, *Phenomenology,* p. 379.

8. Wagner, "A Communication to My Friends," in *Richard Wagner's Prose Works,* p. 289.

9. Cooke, *I Saw the World End,* pp. 18–19.

10. Feuerbach, *Thoughts,* pp. 120–21.

11. Adorno, *In Search of Wagner,* p. 146.

12. Porges, *Wagner Rehearsing the "Ring,"* p. 130.

13. Feuerbach, *Thoughts,* p. 122.

14. Porges, *Wagner Rehearsing the "Ring,"* p. 134.

15. Quoted by Dalhouse, *Richard Wagner's Music Dramas,* p. 104.

16. Quoted by McCreless, *Wagner's "Siegfried,"* p. 5.

17. Feuerbach, *Thoughts,* p. 120.

18. Mann, *Pro and Contra Wagner,* p. 188.

19. Charles Taylor, *Hegel,* p. 173.

20. Conrad, *Romantic Opera and Literary Form*, p. 20.

21. Warren Darcy, "The Pessimism of the *Ring*," *Opera Quarterly* 4 (Summer, 1986): 35.

22. Cooke, *I Saw the World End*, pp. 20–22.

23. Friedrich Nietzsche, *The Case of Wagner*, trans. Anthony M. Ludovici (New York: Russell and Russell, 1964), p. 11.

24. Dalhouse, *Richard Wagner's Music Dramas*, pp. 138–40.

25. Horkheimer and Adorno, *Dialectic of Enlightenment*, p. 51.

SELECT BIBLIOGRAPHY

Ackermann, Peter. *Richard Wagners "Ring des Nibelungen" und die Dialektik der Aufklärung.* Tutzing: Hans Schneider, 1981.

Adorno, Theodor. *In Search of Wagner.* Translated by Rodney Livingston. Manchester: NLB, 1981.

Amerongen, Martin van. *Wagner: A Case History.* Translated by Stewart Spencer and Dominic Cakebread. New York: George Braziller, 1984.

Bailey, Robert. "The Structure of the *Ring* and its Evolution." *Nineteenth-Century Music* 1 (July 1977): 48–61.

Bakhtin, M. M. [V. N. Volosinov]. *Marxism and the Philosophy of Language.* Translated by Ladislav Matejka and I. R. Titunik. Cambridge: Harvard University Press, 1986.

Benjamin, Walter. *The Origin of German Tragic Drama.* Translated by John Osborne. London: NLB, 1977.

Burbidge, Peter, and Richard Sutton, eds. *The Wagner Companion.* New York, Cambridge University Press, 1979.

Conrad, Peter. *Romantic Opera and Literary Form.* Berkeley and Los Angeles: University of California Press, 1977.

Cooke, Deryck. *I Saw the World End: A Study of Wagner's "Ring."* London: Oxford University Press, 1979.

———. *The Language of Music.* New York: Oxford University Press, 1959.

Cumbow, Robert C. "The Ring is a Fraud: Self, Totem, and Myth in *Der Ring des Nibelungen.*" *Opera Quarterly* 1 (Spring 1983): 107–25.

Dalhouse, Carl. *Richard Wagner's Music Dramas.* Translated by Mary Whittall. Cambridge: Cambridge University Press, 1979.

Darcy, Warren. "The Pessimism of the *Ring.*" *Opera Quarterly* 4 (Summer 1986): 24–48.

Deathridge, John. "Wagner's Sketches for the 'Ring': Some Recent Studies." *Musical Times* 118 (May 1977): 383–89.

DiGaetani, John Louis, ed. *Penetrating Wagner's "Ring": An Anthology.* Rutherford, N.J.: Fairleigh Dickinson University Press, 1978.

Donington, Robert. *Wagner's "Ring" and its Symbols: The Music and the Myth.* London: Faber and Faber, 1963.

Dowling, William C. *Jameson, Althusser, Marx: An Introduction to The Political Unconscious.* Ithaca, N.Y.: Cornell University Press, 1984.

Engels, Friedrich. *Ludwig Feuerbach and the Outcome of Classical German Philosophy.* New York: International Publishers, 1941.

Ewans, Michael. *Wagner and Aeschylus: The "Ring" and the "Oresteia."* Cambridge: Cambridge University Press, 1982.

202

Feenberg, Andrew. *Lukács, Marx, and the Sources of Critical Theory.* New York: Oxford University Press, 1986.

Feuerbach, Ludwig. *Principles of the Philosophy of the Future.* Translated by Manfred H. Vogel. Indianapolis, Ind.: Hackett Publishing Co., 1986.

————. *The Essence of Christianity.* Edited by E. Graham Waring and F. W. Strothmann. New York: Frederick Ungar Publishing Co., 1957.

————. *Thoughts on Death and Immortality.* Translated by James A. Massey. Berkeley and Los Angeles: University of California Press, 1980.

Furness, Raymond. *Wagner and Literature.* New York: St. Martin's Press, 1982.

Gadamer, Hans-Georg. *Hegel's Dialectic: Five Hermeneutical Studies.* Translated by P. Christopher Smith. New Haven, Conn.: Yale University Press, 1976.

Glass, Frank W. *The Fertilizing Seed: Wagner's Concept of the Poetic Intent.* Ann Arbor: UMI Research Press, 1983.

Gregor-Dellin, Martin. *Richard Wagner: His Life, His Work, His Century.* Translated by J. Maxwell Brownjohn. San Diego: Harcourt Brace Jovanovich, 1980.

Hegel, G. W. F. *The Phenomenology of Mind.* Translated by J. B. Baillie. 2d ed. London: George Allen & Unwin, 1931.

Hegel, G. W. F. *Introduction to the Lectures on the History of Philosophy.* Translated by T. M. Knox and A. V. Miller. Oxford: Clarendon Press, 1985.

Horkheimer, Max, and Theodor W. Adorno. *Dialectic of Enlightenment.* Translated by John Cumming. New York: Herder and Herder, 1972.

Jacobs, Robert L. "A Freudian View of the *Ring.*" In *Penetrating Wagner's "Ring": An Anthology.* Edited by John Louis DiGaetani. Rutherford, N.J.: Fairleigh Dickinson University Press, 1978.

Jameson, Fredric. *The Political Unconscious: Narrative as a Socially Symbolic Act.* Ithaca, N.Y.: Cornell University Press, 1981.

Kamenka, Eugene. *The Philosophy of Ludwig Feuerbach.* New York: Praeger Publishers, 1970.

Kinderman, William. "Dramatic Recapituation in Wagner's *Götterdämmerung.*" *Nineteenth-Century Music* 4 (Fall 1980): 101–12.

Kristeva, Julia. *Revolution in Poetic Language.* Translated by Margaret Waller. New York: Columbia University Press, 1984.

Lacoue-Labarthe, Philippe, and Jean-Luc Nancy. *The Literary Absolute: The Theory of Literature in German Romanticism.* Translated by Philip Barnard and Cheryl Lester. Albany: State University of New York Press, 1988.

Land, S. K. "The Rise of Intellect in Wagner's *Ring.*" *Comparative Drama* 5 (Spring 1971): 21–43.

Magee, Bryan. "Schopenhauer and Wagner." *Opera Quarterly* 1 (Autumn 1983): 148–71; (Winter 1983): 50–73.

Mann, Thomas. *Pro and Contra Wagner.* Translated by Allan Blunden. Chicago: University of Chicago Press, 1985.

McCreless, Patrick. *Wagner's Siegfried: Its Drama, History, and Music.* Ann Arbor: UMI Research Press, 1982.

Newman, Ernest. *The Life of Richard Wagner.* 4 vols. Cambridge: Cambridge University Press, 1933.

Nietzsche, Friedrich. *The Case of Wagner.* Vol. 8 of *The Complete Works of Friedrich*

Nietzsche. Translated by Anthony M. Ludovici. New York: Russell and Russell, 1964.

Nietzsche, Friedrich. *The Gay Science.* Translated by Walter Kaufmann. New York: Random House, 1974.

Norman, Richard. *Hegel's Phenomenology: A Philosophical Introduction.* New York: St. Martin's Press, 1976.

Noske, Frits. "Das exogene Todesmotiv in den Musikdramen Richard Wagners." *Musikforschung* 31 (1978): 285–302.

Porges, Heinrich. *Wagner Rehearsing the "Ring": An Eye-Witness Account of the Stage Rehearsals of the First Bayreuth Festival.* Translated by Robert L. Jacobs. Cambridge: Cambridge University Press, 1983.

Proudhon, Pierre-Joseph. "What is Property?" In *Social Reformers,* edited by Donald O. Wagner. New York: Macmillan, 1949.

Rather, L. J. *The Dream of Self-Destruction: Wagner's Ring and the Modern World.* Baton Rouge: Louisiana State University Press, 1979.

Riley, Helene M. Kastinger. "Some German Theories on the Origin of Language from Herder to Wagner." *Modern Language Review* 74 (1979): 617–32.

Rorty, Richard. *Consequences of Pragmatism (Essays: 1972–1980).* Minneapolis: University of Minnesota Press, 1982.

Rotenstreich, Nathan. *From Substance to Subject: Studies in Hegel.* The Hague: Martinus Nijhoff, 1974.

Shaw, George Bernard. *The Perfect Wagnerite: A Commentary on the Nibelung's Ring.* New York: Brentano's, 1909.

Shklar, Judith N. *Freedom and Independence: A Study of the Political Ideas of Hegel's "Phenomenology of Mind."* Cambridge: Cambridge University Press, 1976.

Stein, Jack M. *Richard Wagner and the Synthesis of the Arts.* Detroit: Wayne State University Press, 1960.

Taylor, Charles. *Hegel.* Cambridge: Cambridge University Press, 1975.

Taylor, Ronald. *Richard Wagner: His Life, Art and Thought.* London: Panther, 1979.

Todorov, Tzvetan. *Mikhail Bakhtin: The Dialogic Principle.* Translated by Wlad Godzich. Minneapolis: University of Minnesota Press, 1984.

Toews, John Edward. *Hegelianism: The Path Toward Dialectical Humanism, 1805–1841.* Cambridge: Cambridge University Press, 1980.

Vygotsky, Lev Semenovich. *Thought and Language.* Translated by Eugenia Hanfmann and Gertrude Vakar. Cambridge: MIT Press, 1962.

Wagner, Richard. *My Life.* Translated by Andrew Gray. Cambridge: Cambridge University Press, 1983.

———. *Richard Wagner's Prose Works.* Translated by William Ashton Ellis. 8 vols. London: Kegan Paul, Trench, Trübner and Co., 1895.

———. *The Ring of the Nibelung.* Translated by Andrew Porter. New York: Norton, 1977.

Wartofsky, Max W. *Feuerbach.* Cambridge: Cambridge University Press, 1977.

Westernhagen, Curt von. *The Forging of the "Ring": Richard Wagner's Composition Sketches for "Der Ring des Nibelungen."* Translated by Arnold and Mary Whitall. Cambridge: Cambridge University Press, 1976.

Windell, George. "Hegel, Feuerbach, and Wagner's *Ring.*" *Central European History* 9 (1976): 27–57.

INDEX